Why Suicide Is Amoral

Why Suicide Is Amoral

A Philosophical Account

Robyn Gaier

LEXINGTON BOOKS
Lanham • Boulder • New York • London

Published by Lexington Books
An imprint of The Rowman & Littlefield Publishing Group, Inc.
4501 Forbes Boulevard, Suite 200, Lanham, Maryland 20706
www.rowman.com

86-90 Paul Street, London EC2A 4NE

British Library Cataloguing in Publication Information Available

Library of Congress Cataloging-in-Publication Data

Names: Gaier, Robyn, author.
Title: Why suicide is amoral : a philosophical account / Robyn Gaier.
Description: Lanham, Maryland : Lexington Books, [2024] | Includes bibliographical references and index.
Identifiers: LCCN 2024012769 (print) | LCCN 2024012770 (ebook) | ISBN 9781793640871 (cloth) | ISBN 9781793640888 (epub)
Subjects: LCSH: Suicide.
Classification: LCC BD445 .G35 2024 (print) | LCC BD445 (ebook) | DDC 179.7—dc23/eng/20240602
LC record available at https://lccn.loc.gov/2024012769
LC ebook record available at https://lccn.loc.gov/2024012770

To my parents, Roger and Beverly, with all my love and gratitude

Contents

Acknowledgments ix

Chapter One: Why the Amorality of Suicide? 1

Chapter Two: Amoral Actions 37

Chapter Three: Actions of Suicide as Amoral 65

Chapter Four: A Few Objections and Replies 93

Chapter Five: The Significance of Charting a New Path 125

Bibliography 143

Index 149

About the Author 159

Acknowledgments

I sincerely thank Jana Hodges-Kluck and Deanna Biondi for their steadfast patience and support in this project. I also wish to thank Lauran Jones, Felicity Tucker, and Arc Indexing, Inc. for making this book possible. Without your help and encouragement on this project, it simply would not exist. Thank you.

I also thank Gannon University in Erie, Pennsylvania for awarding me a Faculty Research Award in May of 2023. The views expressed here, however, are entirely my own. They do not express, or represent, the views of Gannon University.

Some of the ideas put forth here have originated from, or have been benefited by, philosophical discussions and conferences. Most notably, I thank Josefa Ros Velasco for organizing conferences and books on both depression and suicide. My interest in the work of William Styron, for instance, was originally fueled by those conversations and projects.

I also thank the participants at the Rocky Mountain Ethics Conference (especially in 2019 and 2023) and at the Southwestern Philosophical Society's annual meeting (especially in 2014, 2017, and 2023) for helping me to refine some of the ideas presented here. Specifically, I sincerely thank the following people: Scott Aikin, Lydia Barry, Paul Dages, Eric Dart, Katie Dickey, Dale Dorsey, Mylan Engel Jr., Scott Forschler, Robert Garcia, John Greco, Bill Haggerty, Bob Hartman, Dan Haybron, Kay Redfield Jamison, Juliana Kazemi, Aaron Kerr, Scott Klaeser, Justin Klocksiem, Mike Latzer, Lori Lindley, Geo Lyons, Jim McCollum, Andrea Miller, Alastair Norcross, Dave Nordquest, Tyler Perkins, Dom Prianti, Ken Rogerson, Bruce Russell, Chris Stasa, Matthias Steup, Todd Stewart, Eleonore Stump, Mike Tager, Alan Tomhave, Michael Tooley, and Mark Vopat. Thank you. I also thank my students over the years who have inspired me, and who continue to ignite my love of learning. The mistakes that remain here are, of course, entirely my own.

Additionally, I thank the staff and volunteers of Crisis Text Line, the Trevor Project, the La Crosse Area Suicide Prevention Initiative in Wisconsin, and the Western Pennsylvania Chapter of the American Foundation for Suicide Prevention.

For moral support, I am indebted to my sister, Regina Mann, whose encouragement means so very much to me. I also thank Kevin, Raphael, and Meagan Mann for supporting me and for giving me the gift of hope.

Above all, I am so very grateful to my parents, Roger and Beverly (Liette) Gaier. Their gift of unconditional love has brought me the gift of life more times than I can recall. With all my love and gratitude, I dedicate this book to them.

Chapter One

Why the Amorality of Suicide?

Suicide makes words both impotent and vital. Words are impotent regarding suicide because, quite frankly, they reach their communicative limitation. That is, I have long held the mindset that, regarding the subject of suicide, there simply are no words. The irony is that I have not wavered in such thinking, even while writing this little book advancing the idea that suicide is an amoral action. Somewhere along the way, however, I have come to the realization that failing to attempt to discuss the subject of suicide is not as comforting as it may seem. The pain, confusion, misconceptions, and the social stigma against suicide are not at all eradicated when words are left unwritten and unspoken but, rather, they are intensified. So, despite the inadequacy of words, silence is not a safeguard.[1] It is no wonder, then, that the American Foundation for Suicide Prevention refers to one of its educational programs as simply *Talk Saves Lives*™.[2] One aim of this book is to promote conversations about the nature of suicide in both healthy and meaningful ways. I believe that healthy and meaningful conversations about suicide need to begin by jettisoning value-laden ways of framing (and of defining) actions of suicide which, unfortunately, truncate such conversations as soon as they begin.[3]

The thesis that I will argue for in this book is that suicide is an amoral action, which is to say that it falls outside of the moral domain. As such, suicide is an action that ought not to be the subject of moral evaluation. To claim that an action is amoral is neither to endorse nor to condemn the action in question. I will return to discuss amorality in further detail below but, for now, it suffices to note that, if an action is amoral, then it cannot be morally obligatory, morally impermissible, or even morally *permissible*. Additionally, amoral actions are neither morally better nor morally worse than other actions. Moral judgments are only appropriate for actions that fall within the moral domain. My claim here is that suicide falls outside of the moral domain and, therefore, asserting that any action of suicide is somehow morally obligatory, morally impermissible, morally permissible, or even *morally* better or worse than other actions is inaccurate. I will argue that moral evaluations (or moral judgments) regarding actions of suicide are inaccurate because they make a category mistake—namely, they place suicide somewhere within the moral domain, at least on occasion.

This book is not a self-help book for readers who struggle with suicide ideation, nor is it a self-help book for those who know someone who is struggling with suicide ideation, or who have lost someone to suicide. Nevertheless, I strongly encourage such readers to seek support.[4] It takes courage and strength to reach out for help, but please know that both hope and help exist. Additionally, I implore everyone to privilege their self-care, especially when thinking about the multifaceted subject of suicide even in the abstract.

Additionally, this book is not about the neuroscience of suicide. Although I believe that such an inclusion might be helpful with respect to advancing the thesis of this book, it is not the route that I am choosing to take here.[5] As a philosophical book about the amorality of suicide, I will focus upon creating a theoretical framework for understanding the amorality of suicide *as an action*. The theories that I will employ here—namely, those theories pertaining to amorality and to suicide, respectively—are theories that I believe have merit. Nevertheless, additional arguments supporting such theories are deserving of attention elsewhere because such arguments are too tangential to my aim here, and I fear that their inclusion will lead the discussion astray. To clarify, my objective is not to argue for such theories pertaining to amorality and to actions of suicide respectively, but rather to suggest how such otherwise independent theories might intertwine and be illuminating in their constellation. With that objective in mind, my aim here is modest. I simply wish to begin a conversation about what it might look like, and what it might mean, for suicide to be regarded as outside of the moral domain.

Several preliminary points are in order here. For starters, of course, the nature of amoral actions deserves attention. I will briefly explore how such actions are possible and, in doing so, I will evaluate what is being assumed about actions in the moral domain. My aim in this introductory chapter is to give an overview of the types of amoral actions that I have in mind. Next, I will turn my attention to the distinctions among actions, inactions, and acts, with particular attention to the distinction between an action of suicide and a suicidal act. Specifically, I will examine what it means for an action to be an action of suicide, while noting common misconceptions about the nature of suicide that, in part, fuel the social stigma against suicide. I will then proceed to assess what I understand to be comprising the current landscape regarding the relationship between actions of suicide and actions within the moral domain to draw a contrast to the thesis of this book. Finally, I will briefly explain the structure of the argument that I will put forth here along with an outline of the remaining chapters.

AMORAL ACTIONS

Characterizing actions as within the moral domain seemingly happens by default. *Prima facie* it seems that any action that a moral agent could possibly perform at any given time is subject to moral evaluation; or that any action that a moral agent performs reveals virtuous or vicious qualities of one's character; or that any action that a moral agent performs has the potential for causing harm to other living beings, to the environment, to future generations and so on. Furthermore, it might just seem obvious that some actions, such as shopping for a birthday gift for a loved one, are (morally) better than other actions, such as littering, but (morally) worse than still other actions, such as using one's time spent shopping for a birthday gift to volunteer at a local food bank instead. Consequently, it might be somewhat of a challenge to think about what it means for an action to be outside of the moral domain, or to be *amoral*.[6]

Upon a moment's reflection, however, it is commonplace to attribute amoral actions to *non-moral agents*, with non-human animals and young children as paradigm examples of non-moral agents. So, let us start our investigation of amoral actions by paying attention to what non-moral agents lack. While the actions of non-human animals and young children might be commonly regarded as amoral, it is unhelpful simply to claim that their actions are amoral because they are the actions of non-moral agents. More specifically, we need to know *what* makes their actions amoral.

One immediate thought is that non-moral agents do not seem to be able to take ownership of their actions in the way that moral agents take ownership of their actions. Acting based upon instinct or impulse, for example, is different from acting based upon reasons that reflect an agent's will, or choice. The actions of non-moral agents are amoral, I believe, because such agents lack what I will refer to here as *deliberative agency*.

I understand deliberative agency as entailing an agent's ability to reflect upon possible reasons for acting, to imagine possible consequences of their actions, and to weigh their priorities considering both possible actions and their respective, perceived consequences. Agents can exercise deliberative agency to various degrees, of course, and so it is a threshold concept. Non-moral agents can still have varying degrees of deliberative agency. Nevertheless, as a threshold concept, if an agent can exercise a sufficient degree of deliberative agency, then the agent in question can evaluate different reasons for acting and choose among such reasons. When an agent cannot exercise a sufficient degree of deliberative agency, then those actions that are causally attributed to them (as the originator of such actions) cannot be attributed to them in any *moral* sense. The upshot is that the ability to exercise a sufficient degree of deliberative agency and, thereby, to take ownership of one's actions, seems to be foundational for moral agency insofar as it seems to be what non-moral agents lack, and what makes their actions amoral.

Consider the following illustration. Suppose that a very young child (who is incapable of exercising a sufficient degree of deliberative agency) throws their food across the room. I am tempted to say that the action of the child in question is an amoral action since, after all, I have stipulated that the child lacks the ability to exercise a sufficient degree of deliberative agency. The child's action—insofar as it is an action[7]—is amoral.

Intuitions might divide here, however. Some people might claim that the child's action of throwing their food is, in fact, morally *wrong*, or a morally impermissible action, due to the action's potential for harm and its wastefulness. But because the child in question does not yet understand the wrongness of their action, then the child is not blameworthy for their action. The idea here is that the child's lack of understanding of their action and its consequences serves as an excusing condition. That is, in general, an agent (morally) ought not to throw their food.

I believe that such a viewpoint—namely, that the child's action is morally wrong but not blameworthy—is a bit too quick, however. It is too quick because such a viewpoint assumes that the child in question has a sufficient degree of deliberative agency. Specifically, such a viewpoint assumes that the child in question can exercise their deliberative agency *at that moment* (or at the time of their action). But it is not obvious when another agent can exercise their deliberative agency, and appearances can be deceiving.

To be sure, consider the following example. Suppose that, in the wild, a lion attacks a gazelle. The lion is not thought to be doing something morally evaluable, regardless of how horrendous the lion's attack might be. While it is true that the lion in question is not blameworthy for attacking a gazelle, it is also true that the lion did nothing morally *wrong*.[8] Importantly, the example of a lion attacking a gazelle seems to suggest that it is not the harm, or even the potential for harm, that drives the assessment of an action as an action within the moral domain. It is, rather, the *perceived intention* of such harm and, hence, the idea that such harm can be prevented, as in the scenario of a child throwing their food.

My point is that moral wrongness might be attributed to the child's action because a sufficient degree of deliberative agency is attributed to the child. The harm that the lion's action inflicts upon the gazelle in the wild could be deemed tragic, perhaps, but it is not deemed as (morally) wrong. It is not deemed as wrong because it strains credulity to imagine a lion exercising a kind of reflective, deliberative agency about what actions to pursue in any robust sense. My claim here is that the kind of agency that an agent has *at the time of the action* matters with respect to attempts to classify actions within the moral domain.[9]

To clarify, I believe that the tendency to categorize the action of a child throwing their food as morally wrong reflects the degree (albeit a limited degree) of deliberative agency that the child is assumed to have. That is, unlike the lion's attack, I believe that the temptation to claim that the child's action is morally *wrong* stems not only from the need to intervene, or otherwise to prevent the child from continuing to throw their food, but also from the perception that the child in question *could* have some degree of deliberative agency even if the child has no understanding of their action or the harm that they are doing. My point is just that it is not too much of a stretch of the imagination to think about the child in question as understanding, perhaps in some rudimentary way, that their action results (or could result) in harm; and, importantly, it is not difficult to imagine the child in question as intending such harm. The possibility that the child intends harm, at least in some sense, is what is driving the assessment that the action is wrong—namely, that throwing food is an *intentional action*. A young child, for instance, might be able to reflect (or they might soon be able to reflect) upon their intentions in ways that lions cannot.[10]

I aim to establish that *a lack of deliberative agency* alone is sufficient to account for classifying the actions of non-moral agents as *amoral*. To be sure, suppose that the child in the illustration above completely lacks deliberative agency. Further suppose that there is no possibility that the child in question could develop deliberative agency. Perhaps the child in question suffers from a severe cognitive impairment, for instance. In such a scenario, the child's action more closely follows the intuitions that seem to persist with respect to the lion's action—namely, that it seems inaccurate to say that such an action is wrong, but not blameworthy. Rather, it seems accurate to say that the child's action is not wrong, and so, that it cannot be blameworthy. More akin to an event than an action, the child's action—insofar as it is an action—is amoral, or outside of the moral domain.[11] Hence, I believe that the crucial difference between asserting that the child's action is wrong (and, thereby, within the moral domain) whereas the lion's action is not, depends upon their respective, perceived degree of deliberative agency.

The idea that a category of amoral actions can be discerned through attention to deliberative agency is found in the relevant literature. In his paper entitled "Amorality," Dale Dorsey defines amoral actions as "those that lack any moral evaluative status whatsoever."[12] Moral evaluations of any stripe do not make sense with respect to amoral actions because they are not the sort of actions that can be morally evaluated. To make a moral evaluation regarding an action, certain conditions must be met. Actions that fail to meet these qualifying conditions are outside of the moral domain and, hence, are amoral actions.

So, what are these qualifying conditions, and what does it mean for actions to fail to meet such conditions? To sketch Dale Dorsey's account of amoral actions, or of those actions that fail to meet the qualifying conditions necessary to be in the moral domain, attention to the problem of moral requirability is in order. Dorsey explains that the problem of moral requirability "is the problem of determining which actions that one can perform are eligible to become the object of a moral requirement" for the agent in question.[13] Indeed, the range of actions available to an agent to perform at any given time is necessarily limited. The problem of moral requirability, then, is a problem that all ethical theories need to address. Claiming that an agent *should* have acted differently, for example, implies that the agent in question *could* have acted differently in the given situation or circumstance.

To address the problem of moral requirability, Dale Dorsey offers what he calls the *agency view*. According to the agency view, an action is morally requirable at time *t* if and only if the agent in question can do the particular action at *t* as an agent.[14] For Dorsey's part, he aims to make as few commitments here as possible since it is imperative not to assume any ethical theory when discussing actions outside of the moral domain. Indeed, Dorsey writes:

> I remain neutral on such topics as whether moral deliberation is a result of cognitive, conative, or affective pro-attitudes, the nature of autonomy or autonomous action, whether autonomous agents act under the guise of the good, or whether normative judgments are necessarily motivating and so on.[15]

To attempt to pinpoint what such an open view of acting as an agent means, Dorsey concludes that:

> [t]o perform an action as an agent is to perform that action on the basis of one's own deliberative agency. It is, in other words, to see *a reason to perform that action,* and to *perform the action on the basis of that reason.*[16]

Dorsey further qualifies his position regarding what it means to see a reason to perform a certain action. Dorsey claims that "to perform an action as an agent it is not sufficient to see some reason or other to perform the action."[17] Rather, an agent "must support *that action in particular.*"[18]

To take stock, attention to deliberative agency reveals one way to think about amoral actions—namely, to ask whether an agent can exercise their deliberative agency. Or, to borrow from the two criteria of Dale Dorsey's view, we must ask whether an agent can appreciate a reason to perform an action *and* whether they can perform that action for the reason (or reasons) that they have.[19] If an agent is unable to appreciate a reason for acting, or if they can appreciate a reason for acting but cannot act for *that reason*, then their corresponding action (or inaction) is amoral. Actions within the moral domain must be actions attributable to agents who have the capacity to act as a *deliberative agent*. Such a position can account for the notion that, in general, the actions of non-human animals and the actions of young children are amoral.[20]

Yet the exercise of rational deliberation (or the exercise of an agent's deliberative agency) is different from the exercise of their *moral agency*. Since amoral actions are actions outside of the moral domain, then moral agency also needs attention. Whatever moral agency is thought to entail, it seems clear that it must entail more than simply an agent's capacity to exercise deliberative agency. Specifically, moral agency must also entail a responsiveness to *moral* reasons. Recall that, strictly speaking, deliberative agency is about an agent's responsiveness to reasons, in general. So, deliberative agency and moral agency certainly can overlap, but it also seems that they can come apart.

To be sure, if moral agency (at least in part) is about acting upon moral reasons and, hence, if moral agency assumes an understanding of moral reasons (regardless of how an agent acts), then it seems as though deliberative agency is necessary (although not sufficient) for moral agency. So, an agent might have a sufficient degree of deliberative agency but lack moral agency. *Prima facie*, then, it does not seem as though it is possible for an agent to have moral agency but to lack deliberative agency. Nevertheless, as I will explain, it seems possible for a moral agent to be incumbered by situational constraints that can make *acting upon reasons* impossible for the agent in question. A moral agent might not be able to act upon the (moral) reasons that they have, even though they retain their deliberative agency to appreciate such reasons for acting and, perhaps, even to want to be able to act upon those reasons. Therefore, if deliberative agency entails both an appreciation for reasons for acting *and* the ability to act upon those reasons, then it is possible for a moral agent to be unable to act upon the reasons that they have; and, in turn, it is possible for a moral agent to lack deliberative agency. So, moral agency does not necessitate deliberative agency, and deliberative agency does not necessitate moral agency.

The upshot is that it seems possible, then, that an agent can exercise their deliberative agency (at least to some degree) while still falling short in their capacity to exercise their moral agency. So, in addition to amoral actions stemming from deficiencies in an agent's deliberative agency, amoral actions also can result from deficiencies in moral agency. To clarify, it might be helpful to return to thinking about the actions of young children who are still developing both their deliberative agency and their moral agency.

For instance, young children, who are still developing their moral agency, lack the reasoning skills necessary for moral deliberation. They might be unable to foresee potential consequences of their actions and to evaluate reasons for and against different actions. They might be unable to understand how their behavior impacts others, and they might be unable to reflect upon what kind of person they are becoming through their actions. In other words, they might not be able to exercise their deliberative agency about *moral* reasons (even if they can exercise their deliberative agency with respect to other reasons they have). I do not wish to undermine the point that moral deliberation necessitates such reasoning skills. Yet such a deficiency in moral agency closely resembles a deficiency in deliberative agency; and so, I mention it only to set it aside.

What I understand to be an even more salient feature of moral deliberation is the fact that such moral reasoning does not take place in a social, cultural, and environmental vacuum. That is, it is not simply that the actions of young children are amoral because such children lack the reasoning skills required for moral deliberation. Rather, more pointedly, the actions of young children, who are still developing their moral agency, are amoral because such children lack relational knowledge, which is acquired through social interactions. Put simply, actions within the moral domain are fundamentally *relational* and, as such, they demand the acquisition of what I am calling here relational knowledge. So, just as amoral actions can be the result of deficiencies in deliberative agency, it seems that amoral actions also can be the result of deficiencies in relational knowledge, which compromises moral agency.

The idea that morality is fundamentally relational—or fundamentally about how a person ought to interact among other living beings within an environment (and even with the environment itself)—is, perhaps, an obvious, uncontroversial, and uninteresting claim. But what it means to take seriously the relational aspect of morality is another, less obvious matter. Eleonore Stump, in her book *Wandering in Darkness: Narrative and the Problem of Suffering*, describes what she calls a kind of knowledge of persons "which is non-propositional and which is not reducible to knowledge *that*."[21] Following Frank Jackson's well-known thought experiment dubbed as Mary's Room, Stump regards such knowledge as analogous to the perception of color.[22] Just like a person can know *that* some color is called "red" by learning propositions about the color red, a person's *perception* of the color red yields further information not reducible to propositions about the color red. Stump explains that "although there does seem to be an experiential component of some sort" with respect to the kind of knowledge of persons that she has in mind, she further explains that "it is not a matter of special causal contact with the person known."[23] Stories, for example, can reveal the nature of a person without having direct causal contact with the person known through such stories. What seems to matter is that stories are sufficient to provide an impression of a person which communicates what they are like *as a person*. I believe that such a *knowledge of persons*, although often taken for granted, is essential to an agent's ability to have moral reasons for acting and to perform an action based upon such reasons. That is, relational knowledge seems necessary for an agent to exercise moral agency given the relational nature of morality.

Another way of understanding the importance of what is being communicated through social interactions is to examine what Axel Seemann calls person perception.[24] Writing about the unique phenomenal aspect of perceiving persons, Seemann explains:

> what fundamentally distinguishes the perception of a person from the perception of another kind of object is a certain *phenomenal* aspect: to perceive another person (under conditions of mutual attention) is to grasp a particular aspect of that person's psychological life—namely her subjective attitude. It is crucial that the perceiving person is not confined to the role of an observer: it is through an *interaction*—one person responding in kind to a smile directed at him—that the psychological life of the smiling person is apprehended. The interactive element of person perception is so important because it is through the adoption of the other person's facial expression, and thus expressed subjective attitude, that her psychology is understood.[25]

Seemann suggests that another person's psychological life is imparted to oneself (and vice versa) within a social interaction. Such perceptual experiences are not merely indications of another's mood such as, for instance, an agent concluding that another person is happy because the other person is smiling. But, more importantly, another person's psychological life is also communicated in the exchange—such as, for example, recognizing another's smile as reflecting a joyful surprise, or as finding humor within such circumstances or, perhaps, even understanding that another person's smile is sarcastic. I believe that what Stump refers to as a kind of *knowledge of persons* and what Seemann refers to as *person perception* offer insight into understanding what is required of agents to act upon distinctly *moral* reasons.

To be sure, a brief look at autism seems to support the idea that actions within the moral domain necessitate a kind of relational knowledge acquired socially. Autism has been commonly diagnosed by criteria which fall under three headings: (i) "[a] qualitative impairment in reciprocal social interaction," (ii) "[a] qualitative impairment in verbal and non-verbal communication [as well as] in imaginative activity," and (iii) "[a] markedly restricted repertoire of activities and interests."[26] The characteristic of autism which is of interest here is impairment regarding reciprocal social interaction.

One person with autism, Jim Sinclair, describes his experience in the following way:

> [s]ometimes I'm not aware of social cues because of the same perceptual problems that affect my understanding of other aspects of the environment. [. . .] Sometimes I notice the cues but I don't know what they mean. [. . .] Even if I can tell what the cues mean, I may not know what to do about them. [. . .] It's very insulting, and also very discouraging, to be told that if I don't understand someone, it's because I don't care.[27]

Sinclair is calling attention to the fact that a kind of relational knowledge is imparted through social interaction and, specifically, through social cues. More importantly, Sinclair's statements reveal that achieving such social knowledge about what he should do in a situation depends upon his relational knowledge.

Understandably, Sinclair reports feeling discouraged when other people conclude that he does not care. Sinclair describes one such instance as follows:

> [t]he first time I ever realized that someone needed to be touched was during an encounter with a grief-stricken, hysterically sobbing person who was in no condition to respond to my questions about what I should do to help. I could certainly tell that he was upset. I could even figure out that there was *something* I could do that would be better than nothing. But I didn't know what that something was.[28]

Sinclair's failure to act morally, or to help the person in need of comfort, reveals neither a lack of empathy nor a lack of rationality. Indeed, Sinclair seems otherwise capable of acting as a deliberative agent. Nevertheless, Sinclair's condition highlights the fact that being able to perform the action in question—namely, helping someone in need—relies upon more than just deliberative agency. Relational knowledge is also required for an agent to act upon *moral* reasons, which are fundamentally *relational*. So, when an agent lacks relational knowledge, or when such knowledge is compromised through a social impairment, then an agent's ability to act as a moral agent—that is, an agent's ability to act upon moral reasons—is also impaired.

To clarify, both deficiencies in deliberative agency and deficiencies in relational knowledge seem to underlie amoral actions (since deficiencies in relational knowledge compromise moral agency). I have noted that deliberative agency and moral agency can come apart. The capacity to exercise both kinds of agency seem necessary (although they may not be jointly sufficient) for an agent to perform actions within the moral domain. I have further noted that it seems possible for an agent to retain a degree of deliberative agency even though their moral agency is compromised. Jim Sinclair's account seems to illustrate such a possibility. Sinclair knew that he had a reason to act in the situation he described, and he seemingly was able to act upon the reasons that he had. Nevertheless, Sinclair could not determine what he morally was to do in the situation he described. A moral reason for acting was elusive.

Conversely, just as it is possible to retain deliberative agency but to lack moral agency with respect to an action, I believe that it is also possible for a moral agent to retain their moral agency but have their degree of deliberative agency compromised. Indeed, Dale Dorsey illustrates such a scenario in the following way:

> [i]magine, for instance, that Phil stands before a safe, and that opening the safe will prevent a very serious calamity. Phil, however, does not know the combination of the safe, and hence does not know how to open it. It would seem inappropriate to say that *opening* the safe is morally required, given that he doesn't know the combination (though, strictly speaking, he *can* open the safe, by entering the right numbers in the right order).[29]

Per Dorsey's account, Phil's failure to open the safe is amoral. Simply put, opening the safe is not morally requirable for Phil. Hence, Phil's failure to open the safe in question is amoral even though, strictly speaking, Phil *can* open the safe; and, tellingly, it is amoral even though Phil retains his moral agency. Additionally, Phil's inaction is amoral even though a serious calamity ensues. Phil is unable to prevent a serious calamity from happening due to his cognitive and circumstantial limitations. Because Phil cannot (practically speaking) act upon the reason that he has to open the safe in question, then his deliberative agency is compromised. A moral evaluation of Phil's inaction is inappropriate.[30]

Dale Dorsey's account of Phil highlights the fact that *even moral agents sometimes perform amoral actions*. Moral (and non-moral) agents are constrained by their cognitive and circumstantial limitations. Recall that, per Dorsey's agency view, an agent must have reasons for acting *and be able to act upon such reasons*, or as a deliberative agent, for an action to be morally requirable. If an agent is unable to have reasons, or if an agent is unable to act upon the reasons that they have (as in Phil's scenario noted above), then such an action is not morally requirable. If such an action is not morally requirable, then performing (or failing to perform the action) is outside of the moral domain, or amoral.

Admittedly, regarding Phil's *failure* to open the safe as an example of an amoral action might seem a bit unclear because it is, more precisely, an *inaction* that is regarded as amoral. But because inactions, like actions, can be morally significant, amoral inactions are included in what I am simply referring to here as amoral actions. Both *failing to do a particular action* and *doing a particular action* can be of moral significance. Cognitive and circumstantial limitations, to which Dale Dorsey draws attention, might often imply that a moral agent is unable to act in particular ways. But such limitations might also influence what an agent does—not just what they fail to do. So, even though Phil cannot act upon the moral reason that he has to open the safe, his inaction is amoral. In sum, because certain inactions, or failures to act, have moral significance, they will be understood as included in the category of amoral actions.

To recap, then, there are three ways in which I am understanding amoral actions in this project. I do not claim that these three ways are exhaustive of the category of amoral actions, however. It may be that there are further types or varieties of amoral actions worth exploring. Nevertheless, for my purposes here, the three categories of amoral actions are as follows.

First, some amoral actions are amoral because an agent's deliberative agency is either lacking or compromised. That is, an agent either does not have a reason to act, or they cannot act upon the reason (or reasons) that they have. If someone is tempted to say that the actions of young children (who are still developing their deliberative agency) could be morally wrong but not blameworthy, for instance, then it seems that what justifies classifying their actions as within the moral domain is the perception of some degree of deliberative agency. An agent's capacity to exercise a sufficient degree of deliberative agency is necessary for their action to be within the moral domain because, without the capacity to exercise a sufficient degree of deliberative agency, their actions do not belong to them in a morally significant way. The capacity to act upon the reasons that an agent has is what makes their actions morally their own.

Second, some amoral actions are amoral because an agent's relational knowledge (which is required for moral agency) is either lacking or compromised. Deficiencies in relational knowledge compromise an agent's ability to act as a moral agent given the relational nature of morality itself. Relational knowledge is necessary, I believe, for an agent to see moral reasons *as* reasons for acting. When an agent's relational knowledge is lacking or compromised, there is a disconnection between an agent and other members of the moral community. In short, when an agent's relational knowledge is lacking or compromised, *moral* reasons for acting lose their normative force for the agent in question.

Third, some amoral actions are amoral because moral agents can become unable to exercise their deliberative and moral agencies due to cognitive or circumstantial limitations, as illustrated in Dale Dorsey's example of Phil. I noted earlier, in Dorsey's example, that Phil lacked deliberative agency since he could not act upon the reason that he had to open the safe in question. But that does not mean that the third category of amoral actions here simply collapses into the first category of amoral actions noted above. Phil's lack of deliberative agency is not like a young child's lack of deliberative agency. Because deliberative agency entails both having a reason to act and acting upon that reason, then there are at least two ways an agent can lack deliberative agency. For starters, an agent can fail to have a reason for acting, or they can fail to be able to deliberate about such reasons, as in the scenario of the young child throwing their food. The child in question lacks a sufficient degree of deliberative agency. Additionally, an agent can have the capacity to deliberate about their reasons for acting but be unable to act upon their reasons despite their deliberation, as in the example of Phil.

In practice, these latter deficiencies in deliberative agency can look very different from the former types of deficiencies. Indeed, one of the key insights from Dale Dorsey's account of amoral actions is that *moral agents*—not just non-moral agents—can, and do, perform amoral actions. So, an agent's deliberative and moral agencies can be constrained simply by the limited number of actions that a moral agent can perform at any given time. Recall that the problem of moral requirability is a problem for any ethical theory since it is possible that factors external to an agent—such as those dictated by one's situation or circumstance—uniquely constrain a moral agent's ability to act upon the reasons that they have. Actions that a moral agent could not help but do (or could not help but refrain from doing) in a situation are amoral.[31]

There is a common thread that weaves together the three categories of amoral actions that I have suggested here—namely that, when an agent's actions are not properly their own in a morally significant way, then such an action is amoral, or outside of the moral domain. I believe that each of the three categories of amoral actions describes ways in which an agent becomes morally estranged from their action—namely, when their deliberative agency is undermined, when their relational knowledge is compromised, or when situational factors significantly constrain their actions. Causally attributing an action to an agent is different from *morally* attributing an action to an agent, and that is true even when the action in question is regarded as intentional. I will examine each of these three ways of understanding amoral actions in the next chapter. For now, however, I will turn my attention to the difference between actions of suicide and suicidal acts.

ACTIONS OF SUICIDE AND SUICIDAL ACTS

My aim in this section is simply to draw attention to the fact that an action differs from an act insofar as an action is not merely what an agent does. To clarify, an *act* is simply what one does. Acts could entail twitches, falls, or seemingly automatic responses to stimuli in an agent's environment; and, in this way, acts need not be intentional. Acts can be attributed to non-human animals and to young children, as well as to fully rational adult human beings. An *action*, however, consists of willing both an *end*, or a goal, as well as the *means* of accomplishing the end, or goal, in question. Although some actions also might seem automatic, actions are inherently intentional. While non-human animals and young children (as well as fully rational adult human beings) seem able to perform actions and not just acts, there is nevertheless a difference between an act and an action. Put simply, to perform an action is to employ means-ends reasoning.

Suppose, for example, that a friend of yours informs you that they are going out to eat tonight at a new restaurant in town. It is, perhaps, typical to claim that your friend's action is *going out to eat tonight* or, perhaps, that their action is *dining at the new restaurant in town*. Actions described in these ways, however, miss something important that is constitutive of actions—namely, *why* such acts are chosen over other possible, competing acts that an agent could do. A fuller description of an *action* needs to entail both the goal and the means to that goal—that is, both the act and its end—which are unique to the action in question. Simply put, a complete description of an action needs to entail an agent's *intentionality* in their process of means-ends reasoning.

For instance, following the example above, suppose that your friend desires a change of scenery and, therefore, they wish to leave their home. They search among their options to eat dinner tonight, and they decide to try the new restaurant in town. In such a situation, a goal that they have is to enjoy a change of scenery, and they desire to accomplish that goal by eating dinner at the new restaurant in town. Or, alternatively, suppose that your friend just discovered many positive reviews regarding the food at the new restaurant in town, and they form the goal of trying the food at that restaurant. Now their goal is to eat at the new restaurant in town, and they plan to accomplish that goal by changing their scenery tonight through leaving their home. So, the automatic, knee-jerk tendency simply to say that your friend's action is *going out to eat tonight* or, perhaps, *dining at the new restaurant in town* both appear to under-describe the action in question.

To know their *action*, it is imperative to know both the goal and the means that they pursue in effort to achieve that goal. Their goal could be to leave their home, to get food (because they have none at home), to try a new restaurant, to gather with friends, and so on. Of course, it is also possible that your friend has more than one goal in mind, which influences the means that they pursue to accomplish such goals. They might, for instance, decide to meet a friend at the new restaurant where they also wish to dine. For such an action, their goal is both to try the new restaurant's food and to meet with a friend, which they plan to accomplish by going to the new restaurant tonight. To clarify, whether your friend is going to the new restaurant simply for a change of scenery, or whether they are going to the new restaurant because they desire to try the food at that restaurant, or whether they are going to the new restaurant to meet a friend, or some combination of such goals, each difference in their goals, or the means to achieve those goals, importantly expresses *different actions*.

Other examples abound. For instance, consider the following illustration. Suppose that two people, Smith and Jones, get into an argument. Further suppose that, during their argument, Smith pushes Jones with the intention of hurting Jones. Now suppose that, months after their conflict is resolved, Smith and Jones are waiting at a bus stop. A bus driver loses control of a bus, and Smith pushes Jones out of the way of the oncoming bus so that Jones does not get hurt. Smith clearly performed *different actions*, even though they share the same *act*—namely, pushing another person, Jones.

I do not wish to belabor such a simple point about actions, but I fear that it is a point that too often gets lost in discussions about suicide. That is, too often I believe that there is a tendency to claim that suicide *just is* the intentional *act* of killing oneself. Indeed, such a conception of suicide reveals itself in the common ways of speaking about a person who has *attempted* suicide or who has *contemplated* suicide. Presumably, what it is that they have attempted, or what it is that they have contemplated, is the *act of killing themselves*. But, by definition, suicide is inherently more complex than simply the act of killing oneself.

Per Kelly Posner and others, who authored a chapter in the *Oxford Handbook of Suicide and Self-Injury* entitled "The Classification of Suicidal Behavior," state that the word "suicide" is defined as an agent's "death resulting from intentional self-injurious behavior, associated with any intent to die as a result of the behavior."[32] There are, then, at least two ways in which intentions play a role in actions of suicide. Specifically, as an action, suicide entails both *intending* self-injurious behavior and *intending* to die as a result of the behavior. Such a definition of suicide appropriately captures both parts of an action described above—namely, intending an act because an agent also intends some end, or goal, of their act. But there are ambiguities in such a definition of "suicide." I will highlight several such ambiguities.

For starters, if suicide is primarily defined in terms of entailing the above two intentions—namely, intending self-injurious behavior and intending to die as a result of the behavior—then one might ask whether *death* is essential for an action of suicide to be regarded as an action of suicide? Certainly, death is included in the definition of "suicide" given above. Nevertheless, why not consider the possibility that those who intend self-injurious behavior (and who proceed to engage in such behavior), and who further intend to die as a result of that behavior, thereby, are engaging in an action of suicide?[33] For whatever reason or reasons, I recognize that it is not a common practice to define suicide in terms of intentionality alone. If such behavior and intentionality do not result in an agent's death, then it is commonplace to refer to such actions *not* as actions of suicide but, rather, as actions of *attempted suicide*. But notice that, by referring to such actions as attempted suicide, the word "suicide" becomes synonymous with an agent's death. Hence, the word "suicide" is regarded as a noun, not a verb.[34]

I wish to leave it an open question as to whether such actions ought to be regarded as such, or whether the common tendency to regard such actions as instances in which an agent has attempted suicide is an illustration of how language can lead our collective thinking astray. In any case, I am inclined to believe that the fact that we allow the word "suicide" to be a placeholder for an agent's death clouds our thinking about suicide, in general, and about the morality of suicide, in particular. Because I am focusing upon *actions* of suicide here, I will not be considering the word "suicide" as a noun here. Instead, I will regard the word "suicide" as a verb. The intentionality constitutive of suicide is what sets such actions apart, not the outcome.

The primacy of *intentionality* in actions of suicide (over a person's death) is, perhaps, made apparent by the fact that, intentionally engaging in self-injurious behavior without an intention to die because of the behavior, is not an action of suicide *even if the agent in question dies as a result of such intentional behavior*. My aim here, however, is not to take a stance on the usefulness of the language of attempted suicide. Rather, I only wish to highlight the fact that such language tends to align the word "suicide" more with an agent's death rather than with their intentionality.[35]

Although I do not wish to focus upon colloquial language here, I believe that the inadequacy of common ways of referring to suicide is not a trivial matter. Defining "suicide" in terms of an agent's death (or even as an act of intentional self-killing) suggests that the word "suicide" is not defined in a value-neutral way. Reluctance to define suicide in a value-neutral way implies the possibility that actions of suicide are simply *defined into the moral domain*. Believing, for example, that all killing is wrong, or regarding suicide as a homicide of oneself (or as self-murder), is sufficient to account for the social stigma against not only actions of suicide but also against those persons who suffer, or who have suffered, from suicide ideation.

William Styron, in his memoir *Darkness Visible: A Memoir of Madness*, observed a moral double-standard that is in place regarding deaths by suicide.[36] Specifically, Styron suffered from depression as a mental illness, and his own suicidal thoughts arose while in the grip of his illness. It seems clear that he had his personal experience of suicidal ideation in mind when he explained the moral double-standard in the following way:

> [i]t's quite natural that the people closest to suicide victims so frequently and feverishly hasten to disclaim the truth; the sense of implication, of personal guilt—the idea that one might have prevented the act if one had taken certain precautions, had somehow behaved differently—is perhaps inevitable. Even so, the sufferer—whether he has actually killed himself or attempted to do so, or merely expressed threats—is often, through the denial on the part of others, unjustly made to appear a wrongdoer.[37]

As Styron noted, loved ones left behind after a person's death by suicide might wonder whether there was anything that they could have done differently to have prevented their loss. Such questioning is understandable, of course. Yet while feelings of guilt might naturally arise among survivors, to many survivors their loss came by surprise. Their natural feelings of guilt ought not to implicate wrongdoing since they were unable to have foreseen another's death by suicide. Indeed, no one can know the depths of another's pain.

As Styron also noted, however, people are not as quick to attribute the same innocence to the victims of suicide. While there may have been nothing that loved ones could have done to intervene and, therefore, they are not to blame; there is a common belief that those who die by suicide could have acted differently and, therefore, that such actions are believed to be in the moral domain, at least on occasion.

Yet, writing about his own struggles with suicidal ideation in the grip of severe depression, William Styron expressed his "annoyance" with respect to a common misunderstanding about the kind of *choice* that suicide is.[38] Styron wrote that "the pain of severe depression is quite unimaginable to those who have not suffered it, and it kills in many instances because its anguish can no longer be borne."[39] Tellingly, Styron continued,

> [t]he prevention of many suicides will continue to be hindered until there is a general awareness of the nature of this pain. Through the healing process of time—and through medical intervention or hospitalization in many cases—most people survive depression, which may be its only blessing; but to the tragic legion who are compelled to destroy themselves there should be no more reproof attached than to the victims of terminal cancer.[40]

Per Styron, then, there is no more reason to believe that such a victim of suicide is somehow guilty of wrongdoing any more than the unsuspecting and heartbroken persons that they have left behind. Because Styron's account is insightful, I will be returning to it throughout this book.

For now, to help understand the definition of suicide, it is important to note that *suicidal acts* are not the same thing as *actions of suicide*, which is why I am choosing to use the rather clunky language of "actions of suicide" rather than suicidal actions in the hopes of avoiding confusion. An action of suicide must meet the above definition insofar as it must include both kinds of intentions.[41] So, intentional acts of self-killing ought *not* to be equated with actions of suicide. Strictly speaking, intentional acts of self-killing do not meet the above definition of suicide, which will be the definition of "suicide" that I am incorporating here.[42]

Additionally, there is an ambiguity with respect to an agent's *intention to die*. Usually, an agent's intention to die is interpreted as intending death for its own sake and, thereby, also choosing death for its own sake, or even desiring to die. Consequently, an agent's intention to die (as a result of their intentional self-injurious behavior) is often regarded as the end, or goal, of their action of suicide. While having an intention to die seems straightforward, intentionality is nevertheless ambiguous. Indeed, it seems more accurate to regard an agent's intention to die not as their end or goal but, rather, as the perceived *means* for some other goal or aim.[43]

When I claim that an agent's intention to die seems to track their means, rather than their goal, I have in mind actions in which an agent regards their own death as a way—notably the only conceivable way—to end their pain and suffering. Notice that either intending death for its own sake or intending death as a means to achieve some other end, or ends, are both consistent with the above definition of suicide. Even so, there are several reasons that support understanding an agent's intention to die as a *means* to some other end, or ends, in actions of suicide, rather than as an agent's end, or goal, of their action.

To be sure, consider the following illustration. Suppose, for instance, that someone intends to end their life by a drug overdose. So, it could be claimed that their goal is their own death, and that their means of reaching their goal is through a drug overdose. The obvious and difficult question, of course, is what led this person to pursue their own death as their goal? Were they experiencing unimaginable psychological or physical pain? Were they feeling an overwhelming sense of guilt or self-hatred? Were they plagued by relentless and disturbing thoughts that they should pursue their own death? Or, perhaps, were they feeling absolutely nothing at all, and a deep and disturbing sense of nullity took hold? My point here is that seeing one's death as the goal of one's action leaves open the antagonizing question of *why*—why *that goal* and not some other goal. As an account of an action, it appears incomplete.[44]

So, *prima facie*, it may seem as though overdosing is the *means* of the action of suicide, and the *end*, or goal, of the action is that person's death. But, again, if it is believed that such a person is only intending to overdose because they are intending their own death, then that account of their action of suicide is incomplete. It is incomplete because only one intention is identified, not two. In short, it is incomplete because it makes the mistake of regarding an implication of an intention as a separate, distinct intention.

To be clear, consider a couple of other illustrations. Suppose, for example, that a student intends to do well on an upcoming exam. Further suppose that the student in question believes that they will do well on the exam only if they study for the exam. So, the student in question both intends to study for the exam and intends to do well on the exam. But they are only intending to study for the exam because they intend to do well on the exam and, in their minds, doing well on the exam implies that they study for the exam. Indeed, it is difficult to see how intending to do well on the exam in question would not manifest itself in further intentions—such as studying in advance. But, in this illustration, studying is an implication of the student's intention to do well on the exam. It is not a further, stand-alone intention. That is, if the student in question no longer intends to do well on the exam, then they would no longer intend to study for it.

Or consider a person, Joe, who intends to ride a bus downtown. Because Joe intends to ride a bus, then he also intends to purchase bus fare. Suppose that riding a bus necessitates purchasing bus fare. In such a scenario, it might be natural to suppose that the goal of Joe's action is to ride a bus downtown, and that the means of reaching his goal is to purchase bus fare. Yet what is readily overlooked is that Joe *must* intend to purchase bus fare if he intends to ride the bus. Strictly speaking, then, such intentions are not distinct. If Joe no longer intends to ride a bus, then he no longer intends to purchase bus fare. Conversely, if Joe does not intend to purchase bus fare, then he no longer intends to ride a bus. Seemingly, both of Joe's intentions go together insofar as he cannot have one without the other.

Notice, however, that the intentions at issue in actions of suicide can—and, at least sometimes, do—come apart. It simply is not true that, regarding the intentions that constitute actions of suicide, they must go together insofar as a person cannot have one without the other. A person certainly can intend self-injurious behavior without intending to die as a result of that behavior. This is known as nonsuicidal self-injury. Likewise, a person can intend to die but not intend to engage in self-injurious behavior. Such a person might suffer from suicidal ideation, for example. My point is that the intentions involved in actions of suicide are, in fact, distinct, stand-alone intentions. Or, at the very least, an understanding of suicide as an action ought to entail the fact that the two intentions, which define actions of suicide, can come apart.

Hence, it is problematic to assume, for example, that the end or goal of an action of suicide is a person's death whereas the means of their action of suicide is just whatever means they intend to bring about their death. Actions of suicide are more complex than that. Simply framing a person's action of suicide as a person intending their death as the goal of their action, and whatever means brings about their death also happens to be the means to reach their goal, may not yet capture their *action* of suicide because, again, only one intention is identified instead of two.

My point here does not negate the fact that it is pragmatically imperative to separate a suicidal person from their identified means in which they are intending to die. For example, distancing a person from the pills that they plan to take to end their life is a necessary step for intervention. That is, separating such a person from their identified means makes the possibility of intervention possible, and it decreases the risk of such a person dying by suicide *in that moment*. The need to separate a suicidal person from their identified means in which they are intending to die is consistent, however, with the philosophical point that an action of suicide is not captured in a description in which only one intention is present—namely, *intending to die*. Rather, to capture an *action* of suicide, two intentions must be present such as, for example, *intending to end one's pain* and *intending to die* as the way to reach one's goal of ending one's pain.

But notice that intending to end one's pain as the goal of an action is a rather understandable and common intention to have. Taking an aspirin for a headache or an antacid for an upset stomach, for example, are not the sort of actions that are the subject of moral evaluations. Notice further, however, that intending one's death as the goal of an action and intending to relieve oneself of pain as the goal of an action are describing *different actions*. But it is usually only the former action and not the latter, which is often the focus of discussion regarding actions of suicide. My point here is that it must not be assumed that the goal of any action of suicide is that person's death. Rather, it is quite likely that, for any action of suicide, death is regarded as the *means* and not the goal, or aim, of such an action. I will regard actions of suicide, then, as actions which inherently entail both an *act* and an *end*, or goal. Furthermore, I will maintain that an agent's death (in actions of suicide) more accurately reflects the *means* (or the act) rather than the goal (or the end) of any action of suicide.[45]

Upon a moment's reflection, there are several ways in which a person might intend their own death only as a *means* to some other end, or goal, with respect to an action of suicide. Those suffering from depression or other mental illnesses may seek to end their psychological suffering through death. Similarly, persons who have been bullied or endured emotional or physical abuse may simply want the abuse to stop; and, consequently, they could see their death as the means for stopping the violence against them. Furthermore, those who protest for social, political, or religious causes may see their own death as advancing their causes. Likewise, persons who sacrifice themselves in an emergency in effort to save another person or persons might have foreseen their death as a necessary means to saving a life or lives. Each of these actions of suicide have a reactionary nature to them, where death is seen *as a means* to ending one's suffering, or as a means of standing up for one's principles, or as a means of saving the life of another or others. In short, rethinking the moral landscape of suicide necessitates rethinking the common assumptions made regarding actions of suicide. Additionally, rethinking the common assumptions made regarding actions of suicide includes acknowledging the possibility that a person's death does not need to be sought for its own sake in actions of suicide, nor must one's death be sought as the goal, or end, of their action of suicide.

Indeed, there is another conceptual problem that lurks for those who assume that, for any given action of suicide, the end or goal of that action must be that person's own death. To be sure, recall that Epicurus famously insisted that death is nothing among either the living or the dead. The point is that, if "I" cease to exist at my death, then it is difficult to imagine what it would it mean to desire one's own nullity. To be sure, I could not intend death *for myself* because there would be no self to experience death.

It seems possible that a person's beliefs about an afterlife or, specifically, about the kind of afterlife that they believe they will have, could motivate them to intend their death. But even postulating an afterlife does not let a person off the metaphorical philosophical hook. For starters, death would then be a gateway to an afterlife; and, hence, not sought for its own sake but, rather, still as a necessary means to some other end, or goal (namely, one's afterlife). But, more pointedly, a person's conception of the afterlife is something only believed and not known. Socrates made such a point in Plato's *Apology* when he claimed "[t]o fear death [. . .] is no other than to think oneself wise when one is not, to think one knows what one does not know."[46] Per Socrates, whether there is an afterlife and what the afterlife is like are simply unknown. Socrates' point was that, if I do not know what death is like, then I ought not to fear it. In a similar way, if I do not know what death is like, then I simply cannot *intend* it. That is, I cannot intend what I do not know. An agent's death, then, cannot be the end, or goal, of any action of suicide but, rather, it must be a *means* to what an agent perceives as their goal.

One upshot here is simply that the means-ends reasoning, which is characteristic of actions, is not a trivial matter. Indeed, in *Self-Constitution: Agency, Identity, and Integrity*, Christine Korsgaard recognizes that "an *action* [. . .] involves both an *act* and an *end*, an act done for the sake of an end."[47] But such a way of understanding actions of suicide adds complexity to such actions. Offering an interpretation of Immanuel Kant's philosophical standpoint regarding actions of suicide, Korsgaard explains the importance of being clear about both the act and its end. For example, one common interpretation of Kant's position regarding suicide in the *Groundwork for the Metaphysics of Morals* is that it is morally wrong to end one's life when one perceives one's future to be bleak and to include even more suffering.[48] What is morally wrong with dying by suicide in such a situation must be what Korsgaard notes is "the whole package"—namely, dying by suicide to avoid future suffering.[49] But, as Korsgaard further recognizes,

> [t]he question of rightness or wrongness of, say, [. . .] [dying by] suicide in order to save someone else's life, is left open, as a separate case to be tested separately. [. . .] [Dying by] suicide in order to save someone else's life is a *different action* from [. . .] [dying by] suicide in order to avoid the personal troubles that you foresee ahead.[50]

Although, of course, scholars disagree about how to interpret Kant, I believe that Korsgaard's attention to different actions of suicide is insightful. Korsgaard's point here is insightful because actions of self-sacrifice—namely, dying by suicide to save another's life—are *not* commonly thought to be among actions of suicide.

Indeed, the tendency to fail to see such self-sacrificial actions as actions of suicide speaks to the prevailing misconceptions regarding actions of suicide. Previously I noted problems associated with defining suicide, as well as common assumptions made about suicide. Such problems are made clearer when attention is shifted to trying to understand why actions of complete self-sacrifice are not typically regarded as actions of suicide, especially when they meet the definition of an action of suicide as stated above.

To be sure, failing to see an action of complete self-sacrifice (hereafter, self-sacrifice or a self-sacrificial action) as an action of suicide might be, in part, attributed to the tendency to define suicide as simply an *act* of intentional self-killing, which is somehow independent of means-ends reasoning. In short, failing to see an action of self-sacrifice as an action of suicide speaks to the tendency not to regard suicide as an action, but rather, at best, as simply an act. Once again, it confuses "suicide" as a noun with "suicide" as a verb.

Additionally, regarding suicide as simply an act of self-killing not only conflates an act with an action, but it also tends to define the word "suicide" as inherently immoral and, therefore, as within the moral domain. For example, a person might think that it is morally wrong to kill, and that suicide just is the act of killing oneself. Such a person would then conclude that suicide is morally wrong *by definition*. So, excluding self-sacrificial actions from actions of suicide speaks to the pervasiveness of attaching moral condemnation to the definition of suicide. A person's willingness to engage in self-sacrificial behavior for the safety and well-being of others certainly has a positive connotation to it and might even be called admirable. But the common tendency to define actions of suicide in negative, value-laden ways complicates the possibility of regarding actions of self-sacrifice as actions of suicide.

Finally, failing to see actions of self-sacrifice as actions of suicide is an implication of the assumption that *intending to die* must be interpreted as *intending to die for its own sake* and, importantly, not as a necessary means to some other end, or ends. Appreciating the fact that actions of self-sacrifice are to be included among actions of suicide, however, takes seriously the idea that an agent's foreseeable death could be regarded as a means to some other end, or ends, in actions of suicide rather than sought for its own sake.

Again, strictly speaking, dying by suicide in effort to save the life of another or others meets the definition of suicide noted above. Recall that actions of suicide refer to an agent's "death resulting from intentional self-injurious behavior, associated with any intent to die as a result of the behavior."[51] But I have noted the ambiguity here between intending to die for its own sake and intending to die as a means to some other end, or ends. I have further noted that actions of suicide seem to track those actions in which an agent intends to die only as a means to some other end or ends. Therefore, categorizing actions of self-sacrifice as actions of suicide acknowledges the fact that an agent's death could be intended only *indirectly* through an action of suicide (namely as a means to some other end, or ends).

Indeed, Shelly Kagan affirms that actions of self-sacrifice meet the definition of suicide; and he expresses the fact that self-sacrificial actions fall within the category of actions of suicide in his Open Yale Course on Death, where he notes the following:

> consider cases where your life is valuable and satisfying one, but you kill yourself nonetheless so as to help promote a cause that you deeply support or to protect your friends or loved ones. Strictly, it seems to me, cases like this *should also be counted as instances of suicide*, albeit atypical ones; and a complete discussion of suicide would certainly need to consider such cases as well.[52]

So, while it may be atypical to embrace a broader conception of what actions of suicide entail, it is necessary to do so on the pains of consistency. I will follow Kagan here and include self-sacrificial actions as among actions of suicide.

To take stock, I have emphasized that an action consists of both a goal and the means for achieving that goal. Actions of suicide, therefore, entail both a goal and a means for achieving that goal. I have further stressed that different means and different goals express different actions. One upshot is that actions of suicide are not monolithic but, indeed, entail much variation. For instance, per the definition of actions of suicide, self-sacrificial actions must also be included as actions of suicide.

There is further complexity with respect to understanding the nature of intentionality itself, which is at the heart of actions of suicide. Indeed, assuming that self-killing must be willed as the *goal* in actions of suicide fuels further problematic assumptions about actions of suicide—namely, that a person who engages in an action of suicide must *desire to die* or they somehow must be *choosing to die* since self-killing is their *intentional* goal. But notice that a person who sacrifices themselves to save other people, for example, need not desire to die. Yet their action, strictly speaking, meets the definition of suicide. The upshot is that, while actions of suicide cannot be understood independently of a person's intentions, it does not follow that such intentionality must also reflect one's desires and choices.

Intentions, at best, are difficult to identify. To be sure, notice that it is possible for a person to hold conflicting intentions. For example, if I break a window to escape a burning building, am I intending to break the window, or am I intending to escape the burning building, or both? If both, then in one act (namely, in the act of breaking a window) I would have multiple intentions. On the one hand, I do not intend to break a window insofar as I only intend to leave the burning building. Had there been a nearby door and a clear and safe pathway out of the building, then I would have chosen that option instead. On the other hand, however, because another known option is unavailable to me, and because I very much desire to escape the burning building, then I certainly *intend* to break the window, even with the realization that the additional oxygen will literally fuel the fire. The fact that it is possible to have multiple intentions—both to break the window and to leave the burning building—and even the fact that it is possible to have conflicting intentions (both to break the window and not to break the window in this situation) complicates any understanding of intentionality.[53] I will return to such problematic assumptions about intentionality in chapter three.

Lastly, I am employing the language of "actions of suicide" throughout this project. As I have noted above, by "actions" I have in mind both the act and the end to which the action is done. But, just like my reference to amoral actions here includes amoral *inactions*, such language of "actions of suicide" also entails *inactions* of suicide. Persons who die by suicide, for example, might do so through various types of *intentional inactions*—such as personal neglect, or a hunger strike, or by not getting out of the way of an ongoing train, and so on. Indeed, Émile Durkheim defined suicide as "the name given to any death that results indirectly or directly from a positive or negative act by the victim him or herself."[54] So, Durkheim's definition of suicide includes actions rendered "passive." To be clear, I aim to include such "passive" actions—or, rather, inactions—under the umbrella phrase *actions of suicide*. Inactions of suicide still meet the definition of suicide previously noted.

With these few preliminary points in mind, I will now turn to what I take to be the current landscape regarding the relationship between actions of suicide and the moral domain. In doing so, I hope to shed light upon why the amorality of suicide deserves attention.

ASSESSING THE CURRENT LANDSCAPE

I believe that the thesis that actions of suicide are amoral is bound to strike many people as counterintuitive or, at the very least, controversial. The common tendency, it seems, is to regard actions of suicide as actions within the moral domain, at least on occasion. Indeed, the dominant view appears to be that some, if not all, actions of suicide are immoral. The social stigma regarding suicide is evidence of this dominant view.

Furthermore, it is not difficult to see how the dominant view took hold. Likened to homicide, actions of suicide have been criminalized and, in some places, such actions are still criminalized.[55] Indeed, defining "suicide" not just as self-killing, but as *self-murder*, has contributed to regarding such actions as criminal in nature and, thereby, as punishable in some way (or at least as meriting sanctions). The criminalization of suicide is reflected in the use of the word "commit" with respect to suicide, as if a person is committing a crime. Fortunately, there has been a shift away from such language. Stating that someone has died by suicide is replacing talk of a person who has committed suicide, albeit rather slowly. Such a change in language is significant since how we speak of such actions reflects how we think about them and vice versa. Speaking of a value-neutral action as though it were inherently value-laden constrains how we think about the moral status of such an action. Unfortunately, given the prevalence of the dominant view, it seems that "suicide" is commonly defined into the moral domain.[56]

There is already evidence of the dominant view losing some of its appeal and popularity, however. Specifically, the acknowledgement of mental illnesses has called into question the criminalization of actions of suicide and, in turn, the moral status of such actions. While not lessening the stigmatization associated with suicide (since, unfortunately, there is also a social stigmatization associated with mental illnesses), regarding actions of suicide as stemming from a mental illness, or illnesses, has at least diminished the idea that such actions truly reflect a person's agency. A suicidal person needs help—not the threat of some kind of posthumous legal punishment.

In fact, it is perhaps tempting to say that, because actions of suicide are often the result of a mental illness, or illnesses, then those actions do not belong in the moral domain. But I will not be taking that route here for two reasons. First, attributing actions of suicide as stemming from an agent's mental illness may not be sufficient to speak to the morality of their action. That is, it seems possible to regard an action as within the moral domain—or, specifically, to follow the dominant view that suicide is wrong—but still to regard an agent as not blameworthy for their action. Their mental illness, or illnesses, would then be seen as excusing conditions. So, even if all actions of suicide could somehow be attributed either to a known or unknown underlying mental illness, the action itself might somehow still be regarded as inside the moral domain. But that is not my conclusion here. The claim that actions of suicide are amoral means that such actions themselves do not belong in the moral domain.

Second, it just does not seem as though all actions of suicide can be appropriately attributed to a known or unknown underlying mental illness or illnesses. Existential crises and horrendous life events, I believe, can be sufficient to trigger suicidal ideation even among those agents with otherwise healthy minds.[57] Whether the origins of suicidal ideation are rooted in mental illnesses, tragic life events, or some combination of the two remains an open question.

While it might seem obvious to conclude that any agent who engages in an action of suicide must also be suffering from depression (as a mental illness), I believe that we need to resist such a conclusion as universal. In resisting such a claim, I am following Andrew Solomon's lead. In his book *The Noonday Demon: An Atlas of Depression*, Solomon explains that the common assumption that suicidality is a symptom of depression ought to be called into question.[58] Solomon writes: "[a] clinician treating someone who is depressed and suicidal will in general focus on curing the depression. While curing the depression may help to forestall the suicide, it will not necessarily do so."[59] Solomon's cautionary remark regarding the treatment of suicide yields insight about how to understand the relationship between severe depression and suicide.

As Solomon explains, "[o]ne should not assume that suicidality can be lumped in with symptoms such as disrupted sleep; nor should one stop treating suicidality simply because the depression with which it has been associated seems to have lifted. Suicidality is an associated problem that requires its own treatment."[60] In other words, it is a mistake to regard suicidality as a symptom of depression since doing so compromises the treatment of suicidality. But if that is true, then it is a mistake to believe that suicidality ultimately reduces to an underlying depressive disorder. Requiring its own treatment suggests that suicidality is not merely a symptom of an underlying illness, or illnesses.

The idea that suicide ought not to be regarded as a symptom of a diagnosed or of an undiagnosed mental illness was noted by Émile Durkheim. Since Durkheim looked to social factors and conditions in his study of suicidality, it is unsurprising that he would reject the idea that the presence—or the possible presence—of a mental illness was the common thread that held together the varied reasons for why people die by suicide. Durkheim expressed his concern with understanding suicidality exclusively in terms of an underlying mental illness in the following way:

> while there are some actions of the insane that are peculiar to them and can serve to characterize madness, there are others which, on the contrary, they have in common with sane people, even though they appear under a particular guise in the mad. There is no reason, *a priori*, to put suicide into the first of these two categories. Of course, alienists proclaim that most suicides that they have known present all the signs of mental illness, but this evidence is not sufficient to resolve the matter. [. . .] In any case, one cannot derive a general law from such narrowly specialized evidence. From those suicides that they have known—who were, naturally, mentally ill—one cannot conclude anything about those that they have not observed—who are, moreover, far more numerous.[61]

Durkheim's claim here is insightful. He acknowledged, of course, that some persons who have died by suicide were, in fact, persons suffering from a mental illness. But he refused to make the hasty generalization of concluding that, because some persons who died by suicide suffered from a mental illness, then all such persons who die by suicide also must have been suffering from a mental illness.

There is a subtle difference between the views of Solomon and Durkheim as expressed above. Per Solomon, suicidality requires its own treatment, even when coinciding with a mental illness, such as depression. Whereas, according to Durkheim, suicidality simply does not need to coincide with either depression as a mental illness, or with any other mental illness. I do not see these views as in tension with each other, however. In fact, I aim to honor both insights. In doing so, I will not assume that suicidality is a symptom of depression, or any other mental illness, or illnesses, even while acknowledging that some persons who suffer from suicidality also suffer from a mental illness, or illnesses. Mere correlation, of course, is not causation. Furthermore, I will not assume either that suicidality is itself a mental illness, or that an underlying mental illness must be present—regardless of whether an illness has been diagnosed. Of course, these cautionary notes about suicidality are consistent with recognizing that some persons who engage in actions of suicide are also persons who suffer from a mental illness; and, furthermore, that at least some such persons who engage in actions of suicide do so due to suffering from a mental illness, or illnesses.

Thus far, I have characterized the current landscape regarding the relationship between actions of suicide and the moral domain in terms of the moral wrongness of actions of suicide as well as attributions of mental illness. While I believe that such views capture the most common and current views regarding the moral status of actions of suicide, it would be a mistake to present these two views as encompassing the entire landscape. There are other views that place actions of suicide as within the moral domain—namely, for instance, the view that all actions of suicide are morally permissible. In sum, such a view maintains that prohibitions against suicide are essentially prohibitions against bodily autonomy. Actions of suicide, therefore, are morally *permissible* out of respect for personal, bodily autonomy. I will return to address the idea that an action of suicide is morally permissible in chapter five. Additionally, in chapter five, I will briefly explore how the amorality of suicide can be sustained even in other, non-deontic ethical frameworks. In the meantime, however, I will focus upon seeing the amorality of suicide as countering the dominant view—namely, that suicide is morally wrong, at least on occasion.

CHARTING A NEW PATH

I will begin with a more thorough examination of amoral actions, which are actions outside of the moral domain. Again, I do not understand the account of amoral actions that I present here to be an exhaustive account of the category of amoral actions, as I recognize that there could be other amoral actions not accounted for here. Nevertheless, there are amoral actions in which an agent's deliberative agency is either lacking or compromised. Such actions are not done by an agent *as a deliberative agent*. It might be helpful to think of such actions as more akin to events. When the actions of young children and non-human animals are regarded as amoral, it seems that what they are lacking is such deliberative agency in their means-ends reasoning. Simply put, their actions are not their own, morally speaking.

Second, even with deliberative agency, an agent might lack the ability to appreciate moral reasons for acting. I have suggested here that relational knowledge, which is acquired socially, is essential to appreciating moral reasons. Hence, when an agent's relational knowledge is either lacking or compromised, then they will be unable to act as a moral agent, *even if* they retain their ability to act as a deliberative agent.

Third, even moral agents who can exercise their deliberative agency might find their circumstances constrained. The actions available to them to perform could be so severely limited (or perceived to be so severely limited) such that they do not have a choice about what to do. Circumstantial and cognitive limitations, therefore, can impede an agent's ability to do, or to refrain from doing actions that align with their will. Phil, for example, did not choose to keep the safe closed. Rather, Phil's circumstances impeded his ability to open the safe in question. In chapter two, I will explore each of these three ways an action is amoral in more detail.

In chapter three, I will turn my attention more explicitly to actions of suicide. I follow Edwin Shneidman and, in turn, Thomas Joiner to make the point that the frustration of psychological needs lies at the heart of actions of suicide.[62] As social beings, we have several psychological needs. But, following Shneidman and Joiner, I will focus upon only three—namely the need for autonomy, belonging, and competence.[63] Despite variations in actions of suicide, the commonality of such actions is seen in the ways in which these psychological needs are experienced, or perceived, as being either lost or severely threatened.

Exploring each of these three psychological needs individually mirrors the three categories of amoral actions explained in chapter two. For example, the frustration of the need for autonomy (which seems to be at root with respect to some actions of suicide) is an indication that an agent's deliberative agency is lacking or compromised.[64] Likewise, when an agent's psychological need for belonging is lacking then, so too, is their relational knowledge. That is, an agent's psychological needs for autonomy and belonging seem to be able to build deliberative and moral agency, respectively, when they are met, and to compromise such agencies when they are unmet. Additionally, actions in which an agent experiences or perceives their options to be severely limited frustrates an agent's need for competence. The upshot is that, when these psychological needs are unmet in significant ways (namely, in ways that lead an agent to consider engaging in an action of suicide), then an agent's ability to act upon moral reasons as a deliberative, moral agent is also undermined in some way or ways. Hence, actions of suicide are amoral.

In chapter four, I will explain, and respond to, several objections to the thesis that actions of suicide are amoral. Although I will be unable to anticipate and to respond to all such objections, my hope is that some of the main concerns will be addressed. Lastly, in chapter five, I will explore the implications of my thesis. I will also suggest further areas of research.

My objective here is to promote discussions of actions of suicide in meaningful and healthy ways—namely, in ways independent of moral evaluations. It is my hope that regarding actions of suicide as outside of the moral domain, or as amoral, helps to promote compassion and humility, as well as those conversations that can save lives. Toward that end, if this book advances healthy and meaningful conversations about suicide outside of the moral domain and, thereby, free from moral judgment, then it will have been successful.

NOTES

1. The avoidance of discussing suicide might be explained (at least in part) to a myth that discussing suicide with someone is somehow giving them the idea to die by suicide. For example, in the United States, the National Institute of Mental Health published an online series of frequently asked questions about suicide. Among those questions appeared the question, "[d]oes asking someone about suicide put the idea in their head?" The response to this question is "no." Furthermore, the response to the above question also stated that "[a]sking someone directly, 'are you thinking of killing yourself?' can be the best way to identify someone at risk for suicide." Please see: https://www.nimh.nih.gov/health/publications/suicide-faq

2. For more information regarding the American Foundation for Suicide Prevention's educational program, *Talk Saves Lives*™, please see: https://afsp.org/talk-saves-lives/

3. I am not alone in thinking that a value-neutral approach to suicide is needed. For example, Michael Cholbi also suggests a need for a value-neutral way of speaking about the topic of suicide. In his 2011 book *Suicide: The Philosophical Dimensions* (Buffalo: Broadview Press), Cholbi writes: "I propose [. . .] that a suitable characterization of suicide needs to [. . .] aspire to being descriptive rather than value-laden" (19). But Cholbi immediately cautions readers that such a shift "is easier said than done" (Ibid.).

4. For example, a couple of the resources available in the United States for such support include the National Suicide Prevention Lifeline (988), Crisis Text Line (text "Home" to 741741), and, for LGBTQ+ youth, there is the Trevor Project, (Trevor Lifeline 1-866-488-7386; TrevorText 678–678; and TrevorChat https://www.thetrevorproject.org/). The American Foundation for Suicide Prevention (AFSP) and the National Alliance on Mental Illness (NAMI) are further resources.

5. For more on the neuroscience of suicide, please see: Kees Van Heeringen's *The Neuroscience of Suicidal Behavior* (2018).

6. That is, there seems to be a common tendency to regard all actions that moral agents do (or can do) as either morally impermissible or morally permissible. In other words, there seems to be a common tendency to regard *all* actions as within the moral domain. But I wish to challenge this idea. Regarding all actions as either morally impermissible or morally permissible, for example, overlooks an important aspect of actions themselves—namely, that actions are done by *agents* employing some kind of means-ends reasoning. Therefore, some attention to agency is necessary with respect to categorizing actions as within the moral domain. Simply put, when determining whether an action falls within the moral domain it is not enough simply to know *what* is done. We also must consider *who* is performing the action in question, as well as *why* they are performing *that* action.

7. I will draw upon the distinction between an *act* and an *action* in what follows. But, arguably, throwing one's food could be an act—not an action—if it is done unintentionally, or without an end, or goal, in mind. I, however, will proceed to assume that the child in question could have *some* degree of intentionality. I am proceeding to make such an assumption to motivate the possibility that the child's action could

be regarded as within the moral domain. An (unintentional) act does not belong in the moral domain.

8. Blameworthiness and praiseworthiness are secondary judgments, which means that an action is first evaluated as within the moral domain. An agent is then blamed or praised for their action depending upon several factors, including their knowledge of what it is that they were doing and why they were engaging in the action in question. So, it would be meaningless to assess whether the lion in the example is blameworthy for its action of attacking the gazelle because such an action is not regarded as in the moral domain.

9. One way to think about what it means to be able to exercise a sufficient degree of deliberative agency is by considering the degree to which an agent is regarded as acting voluntarily. That is, if an agent performs an action either unwittingly or unknowingly (and so, non-voluntarily), then it seems that they would not be acting upon a *reason* that they have; and, if they are not acting for any reason that they have, then they are not acting *deliberatively*. Moreover, all involuntary actions are also actions in which agents are not acting deliberatively.

Voluntary actions are not a reliable indication of an agent's deliberative agency, however. A child, for example, could voluntarily throw their food without exercising deliberative agency. So, while deliberative agency appears to presume that an agent acts voluntarily; it is not true that acting voluntarily is an indication that the agent in question is exercising their deliberative agency. Moreover, the possibility that some actions could be non-voluntary, or the possibility that some actions could include a mixture of both voluntary and involuntary features, further complicates ways of discerning whether actions are sufficiently voluntary. Hence, I will be focusing upon an agent's deliberative agency in this project instead of an agent's ability to act voluntarily.

10. Certainly, I am not making any claim about the cognitive capacities of lions here which, of course, is beyond the scope of this project. Rather, my claim here is only that lions—like other non-human animals—are not commonly regarded as being able to exercise the capacity for rational deliberation that is thought to be the hallmark of decision-making among rational, adult human beings.

11. If the child in question completely lacks deliberative agency, then throwing their food across the room is an act, not an action. Furthermore, as an unintentional act, it is outside of the moral domain.

12. Dale Dorsey, "Amorality," *Ethical Theory and Moral Practice*, Vol. 19, No., 2 (April 2016): 330.

13. Dale Dorsey, "Amorality," 331.

14. Dale Dorsey, "Consequentialism, Cognitive Limitations, and Moral Theory," in *Oxford Studies in Normative Ethics*, Vol. 3, ed. Mark Timmons (New York: Oxford University Press, 2013), 190.

15. Dale Dorsey, "Consequentialism, Cognitive Limitations, and Moral Theory," 190.

16. Dale Dorsey, "Consequentialism, Cognitive Limitations, and Moral Theory," 191, Dorsey's emphasis.

17. Dale Dorsey, "Consequentialism, Cognitive Limitations, and Moral Theory," 192.

18. Dale Dorsey, "Consequentialism, Cognitive Limitations, and Moral Theory," 192, Dorsey's emphasis, footnote omitted.

19. Earlier I noted that deliberative agency entails an agent's ability to reflect upon possible reasons for acting, to imagine possible consequences of their actions, and to weigh their priorities considering both possible actions and their respective, perceived consequences. I believe that such a characterization of deliberative agency is consistent with Dale Dorsey's agency view in which an agent must both be able to have reasons and to act upon the reasons that they have. Indeed, I believe that the former characterization of deliberative agency is implied in Dorsey's agency view. So, my adoption here of Dorsey's agency view as the way in which I am understanding deliberative agency is in keeping with my earlier comments regarding what deliberative agency entails.

20. I am making only a generalization here—namely, that there are at least *some* non-human animals and at least *some* young children whose actions are amoral due to lacking a sufficient degree of deliberative agency. The possibility that there are some non-human animals who can exercise a degree (perhaps a sufficient degree) of deliberative agency, or the possibility that there are some young children who can exercise a degree (again, perhaps, a sufficient degree) of deliberative agency, does not undermine the point that I am making here.

21. Eleonore Stump, *Wandering in Darkness*: *Narrative and the Problem of Suffering* (Oxford: Oxford University Press, 2010), 51, Stump's emphasis. For more on Stump's account of the knowledge of persons, please see: Eleonore Stump, *Philosophical Theology and the Knowledge of Persons* (Eugene, OR: Cascade Books, 2023).

22. See Frank Jackson, "Epiphenomenal Qualia," *The Philosophical Quarterly*, Vol. 32, No. 127 (1982): 127–36.

23. Eleonore Stump, *Wandering in Darkness*, 53, footnote omitted.

24. Axel Seemann, "Person Perception," *Philosophical Explorations*, Vol. 11, No. 3 (2008): 245–62.

25. Axel Seemann, "Person Perception," 249.

26. Uta Frith, *Autism: Explaining the Enigma* (Malden: Blackwell Publishers, 1989), 11. There are, of course, degrees of autism.

27. Jim Sinclair, "Bridging the Gaps: An Inside-Out View of Autism (or, Do You Know What I Don't Know?), in *High-functioning Individuals with Autism*, eds. Eric Schopler and Gary B. Mesibov (New York: Plenum Press, 1992), 300.

28. Jim Sinclair, "Bridging the Gaps," 300.

29. Dale Dorsey, "Amorality," 332.

30. I thank Robert Garcia and Juliana Kazemi for raising the point that Phil still needs to *do something*. For example, at the very least he needs to *try* to open the safe, or he needs to warn others of the very serious calamity that is about to ensue. If Phil does not do anything at all, then *that* would be morally evaluable and, hence, within the moral domain. Due to the separability of actions, however, I believe that Dale Dorsey's point remains—namely, that Phil's failure to open the safe in question is

amoral. I believe that Phil's failure to open the safe in question is amoral even though, for example, Phil's failure to try to open the safe, or his failure to warn others, are squarely within the moral domain.

31. To clarify, amoral actions in the first category aim to capture those actions among non-moral agents who lack a sufficient degree of deliberative agency (and, of course, moral agency). Amoral actions in the second category aim to capture those actions among agents with a sufficient degree of deliberative agency, but who lack moral agency. Finally, amoral actions in the third category aim to capture those actions among agents who otherwise have both their deliberative and moral agencies in-tact, but who cannot act upon the reasons that they have due to situational or circumstantial constraints. Hence, technically, the third category of amoral actions more accurately reflects an agent's deliberative agency as compromised, rather than as lacking.

32. Kelly Posner, Beth Brodsky, Kseniya Yershova, Jacqueline Buchanan, and John Mann, "The Classification of Suicidal Behavior," in *The Oxford Handbook of Suicide and Self-Injury*, ed. Matthew K. Nock, 7–22 (New York: Oxford University Press, 2014), 11.

33. For more on defining suicide strictly in terms of intentionality (without emphasis upon external factors, such as an agent's death), please see Gavin J. Fairbairn's *Contemplating Suicide: The Language and Ethics of Self-Harm* (New York: Routledge, 1st Edition, 1995).

34. I thank Geolon (Geo) Lyons for raising this concern about which part (or parts) of speech that the word "suicide" depicts, and whether these different parts of speech are being equivocated in discussions about suicide.

35. Of course, in addition to the language of *attempted suicide*, there are other phrases that are also problematic, such as *failed suicide*, *completed suicide*, and *successful suicide*. Incidentally, such phrases likewise regard "suicide" as simply referring to a person's death at their own hand. The idea of the word "suicide" consists of an agent having two distinct intentions is, unfortunately, lost upon the prevalence of such phrases.

36. William Styron, *Darkness Visible: A Memoir of Madness* (New York: Random House, 1990).

37. William Styron, *Darkness Visible*, 30.

38. William Styron, *Darkness Visible*, 33.

39. William Styron, *Darkness Visible*, 33.

40. William Styron, *Darkness Visible*, 33.

41. I will be focusing upon the two intentions of suicide in my project here since I am focusing upon the amorality of suicide in this project. I will assume the definition of suicide as cited above, namely that actions of suicide refer to an agent's "death resulting from intentional self-injurious behavior, associated with any intent to die as a result of the behavior" (Kelly Posner, Beth Brodsky, Kseniya Yershova, Jacqueline Buchanan, and John Mann, "The Classification of Suicidal Behavior," 11). But, for the reasons noted above, I will largely set aside the issue of whether an agent's death is a necessary component of suicide. Hence, I believe that, if actions of suicide are

amoral, then those actions commonly deemed as *suicide attempts*, for example, are also amoral.

42. It is unclear what *intentional acts of self-killing* might mean. For instance, suppose that a person *intends* to smoke cigarettes knowing the health risks involved in doing so. Further suppose that the person in question dies from health complications caused by them smoking cigarettes. Construing their death as an act of *intentional self-killing* seems inappropriate because they only intended to smoke cigarettes. Such deaths are not at issue in discussions of suicide. Death is neither intended as an end, or goal, of smoking cigarettes nor is death intended as a means to some other end or goal. So, it is problematic to regard actions of suicide as simply intentional acts of self-killing. A more robust understanding of suicide is necessary.

43. For example, Harry Frankfurt in *The Reasons of Love* (Princeton: Princeton University Press, 2004) wrote: "[e]ven of people who [. . .] [die by] suicide because they are miserable, it is generally true that they love living. What they would really like, after all, would be to give up not their lives but their misery" (47).

44. The overdose example is like the restaurant example noted above. Recall that just claiming that your friend's action is dining at the new restaurant in town is incomplete because it does not entail the end or goal of your friend's action—namely, *why* are they dining at the new restaurant. Actions are inherently more complex than acts.

45. One challenge to the idea that, in actions of suicide, an agent's death is more accurately reflected in the *means* of their action rather than in their *end*, or goal, of their action are actions of suicide in which a person reports experiencing a kind of death drive. For example, Clancy Martin reports experiencing something like a repeated drive toward death in his book *How Not to Kill Yourself: A Portrait of the Suicidal Mind* (New York: Pantheon Books, 2023). Specifically, Martin explains his repeated actions of suicide in the Preface of his book where he writes: "I have come to understand that I am addicted to the thought of suicide" (xxiii). Yet I do not regard the possibility that a person might experience a death drive, or an addiction to actions of suicide, as indicating that their death is desired as an end, and not as a means, of their action. Indeed, Martin also writes: "I've lived nearly all my life with two incompatible ideas in my head: *I wish I were dead* and *I'm glad my suicides failed*. I've never once thought, *If only I'd successfully killed myself, I would have been spared all this living I've done*" (xiv, Martin's emphasis). Martin's account suggests that, although he has repeatedly been suicidal, his death is not something that he desires.

46. Plato's *Apology*, trans. G. M. A. Grube, in *Plato: Complete Works*, ed., John M. Cooper, (Indianapolis: Hackett Publishing Company, Inc., 1997), 27, 29a.

47. Christine Korsgaard, *Self-Constitution: Agency, Identity, and Integrity* (New York: Oxford University Press, 2009), 11, Korsgaard's emphasis.

48. Immanuel Kant, *Grounding for the Metaphysics of Morals* (1785), third edition, trans. James W. Ellington (Indianapolis: Hackett Publishing Company, 1993), 30–31. All references to Kant's *Groundwork for the Metaphysics of Morals* will come from this translation; and so, I will reference this work as simply Kant's *Grounding*.

49. Christine Korsgaard, *Self-Constitution: Agency, Identity, and Integrity*, 11.

50. Christine Korsgaard, *Self-Constitution: Agency, Identity, and Integrity*, 11, emphasis added.

51. Kelly Posner, Beth Brodsky, Kseniya Yershova, Jacqueline Buchanan, and John Mann, "The Classification of Suicidal Behavior," 11.

52. Shelly Kagan, *Death* (New Haven: Yale University Press, 2012), 320, emphasis added.

53. Intentionality, of course, is further complicated by the fact that it seems possible that not every intention that a person has will be consciously known to them. Additionally, I originally had incorporated the example of being trapped inside a burning building to illustrate clearly conflicting intentions. Yet it is not lost on me that some persons who have experienced suicide ideation have also reported feeling trapped, or as if they were trying to escape a burning building (for example, see Clancy Martin, *How Not to Kill Yourself*, 201–202 and William Styron, *Darkness Visible*, 50).

54. Émile Durkheim, *On Suicide* (1897) trans. Robin Buss (New York: Penguin Books, 2006), 17.

55. For more on legal issues regarding suicide, please see: Susan Stefan, *Rational Suicide Irrational Laws*: *Examining Current Approaches to Suicide in Policy and Law* (New York: Oxford University Press, 2016).

56. For example, in Jennifer Michael Hecht's book *Stay: A History of Suicide and the Arguments Against It* (New Haven: Yale University Press, 2013), Hecht writes: "I think it is right to say, along with many incisive thinkers throughout history, that suicide is wrong" (226). Hecht seems to be passionate about suicide prevention. Indeed, the wrongness of suicide is construed as fueling an incentive to *stay*. But I question whether maintaining the dominant view that suicide is wrong is either an accurate description of what is happening or a helpful approach to suicide prevention.

57. Arguably, someone might suggest here that, say, horrendous life events might only be triggering to those with an underlying mental illness. Or other people might suggest that, even if something like horrendous life events themselves are sufficient for an agent to engage in suicidal ideation, once they engage in suicidal ideation, they, thereby, have a mental illness (e.g., depression). My aim here is not to take a stance on this open question about which comes first—the illness or the ideation. Rather, my aim here is just to acknowledge the fact that it is, indeed, an open question. To the best of my knowledge, there is a lack of consensus regarding the role of mental illnesses with respect to actions of suicide. My point here is just to acknowledge that the assumption that there is an underlying mental illness among any agent who performs an action of suicide (or even among any agent who might have suicidal ideation) is, in fact, an assumption.

58. Specifically, Andrew Solomon notes in his book *The Noonday Demon: An Atlas of Depression* that "[m]any depressives never become suicidal," and that many people who die by suicide were not also suffering from depression (New York: Touchstone, 2001), 243.

59. Andrew Solomon, *The Noonday Demon*, 243.

60. Andrew Solomon, *The Noonday Demon*, 243–44.

61. Émile Durkheim, *On Suicide*, 39–40.

62. Especially, I will be drawing upon their following works: Edwin S. Shneidman, *The Suicidal Mind* (New York: Oxford University Press, 1996) and Thomas Joiner, *Why People Die by Suicide* (Cambridge, MA: Harvard University Press, 2005).

63. The psychological needs of autonomy, relatedness, and competence comprise what is known as the self-determination theory of human motivation, which stems from the work of Edward L. Deci and Richard M. Ryan. See, for example, Edward L. Deci and Richard M. Ryan "The 'What' and 'Why' of Goal Pursuits: Human Needs and the Self-Determination of Behavior," *Psychological Inquiry*, Vol. 11, No. 4 (2000): 227–68. Yet these three needs also are evident in the works of Edwin Shneidman (*The Suicidal Mind*) and Thomas Joiner (*Why People Die by Suicide*). Specifically, I will appeal to Shneidman's work when focusing upon the psychological need for autonomy, and I will appeal to Joiner's work when focusing upon relatedness and competence. The psychological needs of relatedness and competence are evident in two of the conditions that Joiner attributes to an increased risk for suicide—namely, a thwarted sense of belonging (or the frustration of the need for relatedness) and a perceived sense of burdensomeness (or the frustration of the need for competence).

64. I am not claiming that the frustration of a psychological need of say, autonomy, *causes* a loss of one's deliberative agency. Rather, I am concerned about instances in which an agent is engaging in an action of suicide. If Shneidman and Joiner are correct, then what is lacking is a psychological need. For example, given the lack of the psychological need for autonomy in any given action of suicide, then deliberative agency is compromised with respect to that action. Such an action of suicide is, thereby, outside of the moral domain. Perhaps it is possible that an agent's deliberative agency is first compromised, and, as a result, such an agent is lacking in their psychological need of autonomy. I am not concerned about the direction of causation here as I suspect that the fulfillment of psychological needs on the one hand, and an agent exercising both deliberative and moral agencies on the other hand, are more intertwined than I am suggesting here.

Chapter Two

Amoral Actions

In the previous chapter, I noted that there are three ways in which I am understanding amoral actions. Again, just to clarify, I do not claim that these three ways of understanding amoral actions are exhaustive of the category of amoral actions. There could be other ways in which an action is amoral. Even so, I believe that these three ways of understanding amoral actions outlined here are common ways of understanding amoral actions. I also believe that these three ways of understanding amoral actions help to elucidate the ways in which actions of suicide are amoral. In this chapter, I will explore each of these three ways of understanding amoral actions in more detail. I will begin by focusing upon amoral actions in which an agent's deliberative agency is lacking or compromised. I will then proceed to examine amoral actions in which an agent's relational knowledge is lacking or compromised. Finally, I will turn my attention to those amoral actions that moral agents perform when they are under constraining circumstances or conditions, which make them unable to act upon the (moral) reasons that they have for acting.

DELIBERATIVE AGENCY AND A SENSE OF SELF

Recall that, per Dale Dorsey, deliberative agency entails that an agent not only has a reason to act but also that they can act upon that reason.[1] Because it is thought that non-human animals and young children are either unable, or not yet able, to appreciate reasons for action and to perform actions based upon reasons, then any action that they perform is an amoral action. Notice that I am leaving open the possibility that such agents can perform actions—that is, they can employ some kind of means-ends reasoning. But the ability to employ means-ends reasoning as a *deliberative* agent—that is, the ability to deliberate and to reflect upon the reasons that guide their actions—is believed to be lacking in (at least some) non-human animals and in young children.[2] Hence, their actions are amoral.

My objective in this section is to explain what exercising deliberative agency entails. Specifically, I will suggest here that the ability to exercise deliberative agency with respect to any action entails a sense of self. That is, without a sense of self, an agent cannot act as a deliberative agent. In short, a sense of self provides a framework from which an agent deliberates. The upshot is that when an agent lacks a sense of self, then their deliberative agency is also lacking and, hence, their actions are amoral. Actions within the moral domain must be attributable to agents in a more robust way than simply causally. That is, subjecting an agent's actions to moral evaluation assumes a kind of ownership of those actions. Such actions meaningfully belong to the agent in question.

But what is a sense of self, and how can an agent have a sense of self, especially while philosophers continue to debate about whether there are, in fact, selves?[3] Regarding the latter question, I will follow Simon Blackburn's lead here.[4] In his work on self-love, Blackburn notes that it is regrettable that the phenomenon of self-centeredness, for example, does not "wither because of metaphysical puzzles" about the existence of selves.[5] Blackburn's point is that, while a working definition of a *self* may seem elusive, the phenomenon of creating and maintaining a conception of our-*selves* is not.

To clarify, Blackburn writes that "we talk of self-abasement, self-awareness, self-belief, self-control, self-denial, self-disgust, self-esteem, and so on through the alphabet, past self-hatred and self-love to self-respect, self-searching, self-trust, and self-violence."[6] What is particularly insightful about the extensive list that Blackburn provides is that he uses this list to show that "with a few exceptions we can have just about any attitude toward ourselves that we have toward other people, or even to things in the world."[7] Moreover, taking-up different attitudes toward oneself is a practice so common that it cannot be readily discarded.

Following Blackburn then, it suffices for my purposes here to identify a *self* as an image or a conception that a reflective agent has regarding their life. In reflecting upon one's beliefs, desires, or even upon one's past, the self becomes an "other." Regarding the self as an other is, in fact, a common practice. Indeed, it is through relating to oneself that the experience of guilt becomes possible. Harry G. Frankfurt explained that

> the self-awareness that is characteristic of human beings makes us susceptible to an inner division in which we separate from and objectify ourselves. This puts us in a position to assess the motivating forces by which we happen to be impelled, and to determine which of them to accept and which to resist.[8]

So, Frankfurt understood that it is possible for an agent to relate to themselves given the self-awareness that is characteristic of human beings—namely, reflecting upon one's actions, goals, and values, for instance, entails relating to oneself as an *other*.

Upon a moment's reflection, it is not difficult to see how acting as a deliberative agent requires a sense of self. For starters, an agent's values and their prioritization of their values provides a framework from which they can deliberate. After all, a deliberative agent acts not only *upon* a reason but also *for* that reason, or reasons. It follows that deliberative agency also must require that an agent can reasonably anticipate certain outcomes and to imagine themselves in some future state or time. Furthermore, exercising deliberatively agency assumes that an agent has a way to adjudicate among possible actions. An agent's sense of self, then, is necessary for deliberative agency because it makes possible such adjudication. The ability to conceive of different possible consequences, and the ability to imagine themselves in some future state, as well as the ability to adjudicate among such options, demands higher-order reasoning which, understandably, some agents seem to lack. Actions, then, done in which an agent is unable to anticipate certain outcomes, or unable to imagine themselves in a future state, or unable to adjudicate among their possible actions are amoral.

Admittedly, someone might object to the quick way in which I am dismissing metaphysical claims about the self. But I believe that such concerns are irrelevant in discussions about an agent *exercising* their deliberative agency. To be sure, consider David Hume's view of the concept of a metaphysical entity denoted by the word "self." Hume's view is postulated as a no-self view since he denied understanding a self as a metaphysical entity. Specifically, as Hume explained,

> when I enter most intimately into what I call *myself*, I always stumble on some particular perception or other, of heat or cold, light or shade, love or hatred, pain or pleasure. I never catch *myself* at any time without a perception, and never can observe anything but the perception.[9]

Nevertheless, Hume seemed to have maintained a view that resembles what I am calling here a sense of self.

Consider, for example, Hume's attitude toward suicide. Specifically, Hume did not appear to believe that suicide could be morally wrong or unreasonable in a situation in which "a malefactor [is] justly condemned to a shameful death."[10] Hume reasoned that such a malefactor's action of suicide does no more harm either to himself or to the society in which he is justly condemned.

Setting aside the morality of suicide for a moment, I wish to draw attention to Hume's reasoning *about* the morality of suicide. Hume assumed that agents (in this case, the malefactor in question) have what I am calling here a sense of self. That is, Hume characterized the malefactor in question as being aware and reflective about their interests, as reasoning about their options, and as imagining *themselves* as further disgraced by such a "shameful death" at the hands of the State. If such an agent lacked what I am calling here a sense of self, then adjudicating among their options as Hume suggested would be impossible. Again, I wish to follow Simon Blackburn here in claiming that having and maintaining a sense of self is a rather common practice. Moreover, having and maintaining a sense of self is a practice that need not demand that there exists a self as a metaphysical entity, or even that an agent's sense of self is somehow constant and unchanging.

So, even if David Hume did not believe in an ontological *entity* of self, it seems clear that he thought that an agent could still exercise what I am calling here a sense of self—namely, that an agent could prioritize their values, anticipate possible actions and their consequences, imagine *themselves* in some future state, and evaluate their options. My point here is that I believe that, while metaphysical discussions about what constitutes a self are very interesting and much needed, such discussions are worthy of attention elsewhere. It is sufficient for my purposes simply to acknowledge that being capable of exercising deliberative agency implies that an agent is also capable of weighing possible courses of action that align most with their desired outcome. When an agent loses their sense of self, then they can no longer weigh possible courses of action that align with their desired outcome. In short, when an agent loses their sense of self, then they can no longer exercise their deliberative agency.

An agent can lack a sense of self in several ways. Perhaps an agent lacks self-consciousness. Or perhaps an agent with self-consciousness lacks the ability to reflect upon alternative courses of action, for instance. Or perhaps an agent lacks the ability to consider what they would want in the future.

An agent's sense of self also can be compromised. For example, perhaps the degree to which an agent can predict and evaluate alternative courses of action is insufficient. Or perhaps the degree to which an agent can prioritize their values falls short of entailing that such an agent can act upon the reasons that they have. When an agent's sense of self is either lacking or compromised, then their deliberative agency is either lacking or compromised. When an agent's deliberative agency is either lacking or compromised, then their corresponding action, or actions, are amoral. The actions of such an agent can be attributed to them only causally, but not morally. The reason why such actions cannot be attributed to them in a moral sense is because such actions do not reflect who they are. Their actions are not the product of them acting upon a reason that they have; or, in other words, their actions do not reflect their choices.

The word "choice" is a loaded term—at least philosophically. By "choice," I do not intend to make any claims about free will. Whether agents have free will (in the libertarian sense) is also a topic worthy of discussion elsewhere. Indeed, I wish to remain neutral in the debate between incompatibilists and compatibilists about free will, as I do not wish to isolate either camp. If it turns out that we have free will (in the libertarian sense) then, of course, "choice" tracks an agent's (libertarian) free will. But if it turns out that we do not have free will (in the libertarian sense), then "choice" tracks only our presupposition of free will. So, making a *choice* does not need to entail that an agent could have done otherwise, or even that there were several options for the agent in question to choose from. Indeed, Harry G. Frankfurt famously proposed cases in which one's ability to do otherwise is compromised, and yet moral evaluations of such actions seem appropriate.[11] All that is necessary to make a choice is that an agent can act upon a reason that they have and, importantly, to act for *that* reason. Such an action reflects an agent's sense of self because such an action is the product of an agent's deliberative agency.

So, exercising deliberative agency *makes an agent's action their own* since it reflects their sense of self and what it is that they care about. An agent needs to be able to exercise their deliberative agency for their actions to be in the moral domain and, hence, the proper subject of moral evaluation. The ability to exercise deliberative agency—though not a sufficient condition for an agent's action to be in the moral domain—is a necessary condition.

MORAL AGENCY AND RELATIONAL KNOWLEDGE

While deliberative agency is about whether an agent can act upon the reasons that they have and, especially, to be able to act for those reasons, moral reasons have not been addressed explicitly. To clarify, while the ability to act as a deliberative agent is a necessary condition for one's actions to be in the moral domain, it is not yet a sufficient condition.[12] It is not yet a sufficient condition because an agent might be able to act upon reasons (in general) but not yet be able to act upon and for *moral* reasons. There is a similarity between deliberative agency and moral agency, however. Both manifest themselves in terms of degrees. The moral development of an agent is a process. Akin to deliberative agency, there is also a threshold in which an agent's degree of moral agency is sufficient to regard their actions as within the moral domain.[13]

Since moral agency tracks an agent's ability to act for moral reasons, then what it means to act upon moral reasons deserves attention. Moral reasons are unique insofar as they are normative, which is to say that an appreciation of such reasons implies that they provide a reason for acting. For example, to say that lying is morally wrong is to say that one ought not to lie. There is debate among philosophers as to whether the normative force of moral reasons is inherent in the reason itself—that is, understanding that it is wrong to lie *just is* understanding that I ought not to lie—or whether it is possible to understand that it is morally wrong to lie without also understanding that I ought not to lie. The former is known as motivational judgment internalism (hereafter "internalism"), while the latter is known as motivational judgment externalism (hereafter "externalism").[14]

I wish to remain neutral here regarding the ongoing debate between internalists and externalists. Indeed, I wish to focus upon what both parties in the debate recognize—namely, they recognize that what it means to appreciate moral reasons somehow must also entail an appreciation of the normative force of such reasons. So, while internalists and externalists tell different stories about how the normative force of moral reasons comes about, they both acknowledge that a moral agent is somehow to regard moral reasons as providing reasons for action. That is, both parties recognize that, for moral agents, moral reasons are normative.

In chapter one, I noted that relational knowledge seems necessary with respect to a moral agent's ability to appreciate a moral reason for action. I believe that relational knowledge is necessary in order for a moral agent to recognize moral reasons as normative.[15] Relational knowledge seems necessary since I believe that morality is fundamentally relational. To be sure, reconsider Simon Blackburn's proclamation that with a few exceptions we can take up an attitude about ourselves that we take toward other people or things in the world.[16] If Blackburn is correct, then it is possible to harm or to wrong ourselves just as it possible to harm or to wrong others. Self-deception is one illustration. Just as it is wrong to intend to deceive others, it is also wrong to intend to deceive ourselves.[17] So, moral reasons for acting are not wholly other-regarding. Moral reasons for acting can be self-regarding, too. My point in calling attention to the fact that moral reasons are both other-regarding and self-regarding is to highlight the idea that not only is morality relational, but also that morality is relational *all the way down*.

Therefore, an agent's sense of self (and, specifically, relating to oneself as an other), which is necessary for deliberative agency, is also foundational for moral agency. In the *Sources of Normativity*, for example, Christine Korsgaard captures the importance of a self-conception with respect to morality in the following way:

> [t]he conception of one's identity [. . .] is [. . .] understood as a description under which you value yourself, a description under which you find your life to be worth living and your actions to be worth undertaking. So I will call this

> a conception of your practical identity. Practical identity is a complex matter and for the average person there will be a jumble of such conceptions. You are a human being, [. . .] an adherent of a certain religion, a member of an ethnic group, a member of a certain profession, someone's lover or friend, and so on. And all of these identities give rise to reasons and obligations. Your reasons express your identity, your nature; your obligations spring from what that identity forbids.[18]

Korsgaard's understanding of an agent's practical identities expresses the kind of connection between an agent's sense of self and their moral obligations that I have in mind here. An agent's sense of self both informs and shapes their social interactions and, in turn, their social interactions both inform and shape their sense of self, or what (and who) they care about.

As social beings, our social interactions fundamentally shape how we see ourselves—including the obligations that we believe ourselves to have. Korsgaard observes that "an obligation always takes the form of a reaction against a threat of a loss of identity."[19] So, if an agent's relational knowledge is lacking or compromised, then it seems correct to say that such an agent also experiences a loss of what I am calling here a sense of self.

For example, recall Jim Sinclair's description in chapter one of a situation in which he did not know what he should do, morally speaking. Sinclair experienced both a need to act as well as not knowing how he (morally) should act. While Sinclair's ability to perceive the emotional and intentional states of others is compromised due to his autism, it is involuntarily compromised. Sinclair's description of his frustration regarding the situation reveals that he is open to the psychological states of others which enables him to act in caring and loving ways. Consequently, Sinclair and other persons with autism face the difficult task of learning moral and social norms in ways independent of what I am referring to here as relational knowledge. Interpreting social cues through means other than social interactions or relational knowledge requires considerable effort, patience, and persistence. Indeed, the very fact that many persons with autism learn how to interpret social cues through means alternative to relational knowledge acquired socially is a testament of their will to be open to the psychological states of others.

It is understandable, then, that Sinclair voiced his frustration at being regarded by others as someone who does not care. Sinclair knows himself to be someone who cares about others; and so, not knowing how he should act in the situation he described was particularly disturbing to him as it undermined his sense of self. The idea that a loss or a deficiency of relational knowledge can also implicate a loss or a deficiency of an agent's sense of self is a point that I will return to in chapter three. For now, however, my aim in this section is to explain how a loss or a deficiency of an agent's relational knowledge compromises their moral agency.

One way to see how a loss, or deficiency, of relational knowledge compromises moral agency is by considering what it means to suffer a moral injury. Psychiatrist Jonathan Shay, who treated military veterans in his clinical practice, recognized that some of his patients suffered from what was neither reducible to, nor symptomatic of, known mental health disorders such as Major Depressive Disorder (MDD) and Post-Traumatic Stress Disorder, or PTSD.[20] Using the phrase "moral injury" to describe what some of his patients experienced, Shay presents moral injury as impacting the entire moral agent in a variety of ways. Determining whether a moral agent is suffering from a moral injury involves an investigation into that individual's background, worldview, physical well-being, social environment, and relevant relationships. Focusing upon military veterans, Shay defines a moral injury as "a betrayal of what's right by someone who holds legitimate authority in a high stakes situation."[21]

Brett T. Litz and his co-authors offer a more robust understanding of moral injury insofar as they define morally injurious experiences as "perpetrating, failing to prevent, bearing witness to, or learning about acts that transgress deeply held moral beliefs and expectations."[22] Litz and his co-authors further explain that:

> [m]oral injury requires an act of transgression that severely and abruptly contradicts an individual's personal or shared expectation about the rules or the code of conduct, either during the event or at some point afterwards [. . .]. The event can be an act of wrongdoing, failing to prevent serious unethical behavior, or witnessing or learning about such an event. The individual also must be (or become) aware of the discrepancy between his or her morals and the experience (i.e., moral violation), causing dissonance and inner conflict.[23]

There are enough similarities between these two ways of defining moral injury that even Shay refers to these definitions as picking out two "flavors of moral injury."[24] Shay notes, however, that "in their definition the violator is the self, whereas in [. . . his definition] the violator is a powerholder,"[25] and "that they report that physiological arousal is not part of moral injury."[26] But I understand these differences to be inconsequential.[27] Both conceptions of moral injury help to elucidate the fact that a moral injury is global, insofar as it disrupts one's moral framework, or worldview. Moreover, I will draw upon both accounts of moral injury and maintain that, with respect to such betrayals, the violator can be either oneself or a powerholder.

Moral injury, I believe, can vary in degree—just as the violation of one or more of a person's moral beliefs could vary in their significance. The betrayal inherent in a moral injury, however, undermines a person's moral compass. The ability to trust in oneself, or in one's judgment, becomes lost. Peace from one's internal conflict is desperately sought, and there can be an overwhelming need to be unified around something—even if that *something* is one's pain. In some situations in which a person suffers a moral injury, there also can be a need to restore a sense of control or power over one's life, which is in response to the sense of powerlessness and hopelessness felt in one's life.

For my purposes here, I will focus upon the most severe kind of moral injury. The idea that at least some persons suffering from a moral injury die by suicide is evident in the book *Soul Repair: Recovering from Moral Injury after War* by Rita Nakashima Brock and Gabriella Lettini.[28] They explain that a "[m]oral injury results when soldiers violate their core moral beliefs, and in evaluating their behavior negatively, they feel they no longer live in a reliable, meaningful world and can no longer be regarded as decent human beings."[29] So, some people who experience moral injury might also experience a loss of a sense of self insofar as they no longer have an identifiable self-conception. Brock and Lettini further explain that:

> [s]eeing someone else violate core moral values or feeling betrayed by persons in authority can also lead to a loss of meaning and faith. It can even emerge from witnessing a friend get killed and feeling survivor guilt. In experiencing a moral conflict, soldiers may judge themselves as worthless[. . .].[30]

In short, suffering a moral injury can impact an agent's ability to see moral reasons as providing a reason for acting.

For some people, while suffering a moral injury could be a precursor to death by suicide, it is not itself a mental illness.[31] Johnathan Shay's work paved the way for recognizing and, ultimately, for treating a moral injury as separate from whatever else a person might be enduring—including, but not limited to, PTSD, depression, and anxiety. A moral injury can fragment a person's understanding of themselves and what it is that they value. Persons who suffer a severe moral injury are at risk of losing both their sense of self and their sense of place in the world.

Brock and Lettini highlight the relationship between a severe moral injury and the possibility of dying by suicide by noting that a person's guilt or shame can be so intense as to threaten a coherent understanding of oneself, or a person's self-conception. As Brock and Lettini explain:

> [a]ny person with a conscience feels occasional guilt or shame for something [. . . they] did, but war can require extreme actions that violate the very basis of moral identity. The life or death urgency of war forces untenable actions that

> can elicit profound guilt or shame. When we feel that what we did was wrong or unforgiveable and that our lives and our meaning system no longer make sense, our reason for living is in tatters. The shattering of the soul challenges what holds life together, and the anguish of moral injury begins.[32]

The idea of a person's reason for living as being torn or in tatters fits the idea that one's ability to function as a deliberative, moral agent is also, and consequently, fragmented. Additionally, Brock and Lettini warn that "[o]ne of the most dangerous aspects of moral injury is the collapse of meaning and the loss of a will to live."[33] In short, a moral injury can be fatal.

Illustrations of moral injury are certainly found in a wide variety of contexts and are more commonplace than what Shay's focus upon military veterans seems to suggest. Carol Gilligan, for instance, notes applications of Shay's conception of a moral injury in the context of childhood development and socialization.[34] Particularly, Gilligan focuses upon how "the internalization of the gender binary" in a patriarchal society can fragment one's sense of self.[35] Take, for example, the socialization of female children to serve in caring roles and to distrust their own voice and ability to problem-solve, while male children are socialized not to show their emotions (with, perhaps, the exception of anger). Moral injury happens, then, whenever the internalized socialization runs counter to oneself, and one acts upon their social expectation at the cost of betraying themselves.

While the degrees of moral injury certainly can vary, Gilligan's point is that none of us are able to escape them completely. That is because the internalized social roles simply do not always apply. To illustrate, Gilligan writes:

> [w]hen it becomes seemingly impossible to have a voice and also to have relationships, some form of psychic splitting is inescapable. 'I don't know,' girls say; 'I don't care,' boys say. Yet the research shows that girls do know and boys do care, although they may need not know or to show this.[36]

To maintain relationships and to garner social acceptance, which is a psychological need, most people will do what is socially expected of them even at the price of betraying themselves. Such common betrayals are further examples of what it means to suffer a moral injury.

Citing such common examples is not to trivialize what it means to suffer a moral injury but, rather, to appreciate the scope of such injuries. The severity of a moral injury varies, of course, but it seems possible that even suffering a relatively minor moral injury repeatedly could have the same severity as suffering a severe moral injury, like those that Jonathan Shay noticed among military veterans. Following Gilligan, then, it is of little wonder that persons who identify within the LGBTQ+ community, for example, might especially suffer moral injury in a patriarchal society, insofar as there is simultaneously both a need for social acceptance as well as simply a need to be oneself.[37]

It seems possible, then, that some agents who suffer a severe moral injury lose a sense of themselves—or an identifiable self-conception. In this respect, such agents lose their ability to perform moral actions as a deliberative agent, and they are like those agents mentioned in the previous section who lose a prerequisite for deliberative agency (namely, a sense of self). Yet, fundamentally, what is lost through suffering a moral injury is *relational* trust, either with respect to oneself as an *other*, or with respect to a legitimate powerholder. Suffering a severe moral injury, therefore, compromises an agent's relational knowledge and, consequently, moral reasons for acting lose their normative force. Hence, an agent who suffers a severe moral injury is analogous to Jim Sinclair's account of not having a clear *moral* reason upon which to act. An agent's moral framework breaks down.

Additionally, following Carol Gilligan, even societal structures themselves can be a powerholder and a source of betrayal. For instance, the social expectations created by gender roles, which are socially constructed, are commonly regarded as authoritative. The upshot is that suffering a moral injury is indicative of a breakdown in an agent's relational knowledge—not only through the betrayal that is characteristic of moral injury, but also because suffering a moral injury compromises an agent's ability to relate to others who, themselves, are not experiencing *that* moral injury. Suffering a moral injury is a private affair. Again, just as Jim Sinclair did not know what he should do, but he knew that he should do *something* in the situation he described, so too, are sufferers of moral injury internally conflicted and at a loss about how to move forward—questioning their own values and identity, as well as trusted powerholders, or even society itself. Sufferers of severe moral injury are sufferers of trauma.

To recap, deliberative, moral agents can suffer severe moral injury. Suffering a severe moral injury disrupts one's moral compass through a relational breakdown—namely, through a significant betrayal. Consequently, their relational knowledge is compromised. I believe that when an agent's relational knowledge is compromised then, so too, is an agent's ability to appreciate the normative force of moral reasons or, perhaps, even to appreciate moral reasons at all. To be clear, not all persons who suffer a moral injury thereby engage in amoral actions. Rather, my point here is that, when a moral agent suffers a severe moral injury (or its equivalent), then their moral framework becomes unreliable. Moral reasons for acting no longer have normative force because *seeing oneself as part of a moral community* is precisely what becomes lost to sufferers of severe moral injury. Furthermore, I believe that at least some actions of suicide are performed by persons who suffer a severe moral injury (or its equivalent). I will return to the possible link between severe suffering a moral injury and some actions of suicide in chapter three. For now, I will turn to the third and final category of amoral actions that I believe is relevant to conceptualizing actions of suicide as amoral.

LIMITATIONS UPON DELIBERATIVE, MORAL AGENCY

To recap, amoral actions are not limited to the actions of non-moral agents who lack the capacity to exercise deliberative agency. I have further noted that moral agents, who are deficient in relational knowledge, can lose their capacity to exercise their moral agency. That is, a moral agent could suffer a severe moral injury and, thereby, lose their ability to see moral reasons as providing them with a reason for acting. So, the absence or deficiency of deliberative agency, as well as the absence or deficiency of moral agency, seem to provide two ways of understanding how amoral actions are possible. In this section, however, I wish to focus upon amoral actions that deliberative, moral agents perform.

In short, deliberative, moral agents can be constrained by their circumstantial and cognitive limitations. I will revisit the amoral actions that Dale Dorsey draws attention to in his work. Specifically, Dorsey acknowledges that moral agents can (and do) engage in amoral actions. The problem of moral requirability highlights the idea that only some actions (a limited set of actions) are open to an agent at any given time. Among those actions that could be morally requirable, however, there are still other actions that an agent is very unlikely to do even though, strictly speaking, such an agent *could* perform those actions. As such, Dorsey expresses concern that different senses of "can" are seemingly neglected in conversations about what actions are open to a moral agent to perform at a given time.

There are at least two main ways that a moral agent can be limited in their actions at any given time. First, circumstances constrain the actions that are open (and morally requirable) for an agent to do. Second, a moral agent's cognitive and physical abilities, as well as their identities and temperament, can put in place further constraints regarding what actions within the set of possible actions are truly possible for the agent in question. Yet, if the idea were simply that moral agents are constrained in their actions by a variety of limitations, then the idea is unilluminating. What is of interest here, however, is when such limitations are so constraining that a moral agent is no longer able to exercise their (deliberative) moral agency in any morally significant way.

Recall Dale Dorsey's illustration of Phil noted in chapter one. Phil is unable to open a safe because he does not know the combination to the safe. Phil not knowing the combination to the safe (through no fault of his own) is a cognitive limitation of Phil's. Consequently, Phil is unable to prevent a very serious calamity from happening due to not opening the safe in question. Phil's inability to prevent a serious calamity from happening due to not opening the safe is also a circumstantial limitation. Even supposing that Phil is not a moral monster, and that he desperately wishes to open the safe in question and, thereby, that he wishes to prevent a very serious calamity from happening, the unforgiving circumstances and his cognitive limitations prohibit Phil from acting in the way he believes that he should act and in the way that he desires to act.

The limitations that Phil encounters are enough to make his moral agency meaningless—that is, even though Phil is still a moral agent, he is *unable to act as a moral agent*; and, for that reason, his plight is similar to that of non-moral agents.[38] Phil's inaction is amoral, according to Dorsey, because Phil's moral agency is compromised with respect to that inaction. Phil is *not choosing* to leave the safe unopened. His inability to open the safe is constrained by circumstantial factors (namely, that somehow failing to open the safe in question will result in a very serious calamity) and by his cognitive limitations (namely, not knowing the combination of the safe in question).

It is easy to see how Phil's inaction is *not* a product of his moral agency. Phil's inaction could be likened to accidental actions. For example, suppose that some agent, Smith, opens a door and, unbeknownst to Smith, another agent, Jones, is leaning against the door on the other side. So, by opening the door at that time, Smith accidentally hurts Jones. While Smith intentionally opened the door at that time, Smith did not intend to hurt Jones. So, hurting Jones was not the product of Smith's *moral agency*. Smith's action of opening the door, say, to take a walk outside, is amoral even though Jones was hurt by Smith's action. Accidental actions, then, seem to be good candidates for amoral actions since accidental actions, by definition, are not the product of an agent's moral agency.[39]

So, clearly, both cognitive and circumstantial limitations pose legitimate limitations upon what actions are open to a moral agent to perform at any given time. But they are not the only relevant limitations that a moral agent could face. An additional limitation that a moral agent could face is the fact that a non-moral mode of normativity—such as reasons of love—could make demands upon an agent that overrides their moral reasons for acting.

To be sure, consider the nature of the values that an agent has, which underlie their deliberative agency. More pointedly, how does an agent with deliberative agency *deliberate*? Deliberative agency concerns acting for reasons, in general, which reflect what an agent cares about, or what is important to them. Yet, that is not to say that exercising deliberatively agency necessarily implies that an agent only acts upon egotistical reasons. I wish to follow Harry

G. Frankfurt's lead here in claiming that both egoism and morality are not the only source of normativity for an agent.[40] Specifically, Frankfurt wrote:

> even quite reasonable and respectable people find that other things may sometimes mean more to them, and make stronger claims upon them, than *either* morality *or* themselves. There are modes of normativity that are quite properly compelling but that are grounded neither in moral nor in egoistic considerations. A person may legitimately be devoted to ideals—for instance, aesthetic, cultural, or religious ideals—whose authority for him is independent of the desiderata with which moral principles are distinctly concerned; and he may pursue these nonmoral ideals without having his own personal interests in mind at all.[41]

So, according to Frankfurt, morality is one mode of normativity among others.

Additionally, following Frankfurt, morality also need *not* be the overriding mode of normativity. Frankfurt explained that,

> [a]lthough it is widely presumed that moral claims are necessarily overriding, it is far from clear that assigning a higher authority to some nonmoral mode of normativity must always be—in every circumstance and regardless of the pertinent magnitudes—a mistake.[42]

Prima facie the above passages from Frankfurt's work are a bit jarring for a couple of reasons. First, it is difficult to imagine reasons for acting that are neither egotistic nor moral. Second, it is also difficult *not* to regard moral claims as necessarily overriding—indeed, Frankfurt acknowledged that such a stance "is widely presumed."

But recall that Frankfurt was writing on the reasons of love. Love is a mode of normativity that cannot be reducible to either egotistical or moral reasons for acting. Indeed, Susan Wolf also recognizes reasons of love as a nonmoral mode of normativity in the following passage from her work on *Meaningful Lives*:

> [w]hen I visit my brother in the hospital, or help my friend move, or stay up all night sewing my daughter a Halloween costume, I act neither for egoistic reasons nor for moral ones. I do not believe that it is better *for me* that I spend a depressing hour in a drab, cramped room, seeing my brother irritable and in pain, that I risk back injury trying to get my friend's sofa safely down two flights of stairs, or that I forgo hours of much-wanted sleep to make sure that the wings will stand out at a good angle from the butterfly costume my daughter wants to wear [. . .]. But neither do I believe myself duty-bound to perform these acts, or fool myself into thinking that by doing them I do what will be best for the world. I act neither out of self-interest nor out of duty or any other sort of impersonal or impartial reason. Rather, I act out of love.[43]

I will return to the demands of love in chapter three. For now, I just wish to note that, when an agent exercises their deliberative agency, they are acting for reasons that stem from their sense of self. I further acknowledge that reasons of love are among the reasons that an agent has for acting.

The existence of nonmoral modes of normativity—such as the reasons of love—highlights the idea that deliberative agency is distinct from moral agency. When a deliberative agent acts upon a reason that they have then, fundamentally, they are acting from their sense of self, or who they take themselves to be. What an agent cares most about is reflected in their sense of self. But, again, acting from a sense of self ought not to imply that an agent is acting for egotistical reasons. In fact, acting from a sense of self need not imply that we act upon conscious reasons at all.

For instance, Harry G. Frankfurt noted that we have what he called volitional necessities, or requirements of one's will.[44] Frankfurt's demarcation between the necessities of love and moral requirements is given as follows:

> [t]he necessities of love are not rational, of course, but volitional; love constrains the will rather than the understanding. But just as the moral law cannot be other than it is, so we cannot help loving what we love. Moreover, the dictates of love, like the requirements of the moral law, enjoy an unconditional authority. In radically distinct but nonetheless closely parallel ways, each tells us what we must do.[45]

Frankfurt believed that love makes demands upon us, but what or who we love is itself not a matter of our choosing. One implication here is that an agent might find that there are reasons for acting which stem from what, or whom, one loves. Moreover, these reasons bear a kind of nonmoral normativity—making demands upon the agent in question—as Susan Wolf so eloquently describes above.

To clarify, per Harry G. Frankfurt, we get the following three claims: love is not a matter of our choosing, the necessities of love are volitional, and such volitional necessities (at least sometimes) override moral reasons for acting. Hence, following Frankfurt, it is possible then that the demands of love further limit a moral agent's ability to act upon the moral reasons they have. Moreover, the idea that a moral agent can be constrained, or limited, by their sense of self (or what it is that they care about, or who they take themselves to be) is not limited to Frankfurt's work.

I believe that Bernard Williams offered yet another way to conceive of amoral actions among moral agents who have their deliberative agency intact. In his article entitled "Moral Incapacity," Williams proposed that the incapacity at issue in moral incapacities is the kind of incapacity that is the conclusion of a moral agent's deliberation. It is unlike circumstantial limitations where "we conclude from our knowledge of . . . [an agent's] incapacities how he will deliberate."[46] Moral incapacities work the other way around. For some moral incapacities, we might conclude how another person will act based upon their character—such as, for example, "they would never do *that*" we might say. Bernard Williams noted that usually such an expression regarding another person is a matter of moral commendation, but that it does not have to be.[47]

A moral incapacity, according to Bernard Williams, is a kind of "incapacity to do a certain thing knowingly."[48] It is not as if a moral agent cannot do the action (or inaction) in question strictly speaking, but, rather, that a moral agent would not knowingly do so. As Williams explained,

> in the pure case of moral incapacity [. . .] it is not necessarily true that if I tried I would fail. If I tried, I might well succeed. The moral incapacity is revealed in the fact that for the appropriate kinds of reasons, I will never try.[49]

So, such incapacities are not beyond the realm of what is possible—just like it is *possible* that Phil could correctly guess the correct combination and turn to the right numbers in the right order and in the right way to open the safe. But such incapacities are legitimate incapacities insofar as, for some moral agents, there will be certain actions that they simply will never consider doing, nor ever attempt.[50]

Attention to moral incapacities here is important for two reasons. First, such incapacities are *genuine incapacities*. As Bernard Williams explained,

> I claim that remarks about moral incapacities, about what people cannot or could not do in this sense, are what they seem. These are indeed incapacities, and they are connected with prediction and understanding in some of the same ways as physical, and other psychological, incapacities are.[51]

As genuine incapacities, they are worthy of attention here because such incapacities certainly impact how, or whether, a moral agent can perform certain actions. As such, moral incapacities might themselves further constrain the options available to an agent at any given time. Recall that the problem of moral requirability is the problem of discerning what actions are open to an agent to perform at a particular time. So, moral incapacities merit attention here, too.

Second, moral incapacities are grounded in a moral agent's perceived identity. How a moral agent conceives of themselves and what matters to them is foundational to their moral agency. Yet how a moral agent conceives of themselves and what matters to them is not itself a conclusion garnered from reflection upon moral reasons. Similarly, Bernard Williams noted that,

> [w]ith other incapacities, while the agent cannot remove them at will, he may coherently set about trying to remove or overcome them, but with a moral incapacity he cannot do this, because a fundamental way in which a moral incapacity expresses itself is in the refusal to undertake any such project.[52]

Williams believed that moral incapacities are entrenched in what he called an agent's dispositions.[53] Williams cautioned, however, that with respect to moral incapacities, he did "not intend the notion of 'character' itself to be explanatory."[54] In fact, Williams noted that even a person who is a skeptic about character should still consider moral incapacities.[55]

Bernard Williams' conception of moral incapacities seems to align with Christine Korsgaard's idea of the importance of practical identities, not only with respect to one's *moral* life, but also with respect to one's life in general. Korsgaard powerfully describes what it would mean for a person to violate their practical identities in the following way:

> [i]t is the conceptions of ourselves that are most important to us that give rise to unconditional obligations. For to violate them is to lose your integrity and so your identity, and to no longer be who you are. That is, it is to no longer be able to think of yourself under the description under which you value yourself and find your life to be worth living and your actions to be worth undertaking. It is to be for all practical purposes *dead or worse than dead*.[56]

The primacy of a sense of self is clear in the above passage from Korsgaard. Tellingly, as Korsgaard notes, the psychological suffering of losing "the description under which you value yourself" is akin to a type of death; and it is understandable why someone would wish to avoid it. It is a type of death of which one is all-too-painfully aware. I believe that what Bernard Williams called moral incapacities, and what Christine Korsgaard calls practical identities, both speak to how central a sense of self is with respect to moral agency.

It might be helpful here to revisit Harry G. Frankfurt's notion of volitional necessities. In his essay "Rationality and the Unthinkable," Frankfurt explained:

> a person may be incapable of performing a certain action even though, so far as considerations of these kinds go, he is in a perfectly good position to perform it. It may be, further, that he thinks he should perform the action, and that he has a desire to perform it. If he is nevertheless unable to act because he finds the action unthinkable, then what keeps him from acting is a volitional matter. He cannot perform the action because *he cannot will to perform it*.[57]

Volitional necessities, therefore, place further limitations upon what kinds of actions are open to an agent to perform at any given time. Recall the two criteria that comprise the agency view presented in chapter one—namely, that an agent must have a reason to act and be able to act upon that reason. But, with respect to any action, if an agent is either acting or failing to act *from a volitional necessity*, or solely from their identifiable self-conception or, perhaps, from their practical identities, then such an agent is *not* in the position to consider *moral reasons* concerning the action in question, nor are they able to act upon such reasons. Indeed, to act in any other way is *unthinkable*.

The idea that moral agents can have moral incapacities, I believe, is especially illuminating with respect to actions in which a moral agent sacrifices, or is prepared to sacrifice, themselves through their action or actions. To illustrate the kind of example that I have in mind, I will turn to a common example found in the relevant literature regarding self-sacrifice. Michael Cholbi describes the example of Foxhole Jumper in the following way:

> [a] soldier sees that the enemy has tossed a live grenade into his foxhole. Aware that the grenade's full detonation will kill the other members of his unit encamped in the foxhole, the soldier jumps atop the grenade to absorb the blast with his body. He is killed by the explosion.[58]

The Foxhole Jumper seems to have acted *against* his immediate self-interest. Strictly speaking, while it seems accurate to say that Foxhole Jumper neglected his immediate interests, I believe that it is inaccurate to claim that Foxhole Jumper neglected himself. A desire to adhere to principles, for example, or a desire to adhere to his identity as a soldier, could have motivated Foxhole Jumper to his fate.

My interest in considering the example of Foxhole Jumper stems from the acknowledgment I made in chapter one, namely that actions of self-sacrifice are actions of suicide (albeit atypical actions of suicide). Foxhole Jumper certainly *intends* to jump on the grenade (he is not accidentally falling upon it), and Foxhole Jumper certainly *intends* for his body to shield his comrades. Because Foxhole Jumper's action counts as an action of suicide, then it is an action of suicide in which the agent (Foxhole Jumper) retains his moral agency. But, importantly, retaining his moral agency neither implies, nor necessitates, that Foxhole Jumper acted *from* his moral agency.

It could be that not acting as Foxhole Jumper did would have meant that he sacrificed his personal identity as a soldier and, to borrow from Christine Korsgaard, he thereby could have been in a state *worse than dead*. Not to have tried to save his comrades would have been *unthinkable* to Foxhole Jumper. Construed in this way, Foxhole Jumper's action is amoral. It is amoral because he was acting in effort to preserve his sense of self insofar as he was sacrificing his life to preserve his self-conception, which is imminently at risk (i.e., perhaps the fact that he could not live with himself if he did not try to save his comrades). Recognizing that maintaining a sense of self is, in fact, a necessary condition to act as a deliberative agent means that actions done to preserve one's sense of self are essentially actions in the pre-moral domain.

In short, Foxhole Jumper is *not* acting based upon *moral* reasons—either other-regarding or self-regarding. Instead, in his self-sacrifice, he is acting to *preserve* his self-conception, or who he takes himself to be. Foxhole Jumper is acting from a kind of volitional necessity that aims to satisfy his desire for an identifiable self-conception. Such actions performed in effort to preserve one's sense of self are more basic than actions requiring the exercise of one's deliberative agency. That is, because performing actions based upon reasons implies that an identifiable self-conception is already in place, then Foxhole Jumper cannot be acting based upon reasons discerned through his deliberative agency. As a result, he fails to meet the criteria of Dale Dorsey's agency view, and his action is amoral.

While I will address several objections in chapter four, I wish to address a couple of objections that might surface here. For starters, two immediate questions might be raised here—both of which aim to challenge the amorality of Foxhole Jumper's action. The first question is simply, "why not consider Foxhole Jumper's action as morally praiseworthy?" The second, related question "why not think that Foxhole Jumper's action was, in fact, morally obligatory given his status as a soldier?" I will briefly address each of these questions, respectively, below.

One of the more telling reasons as to why self-sacrificial actions, like Foxhole Jumper's action, are outside of the moral domain is due to reports by persons who have engaged in self-sacrificial actions but survived. Such people typically respond to praise for their actions in surprisingly humble terms—perhaps stating that they only did what anyone else in that situation would have done, or they had to do what they did. Bryan Smyth cites such scenarios as cases of reactive heroism, which he describes as follows:

> cases in which someone engages in an unmistakably selfless action as a more or less spontaneous response to some occurrence or event (e.g., saving someone by running into a burning house, jumping onto a subway track, disabling an active shooter, etc.). A well-known feature of such cases is that in their own accounts after the fact, agents often expressly deny the optionality of what they did. That is, they often claim that they had no choice, that they *had* to act as they did [. . .].[59]

The decision to act in self-sacrificial ways appears to reflect how one conceives of themselves, rather than how they conceive of their moral framework. Smyth notes "what [such an] agent does issues from an existential *must*, not a moral *should*. There is no specifically *moral* agency involved at all, at least as [. . .] usually understood."[60]

Alternatively, some people might claim that Foxhole Jumper's action was, in fact, morally obligatory. He was a soldier and, as a soldier, he must be prepared to give the ultimate sacrifice. Hesitating to save his comrades, or failing to try to save them, is unacceptable. Or so the thought goes. Such a position is not difficult to understand. But notice that such a position relies upon Foxhole Jumper's *identity* as a soldier and ought not to be construed as a claim about whether suicide is in the moral domain *per se*. Believing that Foxhole Jumper was morally obligated *due to his role as a soldier* is, ultimately, to see his identity as a soldier as foundational to his moral obligations. To be sure, there seems to be a common tendency *not* to deem self-sacrifice as morally obligatory in other, self-sacrificial situations or circumstances, or in non-military contexts, such as an onlooker who runs into a burning building to save someone known to be trapped inside.[61] Believing that it is *not* morally obligatory for the onlooker to risk their own life by running into a burning building, reinforces the idea that the alleged moral difference between Foxhole Jumper's action and onlooker's action is their respective *identities*. But, if the issue here is about the Foxhole Jumper's identity—or, more precisely, the extent to which he has internalized his identity as a soldier—then that is a matter in the pre-moral domain.

If my assessment of Foxhole Jumper's action is correct—that is, if Foxhole Jumper felt compelled by a kind of volitional necessity to act in the way he did—then there is a parallel between the circumstantial and cognitive limitations of Phil mentioned previously and the kind of limitation that Foxhole Jumper encountered. Namely neither Phil nor Foxhole Jumper had a *choice* regarding their respective actions in their respective situations. Phil's circumstantial and cognitive limitations meant that he simply could not open the safe, for all practical purposes. Likewise, given Foxhole Jumper's identity (including his volitional necessity and his sense of self), he could not have done otherwise insofar as he was compelled to try to save his comrades by jumping on the live grenade. If Foxhole Jumper acted on reasons of love, for instance, then those reasons are both non-moral and non-egotistical normative reasons for acting.

Yet I suspect that the idea that Foxhole Jumper may not have had a choice in the matter (given what he truly cared about) is precisely what motivates the idea that his action is *not* an action of suicide. I previously noted that such self-sacrificial actions meet the definition of suicide, strictly speaking. But I can imagine an objection that challenges the classification of Foxhole Jumper's action as an action of suicide based upon the definition of suicide previously mentioned.[62]

Recall that an *intention to die* from intentional self-injurious behavior constitutes suicide. Yet it seems that Foxhole Jumper does *not* intend to die. Foxhole Jumper is not choosing to die, nor is Foxhole Jumper desiring to die. As noted above, Foxhole Jumper intends to save his comrades and, in doing so, he intends to preserve his self-conception, or his identity as a soldier. Certainly, it seems that, if there had been another action for Foxhole Jumper to perform that would have saved his comrades and preserved his self-conception without also knowingly ending his life, he would have performed that action instead. Without an intention to die, then, it could be argued that Foxhole Jumper's action fails to satisfy the definition of suicide noted above.

I believe that Foxhole Jumper's action constitutes an action of suicide. But the idea that actions of suicide are amoral does not necessitate that Foxhole Jumper's self-sacrificial action is an action of suicide. If it turns out that Foxhole Jumper's action is *not* an action of suicide, then it is no longer of concern here, as the moral status of such an action would then be irrelevant to the discussion about the amorality of suicide. Instead, however, following Shelly Kagan's assessment that self-sacrificial actions are actions of suicide—albeit atypical actions of suicide—then an explanation is owed. An explanation is owed regarding how it is possible that an agent's intentionality, which is characteristic of suicide, neither translates into an expression of an agent's choice nor of their desire.

I noted in chapter one that intentionality is complex. A person can have multiple intentions and even contradicting intentions. The idea that intentional actions need not align with a person's desires was clearly articulated by G. E. M. Anscombe who wrote the following.

> suppose I feel an upsurge of spite against someone and destroy a message he has received so that he shall miss an appointment. If I describe this by saying 'I wanted to make him miss that appointment,' this does not necessarily mean that I had the thought 'If I do this, he will . . . ' and that it affected me with a desire of bringing that about which led up to my action. This may have happened, but need not. It could be that all that happened was this: I read the message, had the thought 'That unspeakable man!' with feelings of hatred, tore the message up, and laughed. Then if the question 'Why did you do that?' is put by someone who makes it clear that he wants me to mention the mental causes—i.e., what went on in my mind and issued in the action—I should perhaps give this account; but normally the reply would be so such thing. [. . .] One might shrug or say 'I don't know that there was any definite history of the kind you mean' or 'It merely occurred to me. . . .'[63]

Anscombe noted that the narrator here might have had a desire to cause the man in question to miss his appointment but that such a desire for him to miss the appointment *need not* be present. Hence, it is possible—indeed, perhaps likely—that the action of tearing the piece of paper was an outlet for the anger felt toward the man in question rather than the expression of one's desire that he misses his appointment. It is possible, therefore, that the intentional action of destroying the message did not align with, or express a desire of any sort, that the man misses his appointment. It is also quite possible that in retrospect the action of destroying the message is regretted and an apology is made (especially if the man in question consequently misses his appointment). My point here is simply that Anscombe provided an illustration of an intentional action that need not reflect one's desires. Moreover, if feelings of hatred motivated the action of tearing up the message, then such an action originates from "an upsurge of spite" and not by a conscious choice about the matter. Certainly, a person's intentions might reflect their desires for a particular outcome but, as Anscombe reminded us, *they need not do so.*

Additionally, it seems that some people might contemplate actions of suicide in effort not only to protect other persons—as in the action of Foxhole Jumper—but also to advance causes, principles, or ideals. There are many such examples, but I will focus upon just one such example for my purposes here. Consider Thomas Hart Benton, a former Missouri Senator who served from 1821 to 1851. Benton's willingness to defy popular opinion is highlighted in John F. Kennedy's book *Profiles in Courage* where it is noted that Benton's "devotion to the Union was far greater than his devotion to the South or the Democratic party."[64] One telling illustration of Benton's courage is recounted in an exchange between Benton and Henry Foote, who was then a Senator from Mississippi. Kennedy described the ordeal as follows:

> in the midst of another verbal assault upon him by Foote, Benton advanced toward the Mississippian, then turned back at a colleague's restraining touch. Suddenly Foote whipped out a pistol and pointed it at Benton, who dramatically threw open his coat and cried: "I have no pistol! Let him fire! Let the assassin fire![65]

Benton's action and declaration not only seemingly displayed tremendous courage, but his action also underscored the idea that Benton was a man committed to his principles. Backing down, or giving in, to the threat against his life (when Foote brandished a pistol), was unthinkable to Benton. Fortunately, Foote did not fire his weapon. Yet the reason why Benton is remembered is, in part, because of his strong commitment to his principles.

Benton's willingness to sacrifice his life for his principles might look like he is acting upon moral reasons—indeed, *prima facie*, it seems like he is acting upon his moral convictions. But, if it is true that a sense of self is foundational to deliberative agency, and if it is true that deliberative agency is a necessary condition for the exercise of an agent's moral agency, then whether someone is willing to sacrifice themselves for a cause ultimately depends upon who they take themselves to be. What a person is willing to live for—and to die for—reflects how they see themselves. I believe that Benton was willing to self-sacrifice because a failure to do so would have meant a loss of his sense of self and, consequently, a *loss* of himself. Benton, like the Foxhole Jumper, acted from who he took himself to be. He acted upon what he demanded of himself and not what morality demanded of him.[66] One way to think about such actions, then, is to conclude that they stem from a person's pre-moral agency. Indeed, they stem from the root of an agent's deliberative agency. Thomas Hart Benton, therefore, like Foxhole Jumper, could have engaged in his self-sacrificial action out of a *volitional* necessity that was neither moral nor egotistical.

To take stock, I am following Dale Dorsey's example of Phil to suggest that both circumstantial and cognitive limitations can be at work, and, in turn, they can make a moral agent unable to act upon the moral reasons that they have for acting. Yet there are at least two other ways in which a moral agent could be unable to act upon the moral reasons that they have. First, it seems that a moral agent could act upon their reasons of love—where love is a non-moral mode of normativity. That is, it seems possible that such reasons of love could override moral reasons for acting, at least on occasion. Second, in addition to acting upon reasons of love, it seems possible that a moral agent can act in ways to preserve their sense of self. Because I believe that a sense of self is foundational to exercising both deliberative and moral agency, then it seems that actions to preserve one's sense of self are pre-moral, or outside of the moral domain.

Notice that such a discussion has come full circle, as I began this chapter by noting that a loss of a sense of self undermines an agent's deliberative agency. Actions performed in which an agent has either lost their sense of self, or who perceives their sense of self as lost, are amoral. I have further acknowledged that the severe and immediate threat of losing one's sense of self—as in the case of Foxhole Jumper—are also amoral because they are not the product of a moral agent exercising their deliberative and moral agencies.

Yet so far, I have alluded to actions of suicide only in passing. I now wish to turn to such actions more explicitly in the next chapter. My claim is that actions of suicide are amoral because they appear to fall within one or more of these three categories of amoral actions, broadly construed.

NOTES

1. Dale Dorsey, "Consequentialism, Cognitive Limitations, and Moral Theory," in Oxford Studies in Normative Ethics, vol. 3, ed. Mark Timmons (New York: Oxford University Press, 2013), 191.

2. Of course, some adult human beings are unable to reflect upon reasons that are to guide their actions, but I am leaving that point aside here.

3. If, for instance, my "self" only refers to my present beliefs and desires, then there would not be anything remaining of such a self if, suddenly, I no longer had beliefs and desires. In other words, the question raised here is whether my *self* is picking out something about *me* which cannot be explained by other means. There also are further philosophical worries about the unification that the word "self" implies, as well as whether an individual would have just one self at different times or different selves at different times. For more on the multiplicity of philosophical problems concerning a self, see: Shaun Gallagher, ed., *The Oxford Handbook of the Self* (New York: Oxford University Press, 2011).

4. Simon Blackburn, *Mirror, Mirror: The Uses and Abuses of Self-love* (Princeton: Princeton University Press, 2014).

5. Simon Blackburn, *Mirror, Mirror*, 18.

6. Simon Blackburn, *Mirror, Mirror*, 12.

7. Simon Blackburn, *Mirror, Mirror*, 12.

8. Harry G. Frankfurt, *The Reasons of Love* (Princeton: Princeton University Press, 2004), 18.

9. David Hume, *A Treatise of Human Nature*, ed. L. A. Selby-Bigge (New York: Oxford University Press, 1888, second edition 1978), Book I, Part IV, 252.

10. David Hume, "On Suicide" (1757) in *The Ethics of Suicide: Historical Sources*, ed. Margaret Pabst Battin (New York: Oxford University Press, 2015), 410.

11. Harry G. Frankfurt, "Alternate Possibilities and Moral Responsibility," *The Journal of Philosophy*, 66, no. 23 (December 1969): 829–39.

12. Recall that young children and non-human animals could be capable of exercising a degree of deliberative agency, even though their actions are still regarded as amoral.

13. Suppose, for example, that a young child has some degree of deliberative agency, but that they lack moral agency. A parent or guardian might proceed to evaluate the child's actions morally simply as part of the child's moral development. Even so, the child's actions are not yet within the moral domain.

14. Connie S. Rosati, "Moral Motivation," in *Stanford Encyclopedia of Philosophy*, (Stanford: The Metaphysics Research Lab, 2016). https://plato.stanford.edu/entries/moral-motivation/.

15. My claim that relational knowledge is necessary in order for a moral agent to recognize moral reasons as normative (or as providing a reason for action) is consistent with either an internalist or an externalist framework. Per an internalist account, it could be that relational knowledge is necessary to recognize a moral reason at all; and, per an externalist account, it could be that an agent could recognize a moral

reason but only see such reasons as having normative force if they also have relational knowledge. I wish to leave both possibilities open.

16. Simon Blackburn, *Mirror, Mirror*, 12.

17. One might claim that deceiving oneself for the purpose of, say, overcoming a fear or, perhaps, building more confidence in one's abilities is not morally wrong to do. Hence, I intend my statement here to be a generalization regarding the fact that self-regarding moral reasons for acting are similar to other-regarding moral reasons for acting insofar as we can wrong ourselves in ways similar to wronging others.

18. Christine M. Korsgaard, *The Sources of Normativity* (New York: Cambridge University Press, 1996), 101.

19. Christine M. Korsgaard, *The Sources of Normativity*, 102.

20. Jonathan Shay, "Moral Injury," *Psychoanalytic Psychology*, 31, No. 2 (April 2014): 182–91.

21. Jonathan Shay, "Moral Injury," 183.

22. Brett T. Litz et al., "Moral Injury and Moral Repair in War Veterans: A Preliminary Model and Intervention Strategy," *Clinical Psychology Review*, Vol. 29, No. 8 (2009): 695–706, 700.

23. Brett T. Litz et al., "Moral Injury and Moral Repair in War Veterans: A Preliminary Model and Intervention Strategy," 700.

24. Jonathan Shay, "Moral Injury," 186.

25. Jonathan Shay, "Moral Injury," 184.

26. Jonathan Shay, "Moral Injury," 185.

27. Regarding whether the violator is oneself or a powerholder is a difference in perspective, since Litz and his co-authors include perpetrating, as well as bearing witness to, a moral transgression in their definition of a moral injury. Regarding physiological arousal, it is not immediately clear whether such physiological arousal must be at the time of the violation (on Shay's view), or afterwards, or both. But the claim by Litz and his co-authors that a moral injury entails dissonance and inner conflict seems at least open to the possibility that physiological arousal could be present in some cases, even if Litz and his co-authors do not see it as necessitated through suffering such an injury. Essentially, Litz and his co-authors present a conception of moral injury that is more comprehensive in scope—extending to situations well beyond the context of military service, which is Shay's focus.

28. Rita Nakashima Brock and Gabriella Lettini, *Soul Repair: Recovering from Moral Injury after War* (Boston: Beacon Press, 2012).

29. Rita Nakashima Brock and Gabriella Lettini, *Soul Repair: Recovering from Moral Injury after War*, xv.

30. Rita Nakashima Brock and Gabriella Lettini, *Soul Repair: Recovering from Moral Injury after War*, xv.

31. Just as a mental illness might befall anyone, so too, a moral injury might befall anyone. My point here is just that a person does not need to be suffering from a mental illness to suffer from a moral injury. Furthermore, a person does not need to report suffering from a mental illness because they are suffering from a moral injury. While the two can overlap, of course, it is best to regard any mental illness that a person could suffer and any moral injury that they could suffer as separate and distinct issues.

32. Rita Nakashima Brock and Gabriella Lettini, *Soul Repair: Recovering from Moral Injury after War*, 52.

33. Rita Nakashima Brock and Gabriella Lettini, *Soul Repair: Recovering from Moral Injury after War*, 80.

34. Carol Gilligan, "Moral Injury and the Ethic of Care: Reframing the Conversation about Differences," *Journal of Social Philosophy*, Vol. 45, No. 1 (March 2014): 89–106.

35. Carol Gilligan, "Moral Injury and the Ethic of Care: Reframing the Conversation about Differences," 95.

36. Carol Gilligan, "Moral Injury and the Ethic of Care: Reframing the Conversation about Differences," 95.

37. It is worth noting that certain segments of populations seem to consist of individuals who are, in general, more at-risk of dying by suicide than other members of a population not included in those segments. Jonathan Shay's work among military veterans, for example, is insightful for this very reason—namely, in attempting to recognize the ways in which moral injury poses unique challenges among military veterans, in particular. So, it would be interesting to discern whether—and, perhaps the extent to which—those who are more prone to suffer a moral injury within a given population are also more at-risk of dying by suicide than other members of a population who are, perhaps, not as prone to moral injury.

38. Of course, as noted in chapter one, there are other actions (apart from opening the safe) that Phil could do, or he could refrain from doing, which are in the moral domain.

39. Perhaps accidental actions are more appropriately acts (not actions) because, in the example noted, Smith's goal is to walk outside, and he opens the door as a means of reaching his goal. Smith injuring Jones in the process is neither the goal of Smith's action nor the means of reaching his goal. Nevertheless, I believe that it is common to speak of accidental actions even when, in fact, accidents (by definition) are unintentional.

40. Harry G. Frankfurt, *The Reasons of Love*.

41. Harry G. Frankfurt, *The Reasons of Love*, 8, Frankfurt's emphasis.

42. Harry G. Frankfurt, *The Reasons of Love*, 8.

43. Susan Wolf, "Meaning in Life," in *Meaning in Life and Why it Matters* (Princeton: Princeton University Press, 2010), 4. Wolf's emphasis.

44. Harry G. Frankfurt, "Autonomy, Necessity, and Love," in *Necessity, Volition, and Love* (New York: Cambridge University Press, 1999), 129–41.

45. Harry G. Frankfurt, "Autonomy, Necessity, and Love," 141.

46. Bernard Williams, "Moral Incapacity," *Proceedings of the Aristotelian Society*, Vol. 93 (1993): 59–70, 66.

47. Bernard Williams, "Moral Incapacity," 59.

48. Bernard Williams, "Moral Incapacity," 62.

49. Bernard Williams, "Moral Incapacity," 63.

50. Horrendous circumstances and extreme cruelty, however, might make a person do things that they would not otherwise think of doing. Bernard Williams acknowledged this point when he wrote: "[i]t is plausible to say, with the pessimist, that if

having a moral incapacity implies that there are no circumstances at all in which the agent would knowingly do the thing in question, then there are no moral incapacities. Ingenious coercion or brutal extremity can almost always produce such circumstances" ("Moral Incapacity," 69).

51. Bernard Williams, "Moral Incapacity," 60.

52. Bernard Williams, "Moral Incapacity," 68.

53. Bernard Williams, "Moral Incapacity," 66.

54. Bernard Williams, "Moral Incapacity," 60.

55. Bernard Williams, "Moral Incapacity," 61. Williams understood a person's character to stretch "beyond the matter of incapacities. [. . .]" ("Moral Incapacity," 60).

56. Christine M. Korsgaard, *The Sources of Normativity*, 102, emphasis added.

57. Harry G. Frankfurt, "Rationality and the Unthinkable," in The Importance of What We Care About (New York: Cambridge University Press, 1988), 181, Frankfurt's emphasis.

58. Michael Cholbi, *Suicide: The Philosophical Dimensions* (Buffalo: Broadview Press, 2011), 16.

59. Bryan Smyth, "De-Moralizing Heroism: Ethical Expertise and the Object of Heroic Approbation," *Southwest Philosophy Review*, Vol. 36, No. 1 (January 2020): 65–74, 66.

60. Bryan Smyth, "De-Moralizing Heroism: Ethical Expertise and the Object of Heroic Approbation," 70.

61. It seems that common sense morality maintains that, while we morally ought to make sacrifices for the sake of others, there are legitimate limits to these sacrifices. Efforts to be mindful of our own well-being, for instance, come to mind. For a challenge to the idea that there is such a limit to the requirements of morality, please see Shelly Kagan's *The Limits of Morality* (New York: Oxford University Press, 1989).

62. One possible way of framing Foxhole Jumper's action is by appealing to the Doctrine of Double Effect. In short, the Doctrine of Double Effect maintains that some actions could be morally justifiable even when a bad effect is foreseen by the action. The primary example of employing the Doctrine of Double Effect is with respect to the action of killing in self-defense as a morally justifiable action. Simply put, granting that a person only wishes to escape their attacker, and granting that there is no other way to escape their attacker, then employing lethal means in effort to escape one's attacker may only be done with the intention of escaping the attacker in question whose death is merely foreseen, but unintended. It seems, then, that something similar could be said in the case of Foxhole Jumper's action. Namely, it seems that someone might claim that Foxhole Jumper does not *intend* his death even as a means to the end of saving the lives of others. Rather, he merely *foresees* his death.

But I am not convinced that such an assessment reflects what is happening to Foxhole Jumper. Certainly, it seems correct to say that Foxhole Jumper does not directly intend his death insofar as he does not wish to die. But I believe that much is true regarding actions of suicide in general, in which a person's death is seen as a means to another end. Rather, what is of note in Foxhole Jumper's situation is that he acts as he does *even while foreseeing his death* as an outcome of his action. So, explaining that Foxhole Jumper did not intend his death (even indirectly) but only foresaw his death, ultimately just passes the buck. If Foxhole Jumper was not about to do *any* action in which he foresaw his death, then why did he choose *that* action? I believe that Foxhole Jumper's action reflects *not* the fact that he foresaw his death but only intended to save other lives. Rather, I believe that Foxhole Jumper's action reflects what mattered to him *more than life itself.* His action reflects what he was prepared to give his life *for*. His death, then, was not merely incidental, or foreseen but unintended. Rather, he regarded saving the lives of others as worth the price of his life. Other people would not necessarily come to the same conclusion as Foxhole Jumper, even if they otherwise would intend to save the lives of others. In any case, I will not be entertaining the Doctrine of Double Effect here, which has received a fair share of philosophical criticism. For more on the Doctrine of Double Effect, please see Alison McIntyre's "Doctrine of Double Effect," in *Stanford Encyclopedia of Philosophy* (Stanford: The Metaphysics Research Lab, 2023).

63. G. E. M. Anscombe, "Intention," in *Essays in Philosophical Psychology*, ed. Donald F. Gustafson (New York: Anchor Books, 1964): 30–40, 33.

64. John F. Kennedy, *Profiles in Courage* (New York: HarperCollins Publishers, 1955), Reprinted in HarperPerennial 1992, 87.

65. John F. Kennedy, *Profiles in Courage*, 101–102.

66. Arguably, the title of Kennedy's book, *Profiles in Courage*, suggests that Thomas Hart Benton acted *courageously*, and courage, after all, is a virtue. Yet regarding courage as a virtue, places Benton's action in the moral domain. I believe, however, that it is possible for Benton to have acted from a volitional necessity, or from a necessity of his will. If doing otherwise would have been *unthinkable* to him, for instance, then his actions were not a matter of his choice; and so, he was not choosing to do those actions that appear courageous. In short, there could be another way to explain Benton's actions without appealing to an assessment of his moral character. I will address the worry that actions of suicide might reflect a person's moral character in chapter five.

Chapter Three

Actions of Suicide as Amoral

In this chapter, I will investigate various actions of suicide. Recall that, because actions entail both an *act* and an *end* or goal, actions of suicide are quite diverse. It would be a fool's errand to attempt to account for all such actions of suicide and, of course, I will not attempt to do so. My aim here, however, is to account for several such actions. I believe that the array of actions examined in this chapter provides evidence for thinking that actions of suicide are amoral given what it means for an action to be an action of suicide.

To be sure, I will draw upon Thomas Joiner's interpersonal theory of suicide, which is a relational account of understanding actions of suicide. Given the *relational* nature of morality, it seems fitting to examine a *relational* account of suicide. Joiner's account is also worthy of attention given his expertise in the field of suicidology. In general, per Joiner's account, when certain psychological needs are unmet, a person's risk for suicide increases. I will proceed to connect such psychological needs to instances in which either an agent's sense of self or their relational knowledge is either lacking or compromised. I also will connect Joiner's account to instances in which an agent encounters limitations with respect to exercising their moral agency. The upshot, of course, is that actions of suicide that appear to align with Joiner's account are also amoral actions.

AN INTERPERSONAL THEORY OF SUICIDE

Thomas Joiner's aim in his book *Why People Die by Suicide* is not trying to plot a conceptual framework of what constitutes suicide but, rather, to be able to provide "a deeper account of suicidal behavior [and] to explain more suicide-related phenomena."[1] In short, Joiner proposes the following:

> people desire death when two fundamental needs are frustrated to the point of extinction; namely, the need to belong with or connect to others, and the need to feel effective with or to influence others. When both these needs are snuffed out, suicide becomes attractive but not accessible without the ability for self-harm.[2]

The ability for self-harm is a key component of Joiner's theory. In short, the idea is that persons who have built up a tolerance for pain, or who overcome their fear of death, and who have access to lethal means will have an increased risk of suicidal behavior when they also are experiencing a thwarted sense of belonging and perceived burdensomeness.[3]

For my purposes here, however, I will just acknowledge the lethality component of Joiner's theory only to set it aside in the remaining discussion. Instead, I wish to focus upon what it means to have a thwarted sense of belonging as well as perceived burdensomeness (or a loss of the need to feel competent) which, I believe, could negatively impact a person's ability to have reasons for acting and to be able to act upon such reasons. The frustration of psychological needs also inhibits an agent's ability to see a moral reason as providing a reason for acting. In short, I believe that it makes sense to regard a person's deliberative agency and moral agency as dependent upon the fulfillment of certain psychological needs.

What is insightful about Joiner's theory is that, as an interpersonal theory, it is inherently relational. As such, Joiner's theory preserves the wisdom of Émile Durkheim's sociological approach in his understanding of suicide.[4] Joiner, more specifically, credits the work of Edwin Shneidman and Shneidman's predecessor, Henry Murray, who focused upon underlying psychological needs as contributing factors to deaths by suicide.[5]

In this project, I will focus upon Edwin Shneidman's work, as Thomas Joiner's main predecessor. Shneidman focused his attention on what he called *psychache*, which he explained as follows:

> [p]sychache is the hurt, anguish, or ache that takes hold in the mind. It is intrinsically psychological—the pain of excessively felt shame, guilt, fear, anxiety, loneliness, angst, dread of growing old or of dying badly. When psychache occurs, its introspective reality is undeniable. Suicide happens when the psychache is deemed unbearable and death is sought to stop the unceasing flow of painful consciousness. Suicide is a tragic drama in the mind.[6]

Psychache is a deeply personal matter. Shneidman continued, "[w]hat my research has taught me is that only a small minority of cases of excessively psychological pain result in suicide, but *every case of suicide stems from excessive psychache*."[7] Assessing the degree of a person's psychache means being attentive to a person's entire worldview.

Shneidman identified different clusters of psychological needs that are undermined in most actions of suicide.[8] Specifically, such needs are identified by the various kinds of psychological pain. Shneidman noted that "thwarted *love*, acceptance, and belonging" is a source of psychological pain as well as "ruptured key relationships."[9] Such pains indicate the frustration of the need for affiliation and nurturance. Additionally, the pains of suffering from fractured control as well as an assaulted self-image frustrate the "needs for achievement, autonomy, order, and understanding" as well as the need to avoid shame.[10] Furthermore, excessive hostility and rage, as stemming from the frustrated need for dominance, represents another cluster.[11] In commenting upon the psychological needs that Shneidman identified, Thomas Joiner observes that "Shneidman's [. . .] needs are important, but they are collapsible into two major categories of thwarted belongingness (i.e., thwarted love, ruptured relationships) and perceived burdensomeness (assaulted self-image, fractured control, [and] anger related to frustrated dominance)."[12]

While it is understandable to generalize psychache in terms of perceived burdensomeness and a thwarted sense of belonging as Joiner does, there seems to be something important that Shneidman intended to capture in psychache that is missing in Joiner's theory. Specifically, Shneidman noted that there is a psychological need to maintain one's self-image and that, when one's self-image is assaulted, then they could have an increased risk for suicide depending upon other factors. Joiner recognizes that a person's self-image can be assaulted or compromised in his interpersonal theory of suicide. Nevertheless Joiner groups this need under the broad heading of perceived burdensomeness. A person might perceive themselves as a burden if they lose (or if they perceive themselves to have lost) certain competencies. The need to maintain basic competencies and to be effective in one's life are deemed as psychological needs which, if lost, will be an assault to a person's self-image. So, it makes sense to believe that, when a person perceives themselves as a burden to others, then their self-image is assaulted.

But I believe that a person's self-image can be assaulted even more fundamentally than how they believe that they are perceived by others. For instance, consider William Styron's description of slipping into suicidal behavior while in the grip of his depression and as expressed in his memoir *Darkness Visible: A Memoir of Madness*.[13] Again, Styron was not suffering from depression as a natural and a healthy response to disturbing life events; but rather, Styron was suffering from depression as a mental illness. Tellingly, Styron wrote:

> [l]oss in all of its manifestations is the touchstone of depression—in the progress of the disease and, most likely, in its origin. [. . .] I felt loss at every hand. The

> loss of self-esteem is a celebrated symptom, and my own sense of self had all but disappeared, along with any self-reliance.[14]

Styron's focus upon loss is insightful because he conveyed a connection between an acute sense of loss that is characteristic of depression with the loss of life. Indeed, Styron continued:

> [t]here is no doubt that as one nears the penultimate depths of depression—which is to say just before the stage when one begins to act out one's suicide instead of being a mere contemplator of it—the acute sense of loss is connected with a knowledge of life slipping away at accelerated speed.[15]

Styron expressed his sense of self "had all but disappeared" and, thereby, indicating that his self-conception, or the degree of his internal integration, was unrecognizable. So, I believe that Edwin Shneidman paid attention not only to how a person believes they are accepted *by others*, or even the degree to which their life is perceived to be a burden *to others*, but also how a person relates *to their sense of self*.

William Styron's account of experiencing a loss of a sense of self is perhaps most evident in his experience of a psychological break or fragmentation of himself. Indeed, the fragmentation was so apparent to Styron that he went so far as describing a second self. Specifically, Styron described a sense of feeling internally divided, as if he was "accompanied by a second self—a wraithlike observer who, not sharing the dementia of his double, is able to watch with dispassionate curiosity as his companion struggles against the oncoming disaster, or decides to embrace it."[16] Styron explained, "I couldn't shake off a sense of melodrama—a melodrama in which I, the victim-to-be of self-murder, was both the solitary actor and the lone member of the audience."[17] Styron's experience of a second self portrays a loss of a sense of self. Neither the actor nor the lone audience member is whole. Moreover, neither the actor nor the lone audience member is the writer of the script.

So, according to Shneidman, among our psychological needs are the needs for "autonomy, order, and understanding."[18] Such psychological needs are compromised, however, by a fragmented sense of self that Styron experienced. My worry then with generalizing psychache to the realm of a thwarted sense of belonging and perceived burdensomeness, as Joiner does, is that it appears simply to assume that agents have a sense of self. On Joiner's account, there is a *self* who is experiencing a thwarted sense of belonging, as well as a *self* who perceives oneself to be a burden. Yet the possibility that *a sense of self* is also a psychological need that can itself be compromised or fragmented (as evidenced by Styron's account) is lost.

To clarify, my worry with respect to Joiner's interpersonal theory of suicide is that by generalizing psychache with respect to how a person sees themselves in relationship with others (namely, either as not belonging or as a burden), then the psychological pain of losing a sense of self is overlooked. That is, I am not convinced that the psychological need to maintain a self-image, which Edwin Shneidman recognized, is reducible to (or collapses into) how a person believes that others perceive them. Indeed, I regard Shneidman's attention to the need to maintain a self-image as similar to the suggestion made in chapter two—namely, that a sense of self is a prerequisite for an agent to exercise their deliberative agency. Hence, maintaining one's self-image (or a sense of self) is a psychological *need.*

Yet there could be a reasonable explanation for why the loss of a sense of self seems missing in Joiner's account. The aim of Joiner's theory is to predict the likelihood of suicidal behavior and, ultimately, to prevent deaths by suicide. Because a person's sense of self is a private matter, it is understandable that it might be excluded from a theory such as Joiner's for pragmatic reasons alone. Simply put, determining whether one's self-image has been assaulted is mysterious from a third-person perspective. Indeed, Styron was able to write about his experiences only in retrospect. Yet persons suffering from a perceived sense of burdensomeness and thwarted belongingness are more likely to be able to express these conditions even if only indirectly. For example, from a third-person perspective, the idea that another person could be suffering from a thwarted sense of belonging or perceived burdensomeness might be inferred from certain life events, such as the ending of a relationship, a job loss, the death of a loved one, the destruction of one's home or property, the loss of physical or financial independence, and so on.

Additionally, some persons suffering from a thwarted sense of belonging and a perceived sense of burdensomeness are likely to experience a loss of a sense of self as well. It is simply unclear that a loss of a sense of self is necessitated by these other conditions. Importantly, it seems possible that one could experience a loss of a sense of self without also experiencing a thwarted sense of belonging or a sense of burdensomeness that might be identifiable from a third-person perspective. In short, a loss of a sense of self, which was regarded as a source of psychache on Shneidman's account, is seemingly absent in Joiner's theory.

I will proceed, then, with attention to a loss of a sense of self which, I believe, is consistent with Joiner's account, since Joiner regards his account as building upon Shneidman's work. In subsequent sections of this chapter, I also will consider what Joiner describes as a thwarted sense of belonging as well as perceived burdensomeness. While actions of suicide are complex and varied, I will draw upon the idea that excessive psychache is the commonality among such actions. Hence, the frustration of psychological needs, which underlie excessive psychache, merits attention with respect to actions of suicide.

ON THE LOSS OF A SENSE OF SELF

"This Is Water" is the title of a well-known commencement speech delivered by David Foster Wallace at Kenyon College in 2005.[19] Suicide is mentioned in passing in Wallace's speech, but its mention is striking since Wallace, who had been suffering from severe depression, died by suicide approximately three years later.[20] Wallace's characterization of suicidal persons who die by firearms is what I wish to focus upon here. As Wallace explained:

> [consider] the old cliché about the mind being 'an excellent servant but a terrible master.' [. . .] It is not the least bit coincidental that adults who [. . . die by] suicide with firearms almost always shoot themselves in: the head. They shoot the terrible master.[21]

Wallace seemed to have been suggesting that, for some people, the action of pulling the trigger may feel as though it is only a formality. Life is already experienced as, or perceived to be, lost.

I believe that some actions of suicide are engaged in by persons experiencing a loss of a sense of self. The idea that one's life is already lost indicates the absence of a coherent and identifiable self-conception. Moreover, without a coherent and identifiable self-conception, it is impossible to act as a *deliberative agent* because there is no unified understanding of *oneself* from which one can deliberate.

Such fragmentation might fuel the ambivalence that accompanies some actions of suicide, as Edwin Shneidman recognized.[22] So, if both Wallace and Styron's accounts are to be taken seriously, then it must be acknowledged that a person might proceed in an action of suicide in ways that do not reflect their will. Their sense of self is lost. Therefore, such actions of suicide are not the product of deliberative agency and are amoral, or outside of the moral domain.

A similar sentiment is found in Naomi Judd's memoir *River of Time: My Descent into Depression and How I Emerged with Hope*. Judd recounted her experience of depression and of suicidal ideation in the following way:

> [o]ne bitterly cold and dreary morning the urgent thought came to me that if I couldn't get myself out of this despair, I should end my misery quickly. Death would be instantaneous relief. [. . .] I imagined that the impact of my body

> hitting the highway would leave me unrecognizable. It would be a logical end, because *I no longer recognized myself.*[23]

Referring to herself as unrecognizable powerfully indicates a loss of a sense of self that is experienced as intolerably disturbing. The scope and depth of such despair that a person can experience ought not to be underestimated. Indeed, further recall from chapter one that William Styron contended that "the pain of severe depression is quite unimaginable to those who have not suffered it, and it kills in many instances because its anguish can no longer be borne."[24] Naomi Judd died by suicide in April of 2022.[25]

Some people might insist that a change of perspective is necessary for those who suffer from excessive psychache, and that, if such persons could just change their perspective, then perhaps their psychache would no longer be so excessive. Yet such excessive psychache can eliminate a person's ability not only to change their perspective but also even just to recognize that there are, in fact, other perspectives. One's pain becomes all-consuming. As David Foster Wallace had reminded us, even the *desire* to change one's perspective can be elusive. In his commencement speech, Wallace challenged his audience to adopt perspectives other than their own default perspective. But with a brave honesty, Wallace admitted that "it's hard, it takes will and mental effort, and if you're like me, some days you won't be able to do it, or you just flat-out won't want to."[26]

The impossibility of being able to adopt another's perspective—to see, for example, one's life from another's perspective—is telling. Such impossibility implies that persons are unable to deliberate about reasons for action.[27] The ability to take up different perspectives is particularly central to appreciating *moral* reasons for acting. Of course, that is not to say that such a person is unable to act, however, or even that they are unable to employ means-ends reasoning. It is just to say that their actions do not reflect their sense of self. Their actions are not their own in an important way.

As Kay Redfield Jamison explains in *Night Falls Fast: Understanding Suicide*, "[l]ove, success, and friendship are not always enough to counter the pain and destructiveness of severe mental illness."[28] Writing more broadly, Jamison also reflects upon the inability of persons struggling with suicidal ideation to adopt a new or different perspective on their lives in the following passage:

> when people are suicidal, their thinking is paralyzed, their options appear spare or nonexistent, their mood is despairing, and hopelessness permeates their entire mental domain. The future cannot be separated from the present, and the present is painful beyond solace.[29]

While I do not believe that all persons, when they are suicidal, have hopelessness permeating their entire mental domain, it is only because I am imagining instances of suicide in broader terms than what Jamison had in mind in the above passage (such as including Foxhole Jumper's action as an action of suicide). Nevertheless, for the kind of actions of suicide that Jamison is referring to, and for the kind of actions of suicide that David Foster Wallace mentioned in his speech, and for the kind of suicidal state of mind that William Styron described, and for the experience of an unrecognizable self that Naomi Judd experienced, attention is owed. Specifically, I believe that regarding such actions of suicide as falling within the moral domain is a travesty of reason and a lack of understanding of the scope and power of severe mental illnesses.[30]

The psychological need to have an identifiable self-conception according to which a person can determine what is of value to them and, ultimately, to prioritize their endeavors is lost. I suspect that such a description of an action of suicide is what constitutes the more typical actions of suicide—namely, those in which a person feels dead long before they pull the trigger. First-personal accounts from persons who have simultaneously suffered from a severe mental illness that was accompanied by suicidal ideation—such as those of Jamison, Wallace, Styron, and Judd—do not also reflect the simultaneous presence of the ability to have reasons for acting and to act upon such reasons *as a deliberative agent.*

When arguing for the amorality of suicide, however, it may seem unfair to start with discussing actions of suicide among persons suffering from severe mental illnesses. I believe that most of the time when people argue that actions of suicide belong in the moral domain, they do not have in mind instances in which a suicidal person is also suffering from a severe mental illness at the time of their action. Such persons clearly need help for their mental illness, or illnesses; and I do not know of anyone who would deny that help is needed.[31] Yet, I maintain that suicide must be thought about in terms independent of mental illnesses, as well. So, a question then arises as to whether a person can experience a loss of a sense of self in circumstances independent of mental illnesses? I certainly believe so.

It is possible, I believe, that one's situation or circumstances can be so horrendous for a person that they lose their ability to feel whole—to have a unified understanding of their self. In his book, *Man's Search for Meaning*, Viktor E. Frankl recounted his experiences at Nazi concentration camps through his lens as a prisoner and a psychiatrist. Frankl wrote:

> [a]n abnormal reaction to an abnormal situation is normal behavior. [. . .] The reaction of a man to his admission to a concentration camp also represents an abnormal state of mind, but judged objectively it is normal and [. . .] typical

> reaction to the given circumstances. These reactions [. . .] began to change in a few days. The prisoner passed [. . .] to the phase of relative apathy, in which he achieved a kind of emotional death.[32]

The emotional death noted here resembles Wallace's claim that many persons who use firearms to die by suicide are dead long before they pull the trigger. Understandably, of course, the people who Frankl described might also have suffered from depression. So, to clarify, certainly it is possible that the people who Frankl described were also suffering from a mental illness, or illnesses. But my point here is simply that their newfound identities as *prisoners* were sufficient to constitute a loss of a sense of self. Following Edwin Shneidman, then, their self-images were assaulted, making it difficult to maintain an identifiable self-conception, or a sense of self.

Witnessing first-hand the horrors of the Nazi concentration camps compelled Frankl to establish logotherapy, as contrasted with traditional psychotherapy. In logotherapy, a "patient is actually confronted with and reoriented toward the meaning of his life."[33] Frankl saw that reconnecting a person to what is meaningful in their life can be more therapeutic than ruminating over the past or being prescribed medications in effort to treat relentless bouts of despair. In fact, Frankl believed that it was a kind of malpractice for psychiatrists to overlook, or to medicate away, the possible existential crises of their patients. Frankl explained:

> [a] man's concern, even his despair, over the worthwhileness of his life is an *existential distress* but by no means a *mental disease*. It may will be that interpreting the first in terms of the latter motivates a doctor to bury his patient's existential despair under a heap of tranquilizing drugs. It is his task, rather, to pilot the patient through his existential crises of growth and development.[34]

Frankl recognized that existential crises could arise in response to life's circumstances and events, and that such crises can arise independently of an underlying mental illness. Experiencing trauma, for example, challenges a person's sense of meaning. When severe, trauma can undermine one's sense of self, including one's desire for their well-being. Indeed, Frankl closely connected a person's sense of meaning in their lives with a person's will to live.

Conversely, lacking meaning in one's life and, thereby, experiencing existential crises, resembles the excessive psychache, which Edwin Shneidman attributed to persons who died by suicide. Actions of suicide by those who have lost their ability to maintain a minimal sense of self are amoral actions. To clarify, I believe that one's inability to maintain a sense of self could be the result of severe mental illness, but that it need not arise from the presence of an underlying mental illness. There may be circumstances or events that undermine one's self-conception, that take away one's autonomy (and so, leave one or more basic psychological needs unmet), or that otherwise destroy one's sense of meaning in life and, thereby, cause excessive psychache.

Actions of suicide stemming from a lack or an absence of a sense of self are, perhaps, the most difficult actions of suicide to identify in practice. No one else knows of another's internal anguish, or their degree of psychache; and, for the sufferer, their loss feels both profound and permanent. Consequently, these are typically the actions of suicide that are the most shocking or surprising. Indeed, these seem to be among the actions of suicide that even those persons dedicated to suicide prevention have difficulty identifying and predicting. When viewed through a moral lens, however, such actions of suicide are perhaps the most obvious actions of suicide that are *amoral*. Like any action, when someone lacks the abilities required to exercise their deliberative agency at the time of the action, then the action in question is amoral.

It might be that all actions of suicide, at least in some way, signify that a person who dies by suicide has already experienced a loss of a sense of self, or that their sense of self is in immediate danger of becoming lost. David Foster Wallace's claim that a person who dies by suicide is dead long before they pull the trigger illustrates the former, while the self-sacrificial action of Foxhole Jumper seems to illustrate the latter. On the one hand, a perceived, felt, or experienced loss of a sense of self could underlie a person's action of suicide insofar as basic psychological needs, such as autonomy and control, are lost. On the other hand, however, it could be that even a severe and an immediate *threat* to one's sense of self is sufficient to jeopardize a person's basic psychological needs. In any case, I believe that it is imperative to examine both a thwarted sense of belonging and perceived burdensomeness—two of the psychological states identified in Thomas Joiner's interpersonal theory of suicide—to gain further clarity not only about the variety of ways in which a person might experience a loss of a sense of self, but also to begin to examine the ways in which both a person's deliberative agency and moral agency can be compromised in actions of suicide. I will proceed to address a thwarted sense of belonging and perceived burdensomeness separately, even though it is their combination (in conjunction with overcoming one's fear of death) that increases a person's risk of suicide per Joiner's account.

A THWARTED SENSE OF BELONGING

One basic psychological need is the need to belong, or the need for affiliation. It certainly makes sense to think that, as *social beings*, some degree of social acceptance is a necessary part of our *being*. Again, just to be clear, a thwarted sense of belonging is not sufficient on its own accord, or by itself, to account for why a person might die by suicide per Joiner's account. Rather, a thwarted sense of belonging is to be understood in conjunction with a perceived burdensomeness and a capacity for self-harm. But, for my purposes here, I wish to focus upon both a thwarted sense of belonging and perceived burdensomeness independently of each other. My aim in doing so is to suggest that when either of these psychological needs—namely, the need for belonging or the need for competence—are severely lacking, then such an agent's actions are no longer in the moral domain. For instance, if a person's deliberative agency is at-risk with the absence of just one of these psychological needs, then *a fortiori* a person's deliberative agency is at-risk when both psychological needs are severely lacking.

A thwarted sense of belonging is different from the experience of a loss of a sense of self. Persons who experience a thwarted sense of belonging seem to have an identifiable self-conception despite the interplay of the fact that an identifiable self-conception both informs one's social connections and is informed by one's social connections. So, it is not a person's understanding of themselves that is lost but, rather, it is their place in the world. More precisely, if a person no longer feels a sense of belonging, then a significant or valued connection with another person, or persons, is lost.

Unfortunately, our human condition provides ample opportunities in which a person might experience a thwarted sense of belonging. Losing a loved one comes to mind as one of the more salient examples. Grief can be a disorienting process in which one attempts to re-navigate their life without their beloved. But a person might lose their sense of belonging in many other ways. The loss of romantic relationships or even the loss of employment threatens to sever a person's connection with others. A sense of belonging can become elusive, at best, through other life experiences, such as bullying, harassment, abuse, and neglect just to name a few. But situations do not need to be extreme or drastic to undermine one's sense of belonging. Prolonged loneliness, for example, is sufficient to undermine a person's psychological need to belong. It is a person's relationships—namely, their connections with others—that are at issue in losing one's sense of belonging.

In chapter two, I noted that moral injuries seem to illustrate how a person's relational knowledge could be compromised. When a person's relational knowledge is compromised, then their ability to have *moral* reasons for acting and to act upon such reasons is compromised as well. Relational knowledge, however, is socially imparted. Experiencing the loss of a relationship, or relationships, could impact a person's relational knowledge and, in turn, their ability to have moral reasons and to act upon such reasons. So, following Joiner's theory, some people who experience their sense of belonging as thwarted, or as suddenly missing in their lives, might be at an increased risk for engaging in an action of suicide (when other conditions are also met).

But if a person's sense of belonging is thwarted, then it seems likely that their relational knowledge is compromised as well since such knowledge is socially imparted. Furthermore, if a person's relational knowledge is compromised, then they are unable to see moral reasons as providing reasons for acting, and their action of suicide is amoral.

Closer attention to a specific moral injury might help to elucidate how losing one's sense of belonging could be a contributing factor for that person to engage in an action of suicide. In William Styron's famous work *Sophie's Choice*, Styron's character, Sophie, suffers a horrifically severe and heartbreaking moral injury. Sophie is captured by the Nazis during World War II and deported to Auschwitz with her two young children, Jan and Eva. Upon arrival at the camp, Sophie is not only separated from her children, but she is also forced to make an impossible choice. Sophie is forced to choose which of her two children is immediately murdered and which child is spared. Refusing to make such an unconscionable choice means that both children are immediately murdered. In unspeakable anguish and relentless tears, Sophie screams "I *can't* choose! I *can't* choose."[35] Styron wrote: "[t]ormented angels never screeched so loudly above hell's pandemonium."[36]

Yet realizing both children will be immediately murdered by her not choosing, Sophie makes the impossible, so-called choice; and her baby girl, Eva, is sent to be immediately murdered. Quite understandably, Sophie's impossible choice breaks her. Sophie is plagued by an immense feeling of guilt. Although Sophie is a victim of horrific circumstances, she is haunted by the idea that she is also an accomplice to her child's murder. Out of her maternal love to *save* at least one of her children, Sophie simultaneously *betrays* her maternal love.

Sophie's suicide is unsurprising, not just because Styron foreshadows it in his novel, but because Sophie's guilt and grief are paradoxically both entirely incomprehensible and yet oddly understandable. Sophie's moral injury reflects the moral injury suffered among some military veterans, as both Rita Nakashima Brock and Gabriella Lettini recognize. Recall that Brock and Lettini maintain that one of the most dangerous aspects of severe moral injuries "is the collapse of meaning and the loss of a will to live."[37] That is not to say that Sophie *cannot* perform actions, or that she is completely incapable of fulfilling the requirements of both deliberative and moral agency. Rather, it is to say that, regarding Sophie's specific action of suicide, she did not proceed to do *that action* as a *deliberative* agent.

When Sophie dies by suicide, it is clear to the audience that her intentions to end her life cannot be separated from her intention to end her profound guilt and grief. Sophie's screams of "*I can't choose!*" are metaphorically echoed in her action of suicide, as if resounding that she *cannot choose* to continue to bear her agonizing pain. Jeffrey Berman describes Sophie's mental state in the following way: "Sophie is severely depressed. [. . .] Her rage toward God is evident [. . .], as is her belief that life no longer holds any meaning or value to her. Sophie presumably chooses suicide, but depression makes the choice for her."[38]

Both so-called choices then—namely, Sophie's *choice* of which child to save at Auschwitz and her *choice* to die by suicide—are misnomers. They draw attention to the simple fact that some so-called choices simply *do not reflect Sophie's will*. That is, the outcomes are not at all *desired* by Sophie. Nevertheless, the idea that actions of suicide are intentional actions fuels the assumption that, as intentional actions, they must be chosen and, furthermore, as chosen actions, they must reflect a person's will. In short, the assumption is that the outcomes of such actions must be desired by the agent in question. But such an assumption is mistaken.

In chapter two, I noted that a person's intentions do not need to reflect their desires by appealing to the work of G. E. M. Anscombe. But there are plenty of examples of intentional actions that are not chosen. For example, suppose that I am driving an automobile along a highway and a child quickly runs out into the street. Further suppose that I cannot stop in time to avoid hitting the child. But I still can swerve to miss the child. So, suppose that I make the split-second decision to swerve to miss hitting the child but, in turn, I run the automobile off the side of the road and hit a fence. It seems correct to say both that I intended to swerve *and* that I did not choose to hit a fence even though my intention to swerve is what drove me (quite literally) into the fence.

I believe that actions of suicide seem to be similar in this respect—namely, that a person can very much intend to end their life without either choosing to die or desiring to die.[39] Indeed, we already saw an example of such an action of suicide in Foxhole Jumper's action of suicide noted in chapter two. Foxhole Jumper's action is an action of suicide. Yet Foxhole Jumper's action of suicide is one in which Foxhole Jumper neither intended death for its own sake nor desired his death. Rather, he saw his death as the only (necessary) means of saving members of his platoon and, thereby, intended his death. So, *prima facie*, self-sacrificial actions, like Foxhole Jumper's action appears to be among the atypical actions of suicide. But I believe that self-sacrificial actions of suicide might be more typical than atypical insofar as they might more closely resemble other actions of suicide than is commonly recognized.

Moreover, explaining Sophie's suicide in terms of depression, as Jeffrey Berman does, certainly does not negate her moral injury. There might be a kind of chicken and egg problem here—insofar as it might make sense to ask, "*which one came first?*" But actions of suicide are complex, and the dichotomy assumed—namely, that either one's moral injury or their depression or some other such singular factor must explain a person's action of suicide—seems misguided. In William Styron's 1988 *New York Times* op-ed piece entitled "Why Primo Levi Need Not Have Died," which was published after Primo Levi, a Holocaust survivor, died by suicide, Styron wrote:

> [t]he origins of depression remain a puzzle, despite significant advances in research. Many factors seem to be involved. Aside from the basic chemical disturbance in the brain and behavioral and genetic influences, psychological reasons must be added to the equation. Mr. Levi may have been bedeviled by buried conflicts unrelated to Auschwitz. Or, indeed, his ordeal at Auschwitz may have imposed on his soul an insupportable burden [. . .].[40]

Styron neither committed to saying that Levi's death was due to his experiences at Auschwitz, or that Levi's death was due to his depression. Styron left both possibilities open; and, in doing so, allowed for a range of factors to play a role in suicidal thinking. As Styron further explained: "what is of ultimate importance to the victim of depression is not the cause but the treatment and the cure."[41] Yet progress in treatments and cures could be hindered by the perpetuation of the idea that, if a person performs an action of suicide, then they must *desire* their death, or that they are somehow *choosing* their death for its own sake.

Indeed, it is long overdue to recognize that actions of suicide, while intentional, do not necessitate that a person desires or chooses death for its own sake. Edwin Shneidman observed that

> [t]he prototypical suicidal state is one in which an individual cuts his throat and cries for help at the same time, and is genuine on both sides of the act. Ambivalence is the common state in suicide: To feel that one has to do it, and, simultaneously, to yearn for intervention. I have never known anyone who was 100 percent for wanting to [. . . die by] suicide without any fantasies of possible rescue. Individuals would be happy not to do it, if they didn't "have to."[42]

So, suppose that Shneidman was correct in his observation that ambivalence is the common state of suicide. Further, suppose that Shneidman was correct to observe that some people felt as though they *had to* die by suicide—that is, that they had no choice in the matter. Notice that neither one of Shneidman's observations bodes well for a person retaining a sufficient degree of deliberative agency. Indeed, both of Shneidman's observations undermine the deliberative agency required for a person's action to be an action in the moral domain.

The severe moral injury that Sophie suffered compromised her deliberative agency with respect to her action of suicide. Sophie took her life without *choosing* to take it. The constellation of her trauma, victimization, grief, guilt, and depression had taken her life from her. Sophie's sense of belonging in the world is shattered, and her action of suicide is amoral. Her action of suicide is *not* a product of her deliberative, moral agency—nor could it have been.

It seems that some persons who are victims of bullying might have experiences resembling the experiences of some persons who suffer from a moral injury. There are degrees of bullying and degrees of moral injuries, of course, but it could be that some persons who are bullied internalize the awful and undeserved transgressions against them. If a person develops a sense of self-hatred or worthlessness because of being bullied, then their sense of self is in danger of being compromised. But if their sense of self is compromised, then they would no longer be in the position to appreciate self-regarding moral reasons for acting, much less to act upon such reasons. If a person, who is unable to appreciate and to act upon self-regarding moral reasons for acting, performs an action of suicide, then *that action* is outside of the moral domain, or amoral. It appears that at least some instances of bullying and that at least some instances of suffering a severe moral injury are similar insofar as both could entail a kind of betrayal that could seriously threaten a person's will to live.

Lastly, some attention to marginalized societal groups seems warranted in a discussion about how a thwarted sense of belonging can play a significant role with respect to actions of suicide. It is no secret that while risks for dying by suicide appear to be evenly spread throughout the entire human population, some persons are more at-risk than others simply by factors such as their culture, their geographical location, their degree of oppression, and their social mobility. Attention to social factors and conditions are needed, of course, because a person develops their self-conception *socially*.

For instance, Leelah Alcorn was only seventeen years old when she died by suicide in 2014; and her story garnered much attention.[43] Leelah posted her suicide note on social media shortly before stepping out in front of a truck near her home.[44] Her note expressed her pain of simply trying to be who she was—to live authentically—as a transgender girl. In her note, she made a plea to "fix society" and that her death needs "to mean something."[45] When a person is unable to be themselves, then their sense of self is lost. Every action to conform to social expectations, then, becomes a moral injury—a form of self-betrayal. Though deeply loved, her psychological need to belong was socially undermined. Carol Gilligan's observation that a person can feel betrayed by social structures seems to capture Leelah's plea to fix society. In sum, some actions of suicide appear to stem from social structures that betray a person's psychological need for belonging.

A person does not need to internalize self-hatred or a sense of worthlessness upon suffering a moral injury or upon being bullied or marginalized in society to lose their sense of self. Without a sense of belonging, a person's sense of self could be perceived as lost. If the ability to have *moral* reasons for acting and the ability to act upon such reasons depends upon a person seeing themselves *as part of a moral community*, then a loss of belonging is sufficient to compromise those abilities. While I maintain that actions of suicide are amoral, actions of suicide stemming from a loss of belonging signifies a different kind of action within the moral domain. Namely, whenever we contribute to, and thereby perpetuate, oppressive societal structures, then we participate in a moral failing.

A PERCEIVED BURDENSOMENESS

The last psychological need that I will consider here is the need for competence, or the need for a sense of effectiveness in one's life. But the need for competence is multifaceted. In fact, as I noted above, Thomas Joiner combines several psychological needs as frustrated under the heading of perceived burdensomeness. Joiner borrows from Edwin Shneidman who noted that some actions of suicide appear to arise from an "assaulted self-image, fractured control, [and] anger related to frustrated dominance."[46] So, according to Shneidman, the psychological needs at issue in some actions of suicide are the need to maintain a self-image, the need for control, and the need for dominance. When these needs are unfulfilled, or when these needs are in serious and immediate danger of being unfulfilled, then a person's way of thinking (and of acting) is narrowly focused upon how to satisfy such needs. After addressing how the psychological need to belong is thwarted in actions of suicide, Joiner writes:

> I would argue that the other bedrock need is effectiveness or a sense of competence. When this need is thwarted, when one perceives oneself as ineffective, it is painful indeed. To perceive oneself as so ineffective that loved ones are threatened and burdened is even worse, so much so that the desire for death could be generated.[47]

Joiner recognizes that a person's desire for death is not sought for its own sake but, rather, to escape the agony of perceiving oneself to be so ineffective that loved ones are threatened or burdened. In any case, just as there are nuances with respect to the need to belong, there are nuances with respect to the need for competence and effectiveness. To be sure, I will briefly re-consider Foxhole Jumper's self-sacrificial action of suicide.

I previously noted that, when Foxhole Jumper jumps on a live grenade to save the lives of his comrades, he acted according to who he took himself to be. To have done otherwise, or to have failed to act, would have been unthinkable to him. He might have lost his psychological need for competence as a soldier, or for effectiveness in his life, if by not acting as he did since Foxhole Jumper would have reasoned that his comrades would perish in the blast by his inaction. The idea is that, if Foxhole Jumper acted from a volitional necessity, then he was not in the position to act upon moral reasons. Rather, he was acting to maintain his self-image or self-conception—that is, to have failed to act as he did would have meant a loss of his psychological need to be effective or to demonstrate his competence as a soldier.

I believe that there are similarities between the Foxhole Jumper's action of suicide and physician-assisted actions of suicide (hereafter, PAS). One similarity between Foxhole Jumper's action of suicide and possible PAS is the severe constraint, or limitations, among the available courses of action. Another important similarity is that, following Edwin Shneidman, it could be that both self-sacrificial actions (like Foxhole Jumper's action of suicide) and PAS become possible when a person understands that their self-image or self-conception is under clear and immediate threat.[48] Before exploring these similarities, however, attention to what constitutes PAS is in order.

Judgments about the quality and quantity, or duration, of one's life are frequently at issue in medical decisions. For example, decisions about what course of action to take among one's treatment options—including, of course, the option of refusing treatment—ideally expresses a patient's informed decision in consultation with their physician. Informed decisions such as refusing life-sustaining treatments or discontinuing a life-sustaining treatment plan are uniquely personal decisions. Making such informed decisions is a standard practice of care that is not routinely questioned nor considered controversial. It would seem odd for informed decisions among patients suddenly to be denied when the treatment plan in question involves the end of one's life. After all, a patient who refuses life-sustaining treatment (e.g., declines life support) or a patient who discontinues a life-sustaining treatment plan (e.g., withdraws from life support) are making decisions that could expedite their passing.[49]

PAS is an action in which a physician aids a patient to end their life—usually by prescribing lethal drugs—and the patient in question performs the act of administering those drugs, which causes their death. To be clear, PAS is neither active euthanasia in which, say, a physician administers the drugs that cause death, nor is PAS passive euthanasia, in which life-sustaining measures are withheld or withdrawn. Furthermore, both active and passive euthanasia can take voluntary and involuntary forms, as well as non-voluntary forms. But I just wish to stress here that PAS is not equivalent to any form or type of euthanasia.

While PAS differs from euthanasia, there is much debate and concern regarding how their conceptual difference works in practice. For example, some people who are against PAS might oppose PAS out of fear that allowing physicians to assist patients in dying will lead not only to euthanasia but also, specifically, to involuntary euthanasia in which a physician hastens a patient's death against their will. Indeed, even the possibility that allowing PAS might also somehow allow, or lead to, non-voluntary euthanasia is an unsettling and an undesirable possibility, to say the very least. Some proponents of PAS, however, might claim that persons without the ability to take a lethal prescription on their own accord are unfairly denied PAS. It is not my aim here is not to resolve such differences, which tend to focus upon a different, though related question—namely, whether PAS ought to be legal.[50] Legality is one matter, and morality is another.

Rather, my aim here is to put forth an understanding of the amorality of PAS. Again, to clarify, claiming that PAS is amoral is neither to support the practice of PAS nor to condemn such actions. If PAS is amoral, then arguments supporting PAS *because it is deemed morally permissible*, as well as arguments opposing PAS *because it is deemed immoral*, are equally misguided. Therefore, if PAS actions are amoral, then we need to jettison legal arguments, either for or against PAS, that rest entirely upon the moral status of PAS.

There are many factors that can lead a person to seek PAS; and places in which PAS is legal have put in place criteria that a person must meet to obtain PAS. Some of the criteria might include that a person has been diagnosed with a terminal illness, have less than six months to live, complete a psychiatric evaluation and be deemed competent to make such a decision, as well as expressing their wishes for PAS on multiple occasions with those expressions being at least two weeks apart, and so on.[51] The criteria of PAS certainly needs critical attention with respect to how PAS is implemented in the places where the practice is legal.

What is at issue here, however, is whether PAS itself—namely, the action of a patient ending their life under the medical supervision of a physician—is an action that belongs in the moral domain at all. I contend that actions of PAS do not belong in the moral domain. There are several reasons as to why actions of PAS are amoral. Before addressing these reasons, however, I will turn to Andrew Solomon's account of the passing of his mother, which he describes in his book *The Noonday Demon: An Atlas of Depression*.

Andrew Solomon's work on depression and suicide is informed by his personal struggles with both. Not only has Solomon reported some of his struggles with depression and suicidality, but he also was a witness to his mother's struggle with depression and, ultimately, a witness to her suicide. Regarding his mother, Solomon recounts: "I think she had suffered from mild depression for years; if I have depression genes, I suspect they came from her."[52] In 1989, Solomon's mother was diagnosed with terminal cancer.[53] The combination of depression and suffering from cancer understandably led

Solomon's mother to convey a kind of emotional numbness, or sense of nullity. Solomon explains his mother's experience of emotional numbness in the following way:

> [m]y mother took Prozac, then a brand-new drug, for a month during her fight with cancer. She said it numbed her too much—and it made her jittery, which, in combination with the side effects of her chemo, was too much to bear. 'I was walking down the street today,' she said, 'and I thought, I am probably dying. And then I thought, should we have cherries or pears at lunch? And the two things felt too much the same.'[54]

Andrew Solomon continues by stating that his mother "had [a] sufficient external reason to be depressed, and she was a great believer in authenticity."[55] Such emotional numbness, however, compromises a person's ability to consider and to weigh moral reasons for acting. Emotional numbness seems inseparable from an indifference to considerations of varying importance, as Solomon's quote above conveys.

To be clear, it is not that those suffering from depression and a terminal illness appear unable to give due consideration to matters of greater importance. Rather, it is that a person's perceived courses of action become so very limited that exercising one's deliberative and moral agencies is no longer a luxury afforded to them. Like Phil's inability to open a safe and, thereby, his inability to prevent a serious calamity from happening, some people who contemplate PAS do so while in the grip of unbearable and relentless conditions.

With brave honesty, Andrew Solomon writes:

> [m]y mother decided to kill herself on June 19, 1991, age fifty-eight, because if she had waited longer, she would have been too weak to take her life, and suicide requires strength and a kind of privacy that does not exist in hospitals. That afternoon, my mother went to see a gastroenterologist, who told her that large tumors were blocking her intestine. Without immediate surgery, she would be unable to digest food.[56]

Solomon's description of his mother's terminal illness, her depression, and her decision to end her life provides several insights regarding PAS. First, Solomon explains that "I would say of suicide not that it is always a tragedy for the person who dies, but that it always comes too soon and too suddenly for those left behind."[57] Solomon's acknowledgement that actions of suicide are not always a tragedy for the person who dies is a simple reminder that actions of suicide do not take place in isolation. Such actions, if they are to be understood at all, must be understood *contextually*. With respect to Solomon's mother's situation, it could be said that what was tragic was, indeed, the terminal cancer that befell her.

Second, Solomon takes aim at the public debate surrounding PAS and casts blame equally upon those of opposing views. Solomon reports that "those who condemn the right to die are committing a grave disservice. We all want more control over life than we have, and dictating the terms of other people's lives makes us feel safe."[58] The desire to have control over the lives of other people could fuel opposition to a legal right to PAS. Yet Solomon proceeds to caution his audience by stating that wanting such control "is no reason to forbid people [of] their most primitive freedom."[59] Indeed, Solomon maintains that "it is up to each man to set limits on his own tortures."[60] I believe that both of Solomon's insights are analogous to insights that can be drawn from self-sacrificial actions of suicide, such as Foxhole Jumper's action of suicide.

To be sure, it seems that Foxhole Jumper's decision to jump on the live grenade to save his comrades is also akin to setting a limit on his own tortures. To have done otherwise would have meant that he sacrificed his self-conception, or who he took himself to be. Similarly, it could be said that a person who engages in PAS likewise has their self-conception hanging in the balance. Losing a sense of self while still alive is its own torture; and so, in this way, persons who engage in PAS are like the Foxhole Jumper. Somewhat ironically, PAS could be construed as an attempt to *preserve* one's sense of self—to remain a person who is both competent and effective and, thereby, not to further suffer the loss of these basic psychological *needs*.

Furthermore, Solomon advises his readers not to assume that PAS is somehow distinguishable from other actions of suicide. As Solomon explains, "I believe that those who, in supporting the right to die, distinguish some suicides [. . .] from others are telling a lie."[61] Just like Shelly Kagan refers to self-sacrificial actions of suicide as atypical actions of suicide, it certainly seems as though PAS also fits the bill here of being atypical actions of suicide, but they are actions of suicide, nevertheless. It seems clear that Foxhole Jumper's action of suicide does not convey that Foxhole Jumper desired to die or that he somehow chose death for its own sake. Rather, it seems that Foxhole Jumper saw his death as a means—specifically, as the only available means—of saving his comrades. In a similar way, persons who engage in PAS also need not have a desire to die, nor must they choose death for its own sake. Instead, it appears that persons who engage in PAS might see their death as a means—specifically, as the only available means—of *preserving* their sense of self; indeed, through PAS, a person can affirm who they take themselves to be.[62] It is reasonable to suppose that both the Foxhole Jumper and those persons who engage in PAS are acting to preserve a psychological need.

In addition to resembling Foxhole Jumper's suicide, persons contemplating PAS are also in a position like Phil's discussed above. Recall that Phil's inability to open the safe and, thereby, his failure to prevent a serious calamity was due to Phil not knowing the combination of the safe in question. So, while Phil could open the safe if he knew the combination, he cannot open the safe because he does not know the combination. Phil's inability to open the safe is imposed on him. In a similar way, a person's serious and excruciating illness or aliment is imposed upon them. Persons who contemplate PAS do so from a vantage point of drastic limitations. Perhaps there are no treatment options. Perhaps only attempts at palliative care are available and, perhaps, even those fall short of resembling the comfort they once knew.[63] The upshot is that, like Sophie's action of suicide, describing PAS as *chosen* is a misleading misnomer.

Consider, for example, the story of Brittany Maynard who, after being diagnosed with terminal brain cancer in 2014, moved from California to Oregon to have the option for PAS (which was not yet authorized in California at that time).[64] Maynard became an advocate for the option of PAS. Nevertheless, she maintained that she was *not choosing* to die. It was *how* she died that deeply mattered to her.[65] Hence, the moral status of actions of PAS—namely, the fact that actions of PAS are outside of the moral domain—becomes indistinguishable from other actions of suicide insofar as claiming that such an action is *chosen* is a misnomer.

A rejoinder, however, might contend that actions of suicide are, by definition, *intentional*. When Solomon's mother took the lethal prescription, she did so knowingly and free of coercion. So, in response, I wish to make explicit two points regarding PAS, which are implicitly stated above. First, the limitations of options imposed upon a person contemplating PAS cannot be divorced from PAS. It is not an irrelevant detail, for instance, that without immediate surgery Solomon's mother would be unable to digest food. Furthermore, a severe limitation of a person's options seems to be a commonality seen among other actions of suicide—such as Sophie's action of suicide and Foxhole Jumper's action of suicide.

One way to think about the perceived necessity behind such a so-called choice to end one's life is to recognize that assent is not the same thing as consent. For example, if a person is robbed at gunpoint, then they may assent to handing over their money to the armed robber. But they are doing so under coercion. They are not consenting to give their money away but, in such frightful circumstances, they are assenting to give up their money.[66] So, their action of handing over their money does not reflect their will to do so but, rather, their desire to be spared by the robber. So, it certainly is possible that a person could assent to something that does not reflect their will, or that does not reflect their desires.

Second, even among a person's limited options, what appears to be most fundamental to a person's agency is who they take themselves to be. When an identifiable self-conception is lost, then a person is unable to exercise their deliberative agency. Persons suffering from severe depression, for example, might be unable to exercise their deliberative agency due to the loss of a sense of self. William Styron's account of his depression and suicidal ideation appear to illustrate such a loss of self. Yet, even when a person has an identifiable self-conception in-tact, there could be circumstances in which their self-conception is under severe and immediate threat. In such cases, a person might do whatever they can to preserve their sense of self, or who they take themselves to be; and, in extreme cases, some people might intend to preserve their sense of self over life itself, as in the action of Foxhole Jumper. Preserving one's sense of self is a need, not a want, which is why people like Foxhole Jumper could very much feel compelled to so act. Again, it appears as though Foxhole Jumper acts from a volitional necessity in his action of suicide, and not as a moral agent acting upon a moral reason, or reasons.

Foxhole Jumper's action of suicide, as well as Andrew Solomon's recollection of his mother's PAS and Britney Maynard's PAS, offer insight into the amorality of suicide. Namely, such actions of suicide are subtle reminders that death need not be sought for its own sake in actions of suicide. Nor might one's death be regarded as the worst thing that can happen to a person. The loss of oneself while still alive is its own tragedy. Indeed, acknowledging his own struggles with depression and suicidality, Andrew Solomon explains, "I expect that I'll go on living so long as I can give or receive anything better than pain, but I do not promise that I will never kill myself. Nothing horrifies me more than the thought that I might at some stage lose the capacity for suicide."[67] Solomon's brave honesty here is a testament to the idea that thinking about suicide only in terms of taking away one's humanity is too narrow-focused, as an action of suicide might also be an expression of one's humanity.

In this chapter, I have attempted to follow Edwin Shneidman and Thomas Joiner's lead in their recognition that unmet psychological needs are at the root of actions of suicide. I believe that the psychological needs identified here—namely, the need for autonomy, belonging, and competence, are significant. These are significant psychological needs because, when they are unmet, they also undermine a person's deliberative and moral agencies. Hence, if actions of suicide are the result of unmet psychological needs, then actions of suicide cannot be actions in the moral domain. In sum, actions of suicide appear to be actions in which a person's deliberative agency or moral agency (or both) is either lacking or compromised. Moreover, death seems to be a means to another end or goal in actions of suicide; and so, death is neither desired nor chosen for its own sake with respect to any given action of suicide. In sum, the amorality of suicide does not depend upon whether an action of suicide stems from a mental illness, an existential crisis, a moral injury, bullying, self-sacrifice, or PAS. Actions of suicide are amoral.

NOTES

1. Thomas Joiner, *Why People Die by Suicide* (Cambridge: Harvard University Press, 2005), 16.

2. Thomas Joiner, *Why People Die by Suicide*, 47.

3. The fact that curbing access to lethal means, such as firearms, could be a way reduce the number of deaths by firearms—including among those who die by suicide—somehow seems to become lost in discussions of suicide prevention. Even so, if Joiner is correct to claim that a thwarted sense of belonging and perceived burdensomeness can increase a person's likelihood of dying by suicide, but only when someone also has acquired lethal capacity and lethal means, then failing to restrict access to firearms among those most at-risk of dying by suicide is a social, moral failing.

4. Thomas Joiner, *Why People Die by Suicide*, 33.

5. Thomas Joiner, *Why People Die by Suicide*, 36.

6. Edwin S. Shneidman, *The Suicidal Mind* (New York: Oxford University Press, 1996), 13.

7. Edwin S. Shneidman, *The Suicidal Mind*, 13, emphasis added.

8. Edwin S. Shneidman, *The Suicidal Mind*, 25.

9. Edwin S. Shneidman, *The Suicidal Mind*, 25, Shneidman's emphasis.

10. Edwin S. Shneidman, *The Suicidal Mind*, 25.

11. Edwin S. Shneidman, *The Suicidal Mind*, 25.

12. Thomas Joiner, *Why People Die by Suicide*, 96.

13. William Styron, *Darkness Visible: A Memoir of Madness* (New York: Random House, 1990).

14. William Styron, *Darkness Visible*, 56.

15. William Styron, *Darkness Visible*, 57.

16. William Styron, *Darkness Visible*, 64.

17. William Styron, *Darkness Visible*, 64–65.

18. Edwin S. Shneidman, *The Suicidal Mind*, 25.

19. David Foster Wallace, "This is Water," Commencement Address at Kenyon College in Gambier, Ohio, 2005. For transcript, please see: http://bulletin-archive.kenyon.edu/x4280.html (accessed April 8, 2022).

20. David Lipsky, "The Lost Years and Last Days of David Foster Wallace," in *Rolling Stone* (September 20, 2019, online; originally published October 30, 2008, in *Rolling Stone* 1064). https://www.rollingstone.com/culture/culture-features/the-lost-years-and-last-days-of-david-foster-wallace-883224/ (accessed April 8, 2022).

21. This passage refers to a part of the David Foster Wallace's Commencement speech that not included in the Kenyon College bulletin archive. It is, however, noted in Tom Bissell's essay (book review) for *The New York Times* entitled "Great and Terrible Truths" (April 24, 2009).

22. Edwin S. Shneidman, *The Suicidal Mind*, 133.

23. Naomi Judd and Marcia Wilkie, *River of Time: My Descent into Depression and How I Emerged with Hope* (New York: Hachette Book Group, Inc., 2016), 1, emphasis added. The idea that Naomi's illness made her no longer recognize herself is a reoccurring theme in the book.

24. William Styron, *Darkness Visible*, 33.

25. Ramon Antonio Vargas, "Naomi Judd Dealing with Bipolar Disorder When She Died by Suicide, Autopsy Says," in *The Guardian* (August 27, 2022).

26. David Foster Wallace, "This is Water," Commencement Address at Kenyon College in Gambier, Ohio, 2005. http://bulletin-archive.kenyon.edu/x4280.html (accessed April 8, 2022).

27. It can be worse than what I am implying here. That is, some persons who suffer from severe depression as a mental illness are not only unable to exercise their moral agency, but they may also be unable simply to do what is expected of them in meeting the demands of everyday life.

28. Kay Redfield Jamison, *Night Falls Fast: Understanding Suicide* (New York: Random House, 1999), 85.

29. Kay Redfield Jamison, *Night Falls Fast*, 93.

30. For more on how depression (as a mental illness) can impair moral agency, please see Julia Driver's chapter "Meta-Cognition, Mind-Reading, and Humean Moral Agency," in *Moral Psychology and Human Agency: Philosophical Essays on the Science of Ethics*, ed. Justin D'Arms and Daniel Jacobson, 123–36, esp. 131–35 (New York: Oxford University Press, 2014).

31. A more contentious point here is whether *all* mental illnesses that a person could suffer are, in fact, *treatable* illnesses. There seems to be a rather common assumption that all such illnesses are treatable—or that if a person only got the right treatment, then they would be fine (or at least that they would be able to go about their everyday lives). But unfortunately, it is simply not true that other (non-mental) illnesses that could befall a person are treatable, and so it seems misguided to believe that *mental* illnesses are somehow different in this respect. For example, as Naomi Judd explained, "I was diagnosed with severe treatment-resistant depression. Meaning they had tried everything they could think of and nothing was working." (Naomi Judd and Marcia Wilkie, *River of Time*, 220). Recognizing that some mental illnesses that could befall a person are treatment-resistant is neither to give up on the possibility of treatment breakthroughs nor is it to believe (falsely) that our present-day resources are adequate to treat all persons who suffer from a mental illness or illnesses. Rather, recognizing that some mental illnesses that could befall a person are treatment-resistant is simply to resist the temptation of claiming that a person with severe depression, for example, *only* needs access to present-day treatment options, and then they would overcome their depression.

32. Viktor E. Frankl, *Man's Search for Meaning* (Boston: Beacon Press, 2006), 20. Originally published in 1959.

33. Viktor E. Frankl, *Man's Search for Meaning*, 98.

34. Viktor E. Frankl, *Man's Search for Meaning*, 102–103. Frankl's emphasis.

35. William Styron, *Sophie's Choice* (New York: Vintage Books, 1976, reprint 1992), 529, emphasis added.

36. William Styron, *Sophie's Choice*, 529.

37. Rita Nakashima Brock and Gabriella Lettini, *Soul Repair: Recovering from Moral Injury after War* (Boston: Beacon Press, 2012), 80.

38. Jeffrey Berman, *Mad Muse: The Mental Illness Memoir in a Writer's Life and Work* (Bingley, UK: Emerald Publishing Limited, 2019), 57.

39. In the automobile example of swerving to miss a child and, instead, hitting a fence, it might be said that hitting a fence is clearly the lesser of the two evils or of the two options at that time. But that is not to say that hitting the fence in question was desirable as an independent event. That is, *ceteris paribus*, one would not wish simply to crash into fences. I believe that there is an important analogy here regarding actions of suicide. If there are outcomes worse than a person's death, then it is simply not true that *the worst thing* that can happen to a person is their own death. Rather, one's own death could be likened to crashing into the fence in the above example. It is not desirable *ceteris paribus*. But it could be desirable as the lesser of two evils given one's limited options in the moment.

40. William Styron, "Why Primo Levi Need Not Have Died," in *The New York Times*, op-ed, December 19, 1988, as reprinted in *My Generation: Collected Nonfiction by William Styron*, edited by James L. W. West III, 189–92 (New York: Random House, 2015), 191.

41. William Styron, "Why Primo Levi Need Not Have Died," 191.

42. Edwin S. Shneidman, *The Suicidal Mind*, 133.

43. Ashley Fantz, "An Ohio Transgender Teen's Suicide, A Mother's Anguish," *CNN*, January 4, 2015, https://www.cnn.com/2014/12/31/us/ohio-transgender-teen-suicide/index.html.

44. Ashley Fantz, "An Ohio Transgender Teen's Suicide, A Mother's Anguish."

45. Ashley Fantz, "An Ohio Transgender Teen's Suicide, A Mother's Anguish."

46. Thomas Joiner, *Why People Die by Suicide*, 96.

47. Thomas Joiner, *Why People Die by Suicide*, 97.

48. Previously in this chapter, I noted how a loss of a sense of self compromises a person's deliberative agency, or the kind of agency needed for their actions to be within the moral domain. In those actions of suicide, a person's self-conception is already lost, such that one's death is regarded as a formality. In this section, with a focus upon atypical actions of suicide—such as Foxhole Jumper's action and PAS—the idea is that a person's self-conception is in severe and immediate danger of becoming lost. Such actions of suicide, then, are actions needed to save one's self-conception, or who they take themselves to be. In both scenarios—either acting from a loss of one's sense of self or acting from a need to preserve one's sense of self—preclude acting in ways responsive to moral reasons for acting.

49. In his book *Being Mortal: Medicine and What Matters in the End*, Atul Gawande explains our current state of affairs in the following way: "[w]e are running up against the difficulty of maintaining a coherent philosophical distinction between giving people the right to stop external or artificial processes that prolong their lives and giving them the right to stop the natural, internal processes that do so" (New York: Henry Holt and Company, 2014), 244.

50. In addition to a debate about the legality of PAS, a debate about the appropriate standards of care (or the aims of healthcare) is a further, ongoing debate. For example, it is commonly taken for granted that a person may refuse medical treatment, even if such a refusal hastens their death. Yet taking a lethal prescription to hasten one's

death is far from being taken for granted as a standard of care. While palliative care is part of healthcare, it seemingly remains an open question as to what it means to care for someone at the end of their life, and whether providing a good death is an appropriate standard of care.

51. This partial listing is from Oregon's Death With Dignity Act (DWDA) as found on "Frequently Asked Questions" page of the Oregon Health Authority (an official website of the State of Oregon in the United States). https://www.oregon.gov/oha/PH/PROVIDERPARTNERRESOURCES/EVALUATIONRESEARCH/DEATHWITHDIGNITYACT/Pages/faqs.aspx

52. Andrew Solomon, *The Noonday Demon*, 282.

53. Andrew Solomon, *The Noonday Demon*, 271.

54. Andrew Solomon, *The Noonday Demon*, 282.

55. Andrew Solomon, *The Noonday Demon*, 282.

56. Andrew Solomon, *The Noonday Demon*, 276.

57. Andrew Solomon, *The Noonday Demon*, 283.

58. Andrew Solomon, *The Noonday Demon*, 283.

59. Andrew Solomon, *The Noonday Demon*, 283.

60. Andrew Solomon, *The Noonday Demon*, 283.

61. Andrew Solomon, *The Noonday Demon*, 283.

62. I do not intend to suggest here that a person who contemplates PAS (in a place where it is legal), but who ultimately decides against PAS is somehow not affirming who they take themselves to be. Quite the contrary. My point here is simply that whether (or not) someone engages in PAS is an expression of who they take themselves to be. A decision about PAS is very much intertwined with a person's sense of self and, as such, it is not an action in the moral domain. Following Andrew Solomon, it is up to each person to set those limits.

63. To be clear, I firmly agree with the view of Atul Gawande with respect to improving treatment options and efforts with respect to palliative care (especially in the United States). Gawande's view is that, if by allowing PAS, we short-change palliative care, then we cease caring both for and about other persons. If PAS is to be allowed (or legalized), then it ought not to undermine opportunities for palliative care. Gawande writes: "[c]ertainly, suffering at the end of life is sometimes unavoidable and unbearable, and helping people end their misery may be necessary. Given the opportunity, I would support laws to provide these kinds of prescriptions to people. About half don't even use their prescription. They are reassured just to know they have this control if they need it. But we damage entire societies if we let providing this capability divert us from improving the lives of the ill. Assisted living is far harder than assisted death, but its possibilities are far greater, as well" (245). Interestingly, Gawande's comments here echo what Edwin Shneidman claimed with respect to other actions of suicide—namely, that "[i]ndividuals would be happy not to do it, if they didn't 'have to.'" (*The Suicidal Mind*, 133).

64. From *The Brittany Maynard Fund*, an initiative of Compassion & Choices, on their "About Brittany Maynard" webpage. https://thebrittanyfund.org/about/ (access date December 10, 2023).

65. From *The Brittany Maynard Fund*, an initiative of Compassion & Choices, on their "Videos" webpage: https://thebrittanyfund.org/videos/ (access date December 10, 2023).

66. Consenting to give away their money would be if the person in question simply decided to give their money to a charitable cause, free of such coercion.

67. Andrew Solomon, *The Noonday Demon*, 283.

Chapter Four

A Few Objections and Replies

My aim in this little book is to advance a discussion about the amorality of suicide. I suspect, however, that there might be several worries that come to mind regarding the thesis that actions of suicide are amoral. I wish to address several of these worries in this chapter, as I further suspect that such worries might prohibit some people from entertaining the idea that actions of suicide are amoral. Nevertheless, I do not pretend to address all such worries or concerns here. Rather, in this chapter, I wish to focus upon some of the main objections that I imagine could be raised regarding the amorality of actions of suicide. Toward this end, each section heading gives some indication about the respective objection. I then will begin each section with an explanation of the respective objection before offering a response, or responses, to the respective objection.

THE FLOODGATE WORRY

One worry about the thesis that actions of suicide are amoral is what I will refer to as, simply, the floodgate worry. The objection that I have in mind takes seriously the idea that some actions of suicide are amoral because the agent in question lacks a sense of self. But one might wonder what is stopping or preventing a person from claiming that *all actions are amoral* due to a person's lack of a sense of self? The idea here is that, even if it is accurate to claim that *some* actions of suicide are amoral because a person's sense of self is lacking and, in turn, their deliberative agency is compromised, it seems that such reasoning about the amorality of suicide might prove too much. For instance, what, if anything, prohibits a person from stating that their action (indeed, any action whatsoever) is amoral and, importantly, *not immoral* because they have lost their sense of self? Or perhaps they wish to claim that their action is amoral due to limitations in their relational knowledge, or due to circumstantial limitations? Simply stated, if the thesis presented here implies that otherwise immoral actions can be amoral across the board, then surely *that* is not an enticing conclusion to draw.

There are a couple of responses that I wish to make regarding what I am calling here *the floodgate worry*. My first response is that I believe that a sense of self, which is necessary for deliberative agency, creates a rather low threshold to meet for deliberative agency. Recall that, to have deliberative agency, a person must be able to have reasons for acting and be able to act upon such reasons. But we see a breakdown of a person's ability to exercise deliberative agency per Thomas Joiner's interpersonal theory of actions of suicide. That is, a loss of a sense of oneself, the loss of belonging, and the loss of competence or effectiveness fundamentally wreak havoc upon a person's ability to exercise their deliberative agency. Therefore, I believe that it would be a serious mistake to regard an action of suicide as somehow on par with other ordinary actions that people make every day. Actions of suicide are quite different; and the lack of a sense of self in such actions is extreme.

There are, of course, degrees in which one's sense of self is lost, but an agent can still maintain a sufficient degree of deliberative agency. The loss of a sense of self sufficient to prompt an agent to consider engaging in an action of suicide indicates an obliteration of their psychological need to maintain a sense of self, or their self-image. My focus here is, of course, upon actions of suicide. If a person were wishing to argue that other actions are amoral, then they would have the task of showing how *those actions* are amoral. In short, I do not regard the thesis that I present here as opening such floodgates.

My second response to the floodgate worry, however, is simply to point out that the usefulness of moral responsibility itself is a contentious point, at least philosophically. That is, if the purpose of regarding actions as within the moral domain is not only to cast moral judgments about those actions but, importantly, if the purpose is to hold persons morally responsible for their actions, then, at best, we need to proceed with caution here. For instance, in his book *Freedom Without Responsibility*, Bruce Waller interestingly proposed the idea that freedom is consistent with the notion that moral responsibility is an archaic illusion that we would be better off without.[1]

I recognize that there is a distinction, however, between believing that an action is within the moral domain and believing that someone is morally responsible for that action. If someone believes that at least some actions of suicide are immoral, for instance, they could still believe that a person who performs an action of suicide is *not* morally responsible for their action of suicide. So, an *action* within the moral domain does not need to be an action in which an *agent* bears moral responsibility. Nevertheless, if moral responsibility itself deserves philosophical scrutiny, as Waller claimed, then I believe that it also seems reasonable to call into question the presumed scope of those actions assumed to be within the moral domain.

INDIRECTLY RESPONSIBLE

A further concern with the claim that actions of suicide are amoral is simply the idea that, even if such actions do not merit moral evaluation, it still seems possible (and perhaps even appropriate) to suggest that such persons are morally responsible for getting the help they need. Proponents here might simply locate moral responsibility more upstream. An analogy can be made here with respect to drunk driving. While it certainly is true that once a driver is drunk, then they have compromised their ability to drive safely; and so, a drunk driver *cannot* drive safely, and it would be unreasonable to maintain the expectation that they can. It is unsurprising, then, that drunk drivers cause automobile accidents. Yet drunk drivers are still both legally and morally responsible for the accidents that they cause because upstream they knowingly engaged in drinking without a safe travel plan in place. Might actions of suicide be similar? That is, while it might be unreasonable to expect that a person who engages in an action of suicide is morally responsible *in that moment*, could it still be fair to claim that their failure to act earlier (or upstream from their action of suicide) has led to the painfully difficult moment in which they find themselves?

I have a couple of responses to the worry that moral responsibility is found upstream; and so, even if it is inappropriate to hold a suicidal person directly responsible, they somehow could be indirectly responsible for their action of suicide. One observation to make at the outset regards the separability of actions. Shifting the conversation to *prior* actions does *not* negate the claim that actions of suicide are amoral, or outside of the moral domain. I believe, then, that there is a disanalogy between the drunk driving case noted above and actions of suicide. The disanalogy is that, in the drunk driving case, there are reasons to believe that a person's intoxication will hinder their driving and be unsafe. Before individuals become suicidal, however, it is far less obvious that a person can recognize—or, importantly, *care* to recognize—what actions will make them unsafe.

To be sure, given the framework that I have sketched here, it would be difficult (to say the very least) to trace one's experiences back in time where they are reflectively aware of their suffering, and where they are further aware that help is available, but they negligently fail to seek help.[2] Moreover, the idea that someone could fail to get the help that they need is an idea that only has specific kinds of suicide in mind—namely, perhaps, when a person is suffering from a mental illness. But even with respect to those persons suffering from a mental illness, such a charge misses its mark. For instance, that William Styron reportedly was unable to be aware of how his illness disrupted his focus, concentration, memory and, ultimately, his decision-making ability, which he referred to as the sinister hallmarks of depression.[3] If depression is likened to seeing the world from behind a grey and heavy veil, then it must be further noted that the veil itself is *unseen*. So, postulating that a person who suffers from severe depression could (somehow) have taken steps earlier to prevent acting upon their suicidal thoughts is a misunderstanding of the nature of depression as a mental illness. Indeed, recall that Naomi Judd, for instance, sought extensive help in her battle with depression.[4]

Another observation to make in response to the worry that a person could be morally responsible upstream is to notice what is being assumed. Declaring that someone could have gotten help earlier assumes not only that there is adequate help available to them (and, implicitly, to all people), but also that those in need of help can place trust in the help that is available to them. There are problems with both assumptions. Limited mental health resources and health insurance obstacles undermine the fairy tale notion that there is adequate help available to all persons in need. Moreover, as noted earlier, it is possible that some forms of mental illnesses are, in fact, treatment resistant.

Additionally, matters that assault one's self-image, cause moral injuries, or otherwise produce what Edwin Shneidman called psychache, are deeply personal, private matters. Furthermore, since those suffering from depression also have markedly low self-esteem and a sense of self-worth, they also might believe (ironically due to their illness) that they are undeserving of help. It is no surprise then, that some persons—regardless of whether they are suffering from a mental illness—come to form the belief that no one *could* help them because no one could possibly understand their pain. As Shneidman observed, "[s]uffering is half pain and half being alone with that pain."[5] So, even in the absence of a mental illness, the suggestion that suicidal persons are indirectly morally responsible for their actions strikes me as ill-informed. If anything, societies that continue to fail to provide adequate mental health care are morally negligent.[6]

IMMORAL MEANS

Another concern with the idea that actions of suicide are amoral is with respect to the methods or the way, or ways, that someone might die by suicide. Suicide bombers, for example, clearly perform *immoral* actions when they take the lives of others. In general terms, actions of murder immediately followed by an action of suicide seem to warrant pause in placing actions of suicide outside of the moral domain. Additionally, suicide-by-cop scenarios also directly involve other people in ways that seem clearly within the moral domain. Choices to involve others directly in one's action of suicide crosses the line, if anything does, rendering at least *those* actions of suicide within the moral domain.[7] Hence, it simply is not true that all actions of suicide are amoral.

Caution is needed, however, in the task of distinguishing among different types of actions, as well as different kinds of actions of suicide. Recall that, in this project, suicide is defined in terms of including two intentions—namely, "intentional self-injurious behavior, associated with any intent to die as a result of the behavior."[8] So, referring to actions of suicide as amoral is only referring to the action of engaging in an activity where one knows, or has reason to believe, that the activity will result in their death. That is, intending self-injurious behavior and intending to die as a result of such behavior is one action. Whereas intending to hurt others because one is motivated by hatred, for example, is another action. I believe that there is conceptual space to regard the method, or manner, as subject to moral evaluation, while the action of suicide is not.

Suppose, for instance, that a person engages in an action of suicide as a suicide bomber, where the blast from the bomb severely injures other people. It seems clear that the suicide bomber in question believed in the cause so much that they were willing to sacrifice themselves for that cause. The suicide bomber, then, identified with (and, thereby, internalized) their cause, just as Foxhole Jumper identified with (and internalized) his role as a soldier. But engaging in an action of hurting another person, or others, in the name of their cause is itself subject to moral evaluation since, after all, such persons still retain their moral agency. That is, even if such a person has no choice but to give their lives for those causes that they have internalized, it is still an open question as to *how* one gives their life for their cause.

Invoking the separability of actions is applicable to other instances where a suicidal person directly involves another person or others, such as instances of homicide-suicide and suicide-by-cop. Therefore, upholding the amorality of actions of suicide and upholding the idea that persons who engage in actions of suicide could still perform other actions within the moral domain are consistent viewpoints.[9]

AN OBJECTION FROM A RELIGIOUS PERSPECTIVE

In general, one main objection to the amorality of suicide seems to come from a religious perspective. For my purposes here, I will focus upon a Judeo-Christian worldview, which can be interpreted as maintaining the belief that actions of suicide are sinful and, therefore, ought not to be done. Certainly, that is not to say that all such religious persons hold the view that actions of suicide are morally wrong. Rather, it is to say that some persons who hold the view that suicide is immoral (at least on occasion) do so because they also maintain a religious worldview that deems all life as a sacred gift from God. Since suicide is viewed as the rejection of the sacred gift of life that a person has been given by God, such an action turns that person away from God and, thereby, is sinful. Moreover, it is insufficient simply to say that some people do not embrace a religious worldview and, hence, that such people who uphold the amorality of suicide might readily dismiss the concerns of those who embrace a religious worldview. Socially and culturally religious perspectives are deeply influential, and they deserve attention.

While there are various interpretations of religious views, it is easy to see why many religious persons would hold the view that suicide is immoral, rather than amoral (again, at least on occasion). After all, God is believed to be the Creator of all life. So, actions of suicide are an affront to God. Indeed, destroying life that one can neither give back nor replace seems especially cruel, irreverent, and disrespectful. Moreover, since a person ought not to take another's life then, *ceteris paribus*, it follows that one ought not to take their own life, either.[10]

I believe that the moral prohibition of suicide for religious reasons may be divided into three different, but related, worries. The first concerns the idea that life is a gift from God and ought not to be rejected. The second concerns the idea that life is sacred. Finally, the third concern rests upon the idea of playing God insofar as a person, or persons, are seeking control of their earthy existence. I will address each of these worries, respectively.

One philosophical problem with the view that suicide is immoral because it is a gift from God is rather straight-forward. It is simply that, by definition, a gift is not chosen by its recipient. As such, a recipient of a gift has no obligation to maintain the gift that they did not themselves choose to receive. A gift that is forced upon another person to accept does not seem to be a gift at all. Indeed, forcing another person to accept one's gift infringes upon their (autonomous) decision-making.

The above common philosophical response to the idea that actions of suicide are wrong because they are a gift from God is understandable; however, I believe that it also misses the point. It misses the point because such a response supports the assumption that persons who die by suicide are *choosing* suicide in a similar way that they choose, for example, when and where to take a vacation. Receiving the gift of an all-expenses paid vacation might suddenly become undesirable if there is no flexibility regarding the details, such as the time or even the destination. If such a gift was undesirable to its recipient (when they learned of the details, of course), then they may reasonably refuse to take the vacation that they did not ask for and that they had no say in planning.

Choosing suicide, however, is *not* like that. It is not like refusing a gift or deliberating about what to do with one. As noted earlier in the discussion of Sophie's moral injury, I believe that referring to any action of suicide as a *choice* is a misnomer. To be sure, let us briefly reconsider the types of actions of suicide. First, there are actions of suicide that are amoral due to a loss of a sense of self. Some persons who experience severe depression, for instance, or an existential crisis, might come to have a loss of sense of self. Their deliberative agency is compromised because they lack an identifiable self-conception. Second, there are actions of suicide that stem from moral injuries, in which there is a betrayal of trust. Some persons who experience forms of bullying, abuse, or neglect might also engage in actions of suicide due to their perceived loss of belonging, which is a psychological need. Their relational knowledge is compromised by such a betrayal and, consequently, their moral agency is compromised, too. Moral reasons no longer entail a reason for acting. Third, there are perceived or actual limitations that can constrain one's thinking about alternative actions. Actions made under such constrained conditions also are not actions that reflect a person's deliberative agency.

In the first category, a person is experiencing oneself as already lost, whereby the action of physical death is but a formality. In the third category, however, the preservation of one's self-conception is threatened if one does *not* proceed in their action of suicide (e.g., self-sacrificial actions or physician-assisted suicide). Their so-called *choice* is pre-moral, or outside of the moral domain. It reflects what they live for and who they take themselves to be. In all categories, then, it is a misunderstanding to suggest that a person is morally responsible for their respective action of suicide, as actions of suicide do not stem from a person exercising their deliberative agency nor from their ability to act upon moral reasons as a moral agent. To borrow again from Edwin Shneidman, actions of suicide become an option of last resort in which a person would not otherwise engage in such an action if they did not feel or believe that their action is somehow necessary.[11] Suicide, therefore, is not akin to making a *choice* to refuse a gift.

Regarding the sanctity of life claim, I will just note that even universal agreement about the sanctity of life would *not* be sufficient to morally condemn actions of suicide. In fact, noting the rather broad definition of suicide that I am focusing upon in this project, it could be that because life is such a sacred gift, one's willingness to engage in self-sacrificial actions also reveals a profound love. That is, the idea that someone would love someone else *more than life itself* or be committed to a cause that they deem to be greater than life itself is a humbling feature of our existence. Indeed, according to the Gospel of John, Jesus had explained "greater love has no one than this, that he lay down his life for his friends."[12] Maintaining the sanctity of life, therefore, is consistent with also maintaining adherence to the demands of love. If Frankfurt was correct to note love as a nonmoral source of normativity, then it seems possible that love might require a person to lay down his life for his friends, as in the example of Foxhole Jumper.

Additionally, however, a person might think that actions of suicide are immoral (at least on occasion) because such actions are regarded as playing God. The idea that actions of suicide could be seen as playing God particularly arises with respect to actions of PAS. The idea is simply that God is in control of one's life and death; such that performing actions such as PAS undermines God's authority because it is taking control of what is in God's hands.

Yet, it is most unclear as to what is and what is not in God's hands. Certainly, the use of medical interventions that have the capability of prolonging a person's life—such as ventilators or dialysis machines—are not commonly cited as instances of playing God. Moreover, a person who legitimately kills another person in self-defense is also not typically accused of playing God since, presumably, they killed only as the necessary means to survive. Persons suffering from a terminal illness and who decide to pursue PAS, however, are like a person who kills in self-defense. Those who decide to pursue PAS could be acting to preserve their sense of self while confronting their mortality. So, the objection that actions of suicide are wrong because such actions are ultimately playing God is, at best, unclear and, at worst, not applicable.

It seems that one possible reason for the moral prohibition of actions of suicide in religious communities was to discourage such actions that otherwise might have appeared as glorified through martyrdom.[13] Yet regarding actions of suicide as a sin fails to consider the complexity of actions of suicide. For starters, it fails to consider suicidality as a mental health concern in its own right (and not merely as a symptom of depression), as Andrew Solomon observes. Furthermore, it fails to consider suicidality as a consequence of either unmet psychological needs or, ironically, as a consequence of an existential (or a faith) crisis, as Edwin Shneidman and Viktor Frankl recognized. It also fails to consider suicidality as representing an impossible choice—that is, a choice that does not reflect a person's will, as the writings of William Styron make clear. Finally, it fails to consider the possibility of suicidality as self-affirming, as opposed to self-denying as noted in the Gospel of John—namely, it fails to consider how an action of suicide could be an ultimate expression of one's love.

At base, I believe that the religious condemnation of suicide is rooted in a genuine attempt to prevent people from engaging in actions of suicide. If so, then it seems open for a person to claim that, even if suicide is not an action in the moral domain, making people believe that it is has positive consequences—namely, the consequence of reducing the number of people who die by suicide. But certainly, there is reason to doubt the extent to which such condemnation succeeds in preventing actions of suicide.

I believe that religious perspectives can play a role in suicide prevention (and intervention) more effectively by refraining from judgment. More compassion and humility are needed here. Indeed, for some people, religious worldviews provide protection against actions of suicide because they can provide a sense of community, belonging, and purpose. Making all persons feel welcome, refraining from judgment, and building stronger communities seem to hold more promise in preventing actions of suicide than either the religious or the moral condemnation of such actions.

SUICIDE AS OBJECTIVELY WRONG

There are some people who may wish to challenge the amorality of suicide by contending that actions of suicide are just *objectively* wrong. They might contend that the argument presented here for the amorality of suicide relies far too heavily upon a person's subjective experience. It might be true, for instance, that someone is at an increased risk for suicide who experiences a loss of a sense of self, a loss of belonging, and a loss of perceived competence or effectiveness. But it seems that there is still room to argue that an action of suicide is morally wrong even though that fact need not necessitate that such persons who perform actions of suicide are either blameworthy or somehow morally responsible. The action itself is wrong. Full stop.

I have a few responses to the worry that actions of suicide are *objectively wrong*. First, it is unclear how such an action can be objectively wrong given both the contextual nature of actions (and, consequently, of morality), as well as the problem of subjectivity. Regarding the contextual nature of actions, recall that variations in either the action's *end* or the *means* to achieve that end constitute *different actions*. Recall from chapter one that the act of pushing someone can be done with the aim of hurting them or with the aim of saving their life. It is insufficient then, morally speaking, to focus only upon an *act*—without knowledge of the *end* of that act and without knowledge of the context in which the act is performed. Contextual factors change the kind of *action* it is. So, my first worry about the idea that suicide is somehow objectively wrong is that it seems to ignore *actions* of suicide and focus only upon an *act*—namely an act of self-killing. Yet, as I noted in chapter one, suicide as an action is inherently more complex than an act. Additionally, if actions of suicide are objectively wrong, then there cannot be distinctions among actions of suicide—and so, it seems that we would need to conclude that actions like Foxhole Jumper's action of self-sacrifice (or laying down his life for his friends) are also objectively wrong, which is absurd.

Regarding the problem of subjectivity, the idea is that what is so-called "objective" is never, strictly speaking, *objective* insofar as all perceptions and judgments are mediated through a perceiver's unique perspective. Even when a statement is accepted as a fact, it is regarded as something that could be true from multiple perspectives, as a kind of shared subjectivity. In short, we cannot escape our unique perspectives about the world and about *how things seem to us* no matter how confident we are in our assertions.

I will assume, then, that when people claim that actions of suicide are objectively wrong, they mean that actions of suicide are horrific and, furthermore, that it being horrific is an undeniable feature of such actions. So, I could understand if a person might agree that we face the problem of subjectively, but also contend that if they were to witness a vicious murder, for example, it might be difficult to proceed to say something like, "*well, I believe that what I witnessed was wrong, but it is perfectly open for someone else to disagree with me on that matter*."[14] My point here is that sometimes actions seem so *obviously wrong* that there might be a temptation to say that, of course, those actions must also be *objectively wrong*. But if a person regards actions of suicide as so obviously wrong that such actions are also objectively wrong, then it seems that they must be defining suicide as such.

For example, murder is objectively wrong *by definition* of the word "murder."[15] Because murder is wrong by definition, it follows that suicide—as defined as self-*murder*—must also be wrong *by definition*. The conversation, then, about the moral status of actions of suicide ceases before it has a chance to start when suicide is deemed to be wrong *by definition*. Defining suicide as wrong, or in value-laden terms, is *not* an argument for the idea that actions of suicide are, in fact, objectively wrong, or even that they belong in the moral domain. In this project, I have adopted the definition of suicide which entails two intentions—namely, "[. . .] intentional self-injurious behavior, associated with any intent to die as a result of the behavior."[16] Hence, suicide, by definition, is value neutral.

Second, a proponent of the view that suicide is objectively wrong might claim that they are not drawing such a conclusion from the definition of suicide. Or, if they are, they at least recognize that suicide is not self-murder but, instead, self-killing. Yet they might proceed to argue that, as such, all actions of suicide involve killing and that killing is objectively wrong.

But, again, actions of killing are contextual. Certainly, a lion killing a gazelle is not regarded as an objectively wrong action on the part of the lion, who lacks deliberative (moral) agency. Even with respect to human beings, however, not all actions of killing are objectively wrong. A physician killing cancer cells in effort to save a person's life, for example, is not an action in which killing is objectively wrong—nor, perhaps, is killing in self-defense when there is no hope of escape and no other way to deter one's attacker.

A rejoinder might insist, however, that actions involving self-killing are actions that ought to be deterred. Sanctions are in order. So, by proclaiming that actions of suicide are objectively wrong, then it might have the pragmatic result of discouraging such actions. The idea is simply that acknowledging actions of suicide as objectively wrong helps to prevent people from performing actions of suicide.

The belief that moral condemnation must be in place if suicide prevention efforts are to be successful in preventing deaths by suicide appears misguided, however. To the best of my knowledge, no one has seriously proposed that the prevention efforts of, say, heart disease in the United States could be enhanced if we began claiming that it is morally wrong to suffer from heart disease. While people may be quick to point out that there is some marginal discretion about one's diet and lifestyle choices which could impact one's chances of developing heart disease, it is simply inaccurate that these are the only contributing factors. A person's hereditary background, environment, stressors, and other underlying health factors play a role, too. Moreover, even if blaming someone will lead them to change their behavior in positive ways (which is doubtful), it is further doubtful that such changes will be sufficient to decrease the number of people dying from heart disease. In an analogous way, death by suicide also has various contributing factors. So, with respect to both heart disease prevention efforts and suicide prevention efforts, the inclusion of moral condemnation may have the unintentional effect of making a person feel even more hopeless about their condition or otherwise undeserving of help.

I do not believe that moral condemnation is necessary to enhance suicide prevention efforts. In fact, I believe that moral condemnation has the unintended effect of producing more stigmatization and, in turn, making it far more likely that persons who struggle with suicide ideation will do so in silence, without reaching out for help. Additionally, my concern here is that, as amoral actions, moral judgments do not make sense when applied to actions of suicide. But I do not wish to make any claims about *non-moral judgments*. In fact, it seems likely that non-moral judgments could still be made regarding some actions of suicide.

The objection that actions of suicide are objectively wrong would be incomplete without some kind of reference to Immanuel Kant's work on the subject. As mentioned in chapter one, in the *Grounding for the Metaphysics of Morals*, Kant seemingly explained how ending one's life is a contradiction of reason.[17] Since Kant thought that moral principles must be derived through reason, it follows that those rules of action that entail a contradiction are immoral. Regarding the question of whether an action of suicide could be derived from reason, Kant wrote:

> [a] man reduced to despair by a series of misfortunes feels sick of life but is still so far in possession of his reason that he can ask himself whether taking his own life would not be contrary to his duty to himself. [translator's footnote omitted]. Now he asks whether the maxim of his action could become a universal law of nature. But his maxim is this: from self-love I make as my principle to shorten my life when its continued duration threatens more evil than it promises satisfaction. There only remains the question as to whether this principle of self-love can become a universal law of nature. One sees at once a contradiction in a system of nature whose law would destroy life by means of the very same feeling that acts so as to stimulate the furtherance of life, and hence there could be no existence as a system of nature. Therefore, such a maxim cannot possibly hold as a universal law of nature and is, consequently, wholly opposed to the supreme principle of all duty.[18]

Accordingly, there is a moral duty not to end one's life, or at least not to do so in the manner Kant described. But I wish to look more closely at the scenario described in the passage above. My objective here is modest. I am concerned about how the above passage has been interpreted, and what it has been thought to imply.

For starters, the above quotation from Kant's *Grounding for the Metaphysics of Morals* seems to be commonly interpreted as a moral prohibition of actions of suicide. It is not. At most, if there is a moral prohibition of suicide here, it would *only* apply to actions that fit the description noted in the passage. I am following Christine Korsgaard's lead in this respect. That is, that other situations or circumstances—say, for example, a circumstance in which a person is suffering from a mental illness—do not apply here. The qualification that the person described is "still so far in the possession of his reason" could be understood as focusing upon instances in which a person's ability to reason is not compromised by an illness. Moreover, the person in Kant's scenario has been "reduced to despair by a series of misfortunes," and so a self-sacrificial action of suicide (such as sacrificing one's life for the life of another or others) is also not intended here. So, one observation to make at the outset is that, even at most, such a passage does not entail a moral prohibition of *all* actions of suicide (at least not according to the broad notion of suicide that I am referring to here); and so, it ought not to be interpreted as though it does.

But, of course, for my purposes here, there is no need to address *all* possible actions of suicide to challenge the idea that actions of suicide are amoral. If there is only one action of suicide that belongs in the moral domain, then that action alone will be sufficient to refute the idea that actions of suicide are amoral. It is unclear, however, that the above quoted passage entails the moral prohibition of an action of suicide. To be sure, I will turn my attention to the description of the action in question.

"Self-love" in Kant's passage above seems to refer to something akin to self-interest; and so, I will replace references to self-love as references to self-interest. The idea, then, appears to be that a person (presumably a rational, adult human being not suffering from a mental illness and meeting the threshold of moral agency) imagines that the "continued duration" of their life "threatens more evil." Wanting what is in their *self-interest*, they wonder whether they should shorten their life. If there is a contradiction here, then presumably it hinges upon the idea that self-interest cannot be rational grounds for self-destruction. But why not? Again, presumably, it is because destroying "life by means of the very same feeling that acts so as to stimulate the furtherance of life" is a contradiction. I believe, however, that it is Kant's concept of self-love, which I am interpreting here rather broadly as self-interest, that is problematic.

To maintain a contradiction, self-interest could be understood as implying self-preservation. What it means to act in one's self-interest *just means* that a person engages in actions that further their preservation. Such a person is concerned with the duration of their life. So, let us suppose that Kant's understanding of self-love—or, rather, self-interest here—is understood to mean something like "doing whatever promotes one's preservation or continued existence." It would seem to be a contradiction of reason, then, that out of a person's desire for their preservation, they wish to destroy themselves. Ending one's life because of one's desire for self-preservation is a contradiction.

But notice that such a contradiction does *not* map onto the person Kant described. Kant did not describe the person considering shortening the duration of their life as desiring to preserve themselves, which seems to be an implied assumption. Rather, such a person is described as "reduced to despair." Insofar as they have an interest in shortening their life, it is due to their despair. Yet *quantity* or duration of one's life is one thing, and *quality* is another. Self-interest in the quantity of one's life alone, such as a person's interest in living a long life, might typically coincide with self-interest in the quality of one's life, such as a person's interest in having more meaningful experiences. But it also *need not do so*. The person Kant imagined desired a quality of life that was lacking, as he was in despair and his future looked bleak. He then pondered the quantity of his life, namely whether it would be more desirable to shorten his life. No contradiction arises between self-interest in the quantity of one's life and self-interest in its quality, as these can come apart.

I suggest that there are different understandings of self-interest at work here. When self-interest is not equivocated (that is, when it is understood as desiring one's self-preservation), then a contradiction is present. Out of a desire for self-preservation it is a contradiction to desire to destroy oneself. But the contradiction that is present fails to speak to the kind of situation that Kant imagined—namely, it is not a contradiction if, out of desire not to live in continual despair, one contemplates shortening one's life. Hence, a Kantian might decide to keep the contradiction, but lose the example here. If they do so, then it is difficult to see how the contradiction picks out real-life scenarios. Or a Kantian might wish to keep the (realistic) example here but, in doing so, lose the ability to say that the maxim upon which such a person acts implies a contradiction.

An analogy from economics may be helpful here. It is in the self-interest of consumers to make their dollar stretch as far as possible, and so they have an interest to purchase goods or services at the lowest possible monetary cost. In short, consumers desire to spend less money, rather than more money, for any given product or service. Nevertheless, consumers also have an interest in acquiring durable products or dependable services in convenient ways. Sometimes such durable products or dependable services cost more money. So, while it is generally true that consumers are interested in purchasing products and services that cost less, the price of a good or service might not be the *only* relevant factor that some financially able consumers consider. Yet it is not a contradiction of reason for such consumers to declare that they wish to spend less money on a product or a service, but do not do so when the opportunity presents itself. In sum, the self-interest of such consumers is not isolated to the cost of goods or services alone but, rather, includes other factors, such as either the ideal or the perceived quality of goods or services, the convenience of obtaining goods or services, the speed in which such goods or services are available and so on. That is to say, the cost of obtaining a desired good or service is not limited to monetary costs. Non-monetary costs must be considered as well.

So, it is probably safe to say that most people most of the time act in ways that preserve themselves when acting in self-interested ways; just like it is probably safe to say that most consumers most of the time purchase a desired good or service that is the least expensive of those available to them. Yet the idea that one's self-interest can (and does) entail *more* than simply self-preservation means that it is not necessarily a contradiction *of self-interest* (or self-love) when a person focuses upon the quality, rather than the quantity or duration, of their life. So, if the contradiction goes through, then it seems to be a trivial contradiction (namely, out of a desire for self-preservation one cannot will to destroy oneself), and one that is not applicable to the case Kant described (namely, when one contemplates the duration of a life that has a diminished quality).

A rejoinder might reply that the moral prohibition against the action of suicide in Kant's *Grounding* is stronger than I have described. They might claim that, by focusing upon the trees, I have neglected to see the forest. Specifically, a rejoinder might assert that it is not simply that when the quality of one's life is diminished (or reduced to despair) then questions about the quantity (or duration) of one's life arise. Rather, it is that suicide is immoral because a person would be using oneself as a *mere means* to the end of avoiding a future that promises more evil than satisfaction.[19] The contradiction that is deserving of attention here is that a person cannot legislate for themselves the eradication of the source of the legislation. Essentially, an action of suicide would consist of a person choosing to do an action that takes away one's choice to act. Viewed in such a light, there is little use for the distinction between the quality and quantity of one's life or even among the competing ways of defining self-love. Such proclamations are missing the point that rational beings have intrinsic value. Suicide is wrong, a rejoinder would argue, because it is a violation of reason. Again, full stop.

While I believe that I understand the rejoinder's concern, I remain unconvinced by Kant's example. If a person is reduced to despair, then their former, autonomous self is lost. When one loses a sense of self, then they have also lost their deliberative agency. So, Kant tried to thread the needle here and claim both that the person in question *is reduced to despair* but that they are also still *in possession of their (faculty of) reason* to wonder whether it would be better to shorten the duration of their life. But how might they be able to engage in deliberative reasoning while reduced to despair? Additionally, even if they are able to engage in deliberative reasoning, does the reason why they wonder whether it would be better to shorten their life matter here? That is, does it matter if one's reason is for their *own* benefit (e.g., to avoid suffering more evil) or for some other reason (e.g., perhaps to save the life of another or others)? According to the rejoinder, it does not. A person can be reduced to despair for any number of reasons and, presumably, ending the duration of one's life for *any reason* would be using oneself as a *mere means* to an end.

In *The Metaphysics of Morals* (1797), however, Kant briefly described a situation in which a rabid dog bit a man. The man then contemplates about what he should do and, upon considering his options, the man wonders whether he has an obligation to end his life before he loses control and hurts others. Kant explained:

> [a] man who had been bitten by a mad dog already felt hydrophobia coming on. He explained, in a letter he left, that, since as far as he knew the disease was incurable, he was taking his life lest he harm others as well in his madness (the onset of which he already felt). Did he do wrong?[20]

Kant, however, was silent regarding his response to the above question, but his silence is telling and, quite frankly, understandable. It is reasonable to postulate that the man bitten by the rabid dog was also a man who was in the grip of despair, and yet still had possession of his reason to foresee his potential for harming others. So, in this scenario, it seems as though Kant could have given one of the following two responses.

On the one hand, if Kant had declared that it was morally permissible for the man to shorten the *duration of his life when its continued duration promises more evil than satisfaction*, then Kant would be opposing the common understanding of his idea noted in his *Grounding for the Metaphysics of Morals* and, at the very least, appear logically inconsistent. The bitten man would be failing in his duty to preserve himself. So, essentially, Kant would need to make an exception to one's duty to oneself, which is inconceivable given his ethical framework.

On the other hand, however, if Kant had declared that it was morally wrong for the man bitten by a rabid dog to shorten his life, then it is also difficult to see how that would be so, given Kant's ethical framework. After all, it seems that the man in the story could universalize what he is about to do—namely to shorten his life not simply because its continued duration promises more evil than satisfaction *for him* but also because he has a legitimate reason to believe that the continued duration of his life poses a threat *to others*. He could universalize his rule of action, it seems, because the continued duration of his life is a threat to the welfare of other people.

Regardless of how self-love is defined, I believe that Kant was correct to consider self-preservation among the priorities of self-love. Nevertheless, I believe that it is a mistake to regard self-love as simply reducible to, or equated with, a desire for self-preservation. Attention to cases of PAS, for instance, reveals the complexity of self-love. After all, Kant's description of the person considering suicide in the *Grounding for the Metaphysics of Morals* and his description in his *Metaphysics of Morals* of a man bitten by a rabid dog could easily share similarities—namely, both people could be suffering from a terminal illness and both people could be experiencing despair.

THE VICE OF SELFISHNESS

One seemingly prevailing reason as to why some people believe that actions of suicide belong within the moral domain is the notion that at least some actions of suicide are selfish acts. To be clear, selfishness as a moral fault implies not only that someone puts their interests above the interest of another or others but also, and importantly, that they do so in a way that is deserving of punishment or blame. All persons are self-interested to varying degrees; and so, the charge of *selfishness* is not equivalent to claiming that a person is merely self-interested. Rather, the charge of selfishness suggests that a person who acts selfishly is putting an undue emphasis upon their own interests at the detriment of the interests of others. Additionally, the charge of selfishness as a moral fault implies that a person who is selfish is aware of, or is at least capable of appreciating, the fact that they are acting selfishly. To clarify, I understand the charge of selfishness to indicate that a person: (1) recognizes their interests, (2) puts an undue emphasis upon their own interests at the detriment of others, and (3) is aware (or is reasonably capable of becoming aware) of the fact that they are placing an undue emphasis upon their own interests for which they are morally responsible. Therefore, the charge of selfishness as a *moral* failure only applies to moral agents.

It is easy to see why the charge of selfishness arises with respect to actions of suicide. Persons who take their own life for presumably deeply personal reasons leave loved ones to endure the pains of heartbreak and grief. *Prima facie* the interests of others often appear to be ignored. But I believe that the charge of selfishness rests upon misunderstandings about actions of suicide. In fact, Thomas Joiner devotes an entire section in his book *Myths about Suicide* to dispelling the myth that suicide is a selfish action.[21] There are several responses that I wish to make concerning the charge of selfishness.

First, consider persons who have their deliberative agency compromised due to a loss of a sense of self. Because there is no unified understanding of oneself, recognizing one's interests is an impossible task. Recognizing one's interests is assumed of persons who act selfishly, however. Hence, when persons who lack a sense of self (and, thereby, they lack deliberative agency) proceed to engage in actions of suicide, they cannot possibly engage in selfish actions.

Second, recall Shneidman's attention to the frustration of psychological needs, or extreme psychache, as underlying actions of suicide. Shneidman's attention to psychache focused upon the perspectives of persons who died by suicide, which Shneidman analyzed through the notes that they left behind.[22] Their first-person perspective is important here since the charge of selfishness is made from another's perspective, or a third-person perspective. Indeed, according to Thomas Joiner, a person perceiving themselves as a burden to other people is acting most *unselfishly* in their action of suicide. Indeed, the appearance of a selfish action is not the same thing as a selfish action.

To be sure, consider an exchange that William Styron recounted in his memoir when he was suffering from depression. In his memoir, Styron described forgetting about a luncheon in his honor and making alternative plans. Although Styron's action may seem like a rather mundane event, Styron recounted that making alternative plans:

> was outrageous; it had been announced months before to me and everyone else concerned that a luncheon—moreover, a luncheon in my honor—was part of the day's pageantry. But my behavior was really the result of the illness, which had progressed far enough to produce some of its most famous and sinister hallmarks: confusion, failure of mental focus and lapse of memory.[23]

To other persons, Styron's decision to make alternative plans might have been easily characterized as a selfish action. Indeed, it had appeared as though he had decided upon what to do without considering whether others would be hurt or slighted by his action. Styron, however, saw his decision as a consequence of his mental illness. Confusion, failure of mental focus, and a lapse of memory compromise a person's moral agency even while (as in Styron's situation) such a person can still exercise a degree of deliberative agency insofar as they can still act for reasons. The charge of selfishness, then, with respect to such actions is mistaken. Actions in which a person's moral agency is compromised are amoral actions.

Additionally, self-sacrificial actions of suicide seem to be more than often characterized as *selfless* actions rather than selfish actions. So, to motivate the worry here, consider someone who is deeply passionate about a political cause. Suppose that, because of their passion for the cause, they proceed to engage in suicidal behavior—say, for example, a hunger strike—with the intention of giving their lives for the cause, if needed. Suppose further that they die as a result of their hunger strike, and that they leave behind a loving family and friends. *Prima facie* it seems that in such a situation the person's family and friends have some grounds to claim that the action of suicide of the person in question was selfish insofar as the person in question seemingly put the political cause ahead of other obligations that they had, or possibly could have had. For ease of reference, call this person Protester.

I believe that regarding the actions of Protester as selfish relies upon a mistaken understanding about the actions of suicide. For an action to be selfish, one puts an undue emphasis upon their interests at the detriment of the interests of others. But the action of Protester is not putting an undue emphasis upon their interests at all. Such actions of suicide are fundamentally about who one takes oneself to be. Through identifying with a political cause deemed greater than oneself, a person can simultaneously give up their life while affirming who they are.[24] An existential must (not a moral should) propels such actions since to do otherwise would mean a loss of oneself, or an emotional or spiritual death. Therefore, if such an action is self-affirming insofar as to do otherwise would mean a loss of one's sense of self, then such an action is not placing an undue emphasis upon one's interests at the detriment of others. Such actions of suicide are not selfish.

With respect to the charge of selfishness, there is a related worry. The related worry is that each person receives benefits from the community and, thereby, has reciprocal responsibilities to their community. Proceeding in an action of suicide negates one's communal responsibilities. So, to be clear, a person would no longer have communal responsibilities when they die by suicide. David Hume questioned what an individual would owe to society when he observed that:

> [a]ll our obligations to do good to society seem to imply something reciprocal. I receive the benefits of society, and therefore ought to promote its interest. But when I withdraw myself altogether from society, can I be bound any longer?[25]

Hume continued by questioning the degrees of an individual's suffering as well as the degree of communal benefit. Specifically, Hume noted:

> I am not obliged to do a small good to society, at the expense of a great harm to myself. Why then should I prolong a miserable existence, because of some frivolous advantage, which the public may, perhaps, receive from me?[26]

Hume's ideas here are two-fold. Not only do communal obligations cease when one is no longer part of the community, but also that one's communal obligations—whatever those may be—are not the kind of thing that overrides all considerations (and types) of harm to oneself.

But why not? Hume's declaration that he is not obligated to do a small good for society at a great expense to himself does not negate the possibility (albeit rare possibility) that a person's contributions to society over the natural course of their lives could outweigh their present suffering. Such reasoning, however, misses the point or, rather, the *perspective* of a person considering an action of suicide. Attempting to weigh advantages and disadvantages to individuals, and then to societies, misses the point of the extreme psychache that Edwin Shneidman saw as characteristic of those who engage in actions of suicide.

If a person continues to insist that moral obligations to others or to the community somehow override or outweigh the need to maintain a sense of self, then consideration of Bernard Williams' criticism of utilitarianism is in order. In general terms, according to a utilitarian worldview, a person ought to do those actions that maximize the overall utility of everyone impacted by one's actions. But as Bernard Williams pointed out, one would be essentially choosing between maximizing utility and preserving their own integrity in such situations. If a utilitarian framework for reasoning about what to do is adopted, then one must neglect preserving their own integrity for the greater good. As Williams explained, "the point here is not, [. . .] that if a project or attitude is that central to his life, then to abandon it will be very disagreeable to him," but, rather, "[t]he point is that he is identified with his actions as flowing from projects and attitudes which in some cases he takes seriously at the deepest level, as what his life is about [. . .]."[27] Understanding that a sense of self is foundational to deliberative (moral) agency creates a conceptual space for recognizing that moral considerations about *how* one should live take as a given that one has addressed the more fundamental questions of *who* one is and *what* is important to them.

Hence, those persons who attempt to make a comparison by weighing one's present suffering against any societal harm miss the larger issue here. For starters, such a comparison fails to recognize the possibility that one's present suffering undermines their deliberative agency. But it also fails to recognize that a person could proceed in an action of suicide from either a loss of one's sense of self (as, for example, William Styron claimed in his struggle with severe depression) or from a desire to maintain one's sense of self (as, for instance, in Foxhole Jumper's suicide). Neither of these extreme cases—nor the spectrum between them—imply that actions of suicide are selfish.

SUICIDE AS A RIGHT

One upshot of the idea that actions of suicide are amoral is that moral evaluations of actions of suicide are inappropriate—including moral evaluations of PAS. Yet if moral evaluations of PAS are inappropriate, then it seems as though decisions regarding PAS are appropriately personal matters between a patient and their physician. Does that thereby make suicide a *right*? The worry here is just that, if suicide is a right, then it does not seem as though it would be outside of the moral domain. After all, rights can be taken away, denied, and violated. Moreover, a person can be harmed by having their rights taken away, denied, or violated. So, if a person is somehow entitled to PAS which, to gain popular support has been referred to as death-with-dignity and physician-aid-in-dying, then at least one kind of action of suicide—namely, PAS—seems to be within the moral domain.

There are two responses that I have to the worry that, if persons have a right to PAS then PAS must fall within the moral domain. The first concern is the general lack of clarity regarding most discussions about "rights." Specifically, it is a bit unclear what the language of rights is tracking with respect to PAS. I suggest, however, that the language of "rights" in discussions of PAS refers more appropriately to *legal* rights rather than to moral rights, which takes me to my second response. My second response is just that if the language of rights is meaningful at all in this context, then I believe it is referring solely to legal rights. Claiming that someone has a *right* to PAS, or to death-with-dignity, or to physician-aid-in-dying is essentially to claim that the government (in conjunction with the appropriate professional medical societies) ought to allow such practices as part of what it means to *care for* and *about* persons seeking such help.

Of course, there may be concerns with the implementation of one's legal right to PAS that are morally questionable. For example, if the criteria are either too relaxed or too stringent, then persons could be harmed. An example of a too relaxed criterion is short-changing any kind of mental health screening. A person suffering from depression could express their wish for PAS and could have their request granted instead of being treated for depression. The opposite problem could arise as well. The criteria could be too stringent as when, for example, the waiting period after a patient's second request for PAS is unduly extended for the purpose of discouraging such practices. What is important to note, however, is that moral issues in these cases are about the *implementation* or the practice of exercising a legal right. They are not about the action of PAS itself.

With respect to the action of PAS, what essentially matters is how a person understands their self-conception and what is of meaning to them based upon the identities that they have internalized. In this way, PAS could be a matter of a person maintaining their self-conception, existing at a pre-moral level of decision-making and, therefore, outside of the moral domain, even for persons whose deliberative agency is otherwise intact. The framework I put forth here allows for the possibility that PAS and other actions of suicide can be a legal right, even though such actions are amoral. Someone also might propose that PAS could be deemed illegal, even though amoral. The scope of my project here is not to address a person's legal rights on this matter. Rather, I just will say that it is my hope that viewing actions of suicide as amoral could be a step in the direction of regarding such actions as private decisions about one's care without the baggage of social stigma attached.[28]

SUICIDE PREVENTION AND INTERVENTION

While less of an objection, the worry here is simply an inquiry about the implications for suicide prevention and intervention if actions of suicide as amoral. For example, if a person regards actions of suicide as an expression of one's autonomy and, therefore, a morally permissible action, then their views would suggest no intervention. Other persons who see persons suffering from a mental illness as in need of treatment would support intervention in the hopes of preventing deaths by suicide. Reportedly, in 1972, Thomas Szasz and Edwin Shneidman engaged in such a debate on the ethics of suicide prevention.[29] As Louis Jolyon West explained, "[f]or Shneidman, it is the healer's duty to treat the suicidal patient, while Szasz considers unethical any treatment that is not specifically contracted for."[30]

Debates like the one between Szasz and Shneidman seem like an instance of persons talking past each other. Granting a rather broad scope of actions that can constitute suicide adds complexity to the task of addressing concerns about the moral appropriateness of intervention and prevention. So be it. The belief that other persons could have a moral obligation to intervene in effort to prevent another's death by suicide is consistent with the belief that actions of suicide are amoral.[31] Shneidman was correct, I believe, to claim that others—especially psychiatrists—have a professional duty to intervene.

Yet I do not believe that the duty to intervene ought to be generalized to include all possible actions of suicide. For example, I believe that it is possible that actively intervening in instances of, say, PAS could cause more harm and distress for such persons who are able to make such a decision on their behalf, such as alluded to in the story of Andrew Solomon's mother. Hence, the belief that other persons ought to refrain from intervening with respect to some actions of suicide is also consistent with the belief that actions of suicide are amoral.

AN OBJECTION FROM SAFETY CONTRACTS

One objection or worry with respect to the amorality of suicide is an objection stemming from the use of safety contracts. Specifically, sometimes persons who are struggling with suicidal ideation and who reach out for help, might be asked by their provider or crisis services team to agree to the terms of a safety contract. The aim of such a contract is to keep a suicidal person safe while their recovery is ongoing. So, for example, a safety contract would ask that the person in question agrees to reach out for additional help from an identifiable provider or crisis services team before they engage in an action of suicide. Setting aside the efficacy of such contracts for the moment, the fact that safety contracts are something that might be utilized in suicide prevention seems to suggest that persons who are suicidal have a sufficient degree of deliberative agency and moral agency. That idea is that, whenever a person agrees to a contract, they presumably have a sense of self. They are entering into an agreement regarding their safety, and they are agreeing to hold themselves accountable. Hence, the existence of such contracts as part of a safety plan appears to count as evidence that, for at least some suicidal persons, the decision as to whether they will engage in an action of suicide is within the moral domain. Specifically, if such a person were to engage in an action of suicide without seeking help first, then they would be violating the agreed upon terms of their contract.

I wish to make a couple of responses here. First, it is important to acknowledge that a person's degree of both deliberative agency and moral agency is subject to change. It is possible, therefore, that a person has a sufficient degree of deliberative and moral agency to agree to the terms and conditions of a contract, but then to have either their degree of deliberative agency or their degree of moral agency compromised. The upshot is that the ability to agree to the terms of a safety contract and the ability to uphold the terms of that contract are separate, distinct considerations.

Second, it seems to be an open question as to whether such safety contracts are effective, and so I will regard the efficacy of such contracts as an open question here. Supposing that safety contracts are sometimes effective, then, does not contradict the thesis that actions of suicide are amoral for at least two reasons. It could be, for instance, that a person simply retains a sufficient degree of their deliberative and moral agencies throughout the entire process—namely, from their suicidal ideation to their seeking of help, to their agreement to the terms of a safety contract, and to following up with others as expressed in the terms of their contract.[32]

Additionally, the efficacy of safety contracts (at least sometimes) could also be explained by simply the formalization that other people care about their safety. If Thomas Joiner is correct that a perceived feeling of burdensomeness can increase a person's risk of dying by suicide, then a safety contract might be an explicit way to communicate to someone that other people are requesting that they seek help when feeling suicidal. I believe that the extent to which safety contracts are effective, then, is because they re-establish a connection with others that might otherwise be perceived as lost or compromised. I acknowledge that, for some people struggling with suicide ideation, a safety contract may be of help to them in their effort just to get through the moment at-hand. Simply being held accountable by another person can be life-saving.

Third, there is some doubt about the efficacy of safety contracts. Yet doubting the efficacy of such contracts is also consistent with the amorality of actions of suicide. To be sure, consider the following account. David A. Jobes, in his book *Managing Suicidal Risk: A Collaborative Approach*, describes such safety contracts as both peculiar and problematic.[33] Specifically, Jobes writes,

> the problem with contemporary use of safety contracts is that they are neither about safety nor truly contractual in any legal sense. Yet they are pervasively used all over the country and probably reflect routine care. In truth, however, safety contracts are all too often used very inappropriately—as a mere ploy or maneuver to move the patient along while still providing the appearance of "protective" documentation within the clinical record. Nevertheless, in my experience as a forensic expert, safety contracts often come back to haunt

> clinician-defendants rather than "protecting" them from malpractice litigation because the contract obviously failed to protect the patient from a suicidal demise.[34]

So, if such contracts are not efficacious, or worse, if they are done with the aim of protecting the *provider* of care, then I do not believe that their use (even as a routine, standard of care) counts as evidence that actions of suicide belong within the moral domain.

In the Prologue to her book *Night Falls Fast: Understanding Suicide*, Kay Redfield Jamison describes a kind of promise that she and a very close friend of hers, Jack Ryan, had made. Admittedly, Jamison acknowledges that she was skeptical of the plan from the start. The plan, in short, was a kind of safety pact aimed at preventing each other's death by suicide. Jamison describes their promise to each other in the following way:

> we agreed, we would meet at Jack's home on Cape Cod. Once there, the nonsuicidal one of us would have a week to persuade the other not to [die by] suicide; a week to present all the reasons we could come up with for why the other should go back on lithium, assuming that having stopped it was the most likely reason for the danger of suicide (we both had manic-depressive illness and, despite the better and often expressed judgment of others, had a tendency to stop taking our lithium); a week to cajole the other into a hospital; to invoke conscience; to impress upon the other the pain and damage to our families that suicide would inevitably bring.[35]

Jamison continues, "[w]e decided that a week was long enough to argue for life. If it didn't work, at least we would have tried."[36] While Jamison agreed to the plan, her first-hand experiences of suffering from her illness and her research on suicide were enough to convince her that such a plan—despite being well-intended and sincerely agreed upon—would not work in practice. Jamison writes:

> [w]ho were we kidding? Never once, during any of my sustained bouts of suicidal depression, had I been inclined or able to pick up a telephone and ask a friend for help. Not once. It wasn't in me. How could I seriously imagine that I would call Jack, make an airline reservation, get to an airport, rent a car, and find my way out to his house on the Cape?[37]

As Jamison highlights, such plans assume that a person could perform tasks that they would typically perform if they were not suicidal—as if being suicidal were merely one factor among many for a person to consider, instead of *the factor* that negates all other considerations.

Jamison's skepticism about the plan was well-founded. She explains that, many years after making such a promise, Jack died by suicide.[38] He had not called her. Jamison recounts:

> [a]lthough shaken by Jack's suicide, I was not surprised by it. Nor was I surprised that he had not called me. I, after all, had been dangerously suicidal myself on several occasions since our [. . . pact] and certainly had not called him. Nor had I even thought of calling. Suicide is not beholden to an evening's promises, nor does it always hearken to plans drawn up in lucid moments and banked in good intentions. I know this for an unfortunate fact. [. . .] I have a hard-earned respect for suicide's ability to undermine, overwhelm, outwit, devastate, and destroy.[39]

I believe that Jamison's insight is too easily lost when actions of suicide are placed within the moral domain. The harsh reality of what it means to be in a suicidal state of mind must not be so readily discounted in discussions about suicide. The philosophical point that I want to stress here is simply that, if an action is within the moral domain, then it is assumed that the agent in question has a sufficient degree of both deliberative agency and moral agency. Yet the fact that actions of suicide can escape the hold of promises made to others, and even those made to oneself, makes the amorality of such actions undeniable.

So, employing safety contracts as part of a safety plan for suicide prevention does not undermine the idea that actions of suicide are amoral. Leaving the efficacy of such contracts an open question, I believe that both the extent to which such contracts are effective, and the extent to which their efficacy is called into question, are consistent with thinking about actions of suicide as outside of the moral domain.

INSIGHTS FROM HINDSIGHT

The objection that I have in mind is as follows. Suppose that someone seriously had contemplated dying by suicide. Suppose further that they might have even gone so far as to develop a plan, find the means for carrying out their plan, and determine their timeframe or have the day and the hour in mind. Now suppose that something happened which changed their mind. Suppose that they persevered through whatever trials or tribulations that they were experiencing at the time. And now suppose, many months or even years later, they reflect upon that time. Specifically, they notice the fact that they are grateful for their lives and the way in which their life has been shaped by their previous experiences. While they still carry their pain (or the memory of their pain) with them, they are glad, if not utterly relieved, that their life did not end many months or even years prior to the present moment. In fact, they are so relieved that they did not act upon their plan that they are convinced that, if they had acted upon their plan at the time, then they would have been *wrong* to have done so. They would have missed so much. Other people would have missed them, too, and the community would have been made worse off had they carried out their plan. In other words, looking back on their previous self, they now believe that they were previously *wrong* for nearly ending their life. That is, it is not difficult to imagine a person claiming that, if they had carried out their action of suicide at the time, then they would have done something morally wrong.

Before responding to this worry, I believe that such a view—namely, that a person's action of suicide could, in hindsight, appear to be so obviously mistaken—is a rather common experience. There are several such stories of hope and of survival. One famous such story is the story of Kevin Hines, who amazingly survived a jump from the Golden Gate Bridge in San Francisco, California. Hines explains that after he jumped, but before he hit the water, he had regretted his decision to jump.[40] Hines is now an author, motivational speaker, and an advocate for suicide prevention.[41]

I have two responses to the legitimate worry that, in hindsight, actions of suicide might be regarded as wrong, or at least as deeply mistaken, by those who have engaged in actions of suicide. First, it seems that a greater sense of compassion is needed here for *a person's perspective at the time of their action*. Taking up the perspective of hindsight is, in fact, taking up a different perspective at a different time and at a different place in one's life. Moral actions as well as amoral actions do not occur in hindsight. They occur in the here and now.

To be sure, consider the following illustration. Suppose that a physician is trying to diagnose a patient who just so happens to have an extremely rare illness. The patient in question is suffering tremendously and, in agony, pleads that the physician *does something*. The physician has two prescriptions that they believe could work, Drug A and Drug B, respectively; but the physician has no idea which one to prescribe. The physician only knows that the two drugs simply cannot be taken together. If they are taken together, then there will be disastrous results. Furthermore, the physician knows that one of the drugs will almost certainly work (and help the patient), whereas the other drug will almost certainly fail (and will add to the patient's agony). Because the patient in question has such an extremely rare illness, the physician simply has no idea which of the two drugs is more likely to help the patient. Yet not prescribing either drug—when one might be helpful to the patient—seems unconscionable to the physician.

So, the physician prescribes Drug A, which (unfortunately) has awful side-effects and contributes to the agony of the patient in question. Seeing the results of Drug A, the physician immediately tells their patient to stop using Drug A, to wait twenty-four hours, and then to try Drug B, instead. Drug B relieves the patient of their symptoms, and the patient in question makes a full recovery. So, it seems reasonable to ask, did the physician do something morally wrong or negligent when they prescribed Drug A to this patient? Of course not. Based upon the information that the physician had *at the time* that they prescribed Drug A to their patient, they had no reason to believe that it would be the drug that increases the patient's agony. In fact, they prescribed Drug A to their patient on the belief that it might help their patient. Certainly, the physician might *regret* that they did not start with Drug B for their patient, but that does not mean that the physician is somehow to *blame* for not starting with Drug B.[42]

Regarding actions of suicide, then, it is imperative to remember that such actions stem from excessive psychache. Basic psychological needs are unmet or under serious threat. There also could be cognitive, circumstantial, and relational factors that limit a person's ability to exercise their deliberative agency. The situation, environment, and psychological state in which a person finds themselves in when they consider actions of suicide cannot be extracted away from an action of suicide. Moreover, if Edwin Shneidman was correct that many people who are suicidal experience ambivalence, then they are like the doctor described above—namely, they do not know what will relieve their suffering, but they are desperately searching for relief from their suffering, which they experience as intolerable. It is understandable, then, to desire to try something—anything—that might bring relief.

William Styron captured the idea of how a sense of desperation might permeate the thought processes of someone who is suicidal, when he explained his experience in the following way:

> it is not an immediately identifiable pain, like that of a broken limb. It may be more accurate to say that despair, owing to some evil trick played upon the sick brain by the inhabiting psyche, comes to resemble the diabolical discomfort of being imprisoned in a fiercely overheated room. And because no breeze stirs this caldron, because there is no escape from this smothering confinement, it is entirely natural that the victim begins to think ceaselessly of oblivion.[43]

So, it seems both unfair and unreasonable to suggest that those who are suicidal can separate their unbearable pain from their decision-making in that moment.

Edwin Shneidman made a similar observation. Shneidman explained:

> [t]he suicidal person's thinking pattern has constricted; often it is dichotomous with only two possibilities: yes or no, [. . .]—the desperation of seeing only two alternatives, and not three or more choices as we do in ordinary life. In the camera of the mind, the suicidal film is limited to stark black and white.[44]

Shneidman's observation that suicidal persons have constricted thinking patterns led him to advise that a person ought not to decide to die by suicide while they are suicidal. Unfortunately, however, he also knew that the soundness of his advice is something that becomes lost in such constricted patterns of thought.

The second reply that I wish to make with respect to the objection that an action of suicide could be seen as morally wrong in hindsight is to note that the objection itself offers hope. That is, the objection suggests that, if only a person can somehow get through the moment at-hand, then they might see their situation quite differently. Granting the truth of that sentiment, the objection supports the idea that actions of suicide are amoral because either they do not reflect one's deliberative, moral agency, or because a person has found themselves in such awful circumstances where they no longer believe that they have a choice in the matter.

The objection is hopeful insofar as it suggests that a person can take up a perspective that they were previously unable to fantom with the advantage of hindsight *and* believe that they would have done something wrong had they acted earlier. I do not believe that such an objection undermines my thesis here; indeed, I believe that it *supports* my thesis that actions of suicide are amoral. It supports my thesis because it provides evidence for believing that persons engaging in actions of suicide have their deliberative or moral agencies compromised. Their actions, though intentional, are not the products of deliberative, moral agency, nor could they be.

In this chapter, I have made a few remarks in response to some of the main objections against the amorality of suicide that I anticipate. Undoubtedly, more objections will either come to mind or be brought to my attention; and I welcome them. While there is more work to do, I sincerely believe that the most promising route toward more effective suicide prevention efforts is increasing our dialogue, humility, and compassion, while decreasing the silence, social stigma, and moral condemnation. Ultimately, I believe that postulating actions of suicide as amoral actions is a philosophically defensible position.

NOTES

1. Bruce Waller, *Freedom Without Responsibility* (Philadelphia: Temple University Press, 1990).

2. Of course, ideally, a person would not wish to trace their steps—or another person's steps—back in time to see what they could have done differently as that has the benefit of hindsight. But, more importantly, such a backward-looking strategy is not helpful in the prevention of actions of suicide. Rather, to be proactive, it would be important to have a forward-looking approach—namely, to get help before one is experiencing a crisis, or to have a safety plan in place to avert such a crisis. I have suggested a backward-looking approach here only to show that, sometimes, even in hindsight, there is no clear point or place where it could have been obvious to a person that they need help. Depression, for instance, can distort even a person's recognition of their own thought patterns such that they believe that how they see things is the truth.

3. William Styron, *Darkness Visible: A Memoir of Madness* (New York: Random House, 1990), 14.

4. Naomi Judd and Marcia Wilkie, *River of Time: My Descent into Depression and How I Emerged with Hope* (New York: Hachette Book Group, Inc., 2016).

5. Edwin S. Shneidman, *The Suicidal Mind* (New York: Oxford University Press, 1996), 119.

6. I believe that continuing to see actions of suicide as within the moral domain perpetuates the tendency to see suicide as a problem that individuals alone face. Recognizing that actions of suicide are outside of the moral domain might help to clarify that actions of suicide are a public health crisis that individuals, as well as communities, face.

7. Of course, all actions of suicide involve other people; and I thank Paul Dages for calling this point to my attention. The objection that I wish to focus upon here, however, are those actions—such as homicide-suicide—that clearly challenge the amorality of suicide as they are actions that combine an undeniably immoral action with an action of suicide.

8. Kelly Posner, Beth Brodsky, Kseniya Yershova, Jacqueline Buchanan, and John Mann, "The Classification of Suicidal Behavior," in *The Oxford Handbook of Suicide and Self-Injury*, ed. Matthew K. Nock, 7–22 (New York: Oxford University Press, 2014), 11.

9. Dale Dorsey's example of Phil (as found in chapter one) also seems to support that claim that I am making here; namely that, even though Phil's failure to open the safe is an amoral (in)action, Phil could still perform other actions within the moral domain. Phil could warn others that a serious calamity is about to happen, for example.

10. The sacredness of life, it seems, ought to extend to all living beings—not just to human beings. After all, God as Creator is believed to have created (or to have made possible the creation of) all living beings. Otherwise, it seems that a person would be committed to holding inconsistent views about the sacredness of life. That is, if the sacredness of life only applies to *human* life, then it is difficult to see how one can resist the accusation of speciesism. But I digress.

11. Edwin S. Shneidman, *The Suicidal Mind*, 133.

12. *The Holy Bible*, The Gospel of John 15:13, New International Version (Grand Rapids: Zondervan Publishing House, 1984), 616.

13. The idea is that the religious condemnation of suicide stems from a concern that martyrdom was having too much appeal. Indeed, in his article "Suicide and Self-Starvation," Terence M. O'Keeffe explains: "[w]hat spurred Augustine and others to condemn suicide was the suicidal mania of many of the early Christian martyrs, and in particular the sect of the Donatists, for whom, taking the high valuation of martyrdom seriously, the most sensible course after baptism was to preserve the state of grace thus gained by instant death, by martyrdom if possible but by suicide if necessary. It was in opposition to this that Augustine stressed the condemnation of suicide as a frustration of God's plan and a rejection of God in rejecting his gift of life. Only in the sixth century did Church law incorporate a ban on suicide. Until that time, the promise of escape from temptation and the guarantee of posthumous glory were powerful inducements to martyrdom *and* to suicide" (*Philosophy*, Vol. 59, No. 229 [July 1984]: 349–63, 352).

14. The nature of normativity alone counts against such reasoning here. Morality, as normative, is *prescriptive* not descriptive.

15. Yet appearances here are deceiving. While "murder" is objectively wrong, reasonable people still disagree as to what constitutes "murder." Is murder *any* unjustified killing? If so, what counts as *unjustified* killing? Is killing in war murder? Is capital punishment murder? Must murder be premeditated? Must the would-be murderer have an evil intent? Does killing a non-human animal for no good reason count as murder? At the very least, the fact that reasonable people disagree with how to respond to such questions lessens the force of the claim that *murder is objectively wrong*.

16. Kelly Posner, Beth Brodsky, Kseniya Yershova, Jacqueline Buchanan, and John Mann, "The Classification of Suicidal Behavior," in *The Oxford Handbook of Suicide and Self-Injury*, ed. Matthew K. Nock, 7–22 (New York: Oxford University Press, 2014), 11.

17. Immanuel Kant, *Grounding for the Metaphysics of Morals* (1785), third edition, trans. James W. Ellington (Indianapolis: Hackett Publishing Company, 1993).

18. Immanuel Kant, *Grounding for the Metaphysics of Morals* (1785), 30–31.

19. To clarify, the appeal to immorality of using a person as a mere means comes from a formulation of the categorical imperative, which is a universal moral principle, namely that moral agents are to "[a]ct in such a way that you treat humanity, whether in your own person or in the person of another, always at the same time as an end and never simply as a means" (as found in Kant's *Grounding for the Metaphysics of Morals* [1785], third edition, trans. James W. Ellington [Indianapolis: Hackett Publishing Company, 1993], 36, translator's footnote omitted).

20. Immanuel Kant, *The Metaphysics of Morals* (1797), as found in *Practical Philosophy: The Cambridge Edition of the Works of Immanuel Kant*, translated and edited by Mary J. Gregor (New York: Cambridge University Press, 1996): (6:424), 548.

21. Thomas Joiner, *Myths about Suicide* (Cambridge: Harvard University Press, 2010), 42–53.

22. Edwin S. Shneidman, *The Suicidal Mind* (New York: Oxford University Press, 1996), 4.

23. William Styron, *Darkness Visible: A Memoir of Madness* (New York: Random House, 1990), 14.

24. Compulsory military service, or the drafting of soldiers in wartime, is a controversial issue, at best. One concern regarding the drafting of soldiers is simply that those would-be soldiers did not volunteer to serve in the military, and so making military service compulsory takes away their freedom of choice. So, some persons might be opposed to the drafting of soldiers as a matter of principle. But the underlying worrisome concern with respect to the drafting of soldiers is that soldiers must be prepared to sacrifice their lives and, what a person chooses to sacrifice themselves *for* is a deeply personal choice. One person, or entity, cannot determine for another person (or persons) what it is that they ought to be prepared to die for.

25. David Hume, "Of Suicide" (1757), as found in *The Ethics of Suicide: Historical Sources*, ed. by Margaret Pabst Battin (New York: Oxford University Press, 2015), 410.

26. David Hume, "Of Suicide" (1757), as found in *The Ethics of Suicide*, 410.

27. Bernard Williams, "A Critique of Utilitarianism" in *Utilitarianism For and Against* by J. J. C. Smart and Bernard Williams (New York: Cambridge University Press, 1973): 75–150, 116.

28. Some people might claim that there is a right to life. I will not purport to examine what such a right looks like or means in practice. But one danger in purporting that there is a right to life is the idea that rights can be waived or given up. So, if there is a right to life, then it seems as though one might freely choose to give up their right to life. Yet it is doubtful that those who espouse a right to life in other public conversations intend for the implications of their view to apply to PAS.

29. Louis Jolyon West, "Reflections on the Right to Die," in *Suicidology: Essays in Honor of Edwin Shneidman* (Northvale, NJ: Jason Aronson Incorporated, 1993), 359.

30. Louis Jolyon West, "Reflections on the Right to Die," 359.

31. To be clear, the thesis that actions of suicide are amoral does *not* preclude moral evaluations of those who assist or who encourage others to die by suicide. These are separate actions performed by *other* people, not the person in question. It is certainly possible that these different actions performed by others are, in fact, subject to moral evaluation.

32. I am assuming here that such a person did not engage in an action of suicide—or, as more commonly phrased, I am assuming that such a person did not *attempt suicide*. If, however, such a person did engage in an action of suicide in the process that I have described, then they would *not* have retained either their deliberative or moral agency at that point in time. For the sake of simplicity, however, I am focusing only upon a person who struggles with suicidal ideation and who sought help before engaging in an action of suicide.

33. David A. Jobes, *Managing Suicidal Risk: A Collaborative Approach* (New York: The Guilford Press, 2006), 3.

34. David A. Jobes, *Managing Suicidal Risk*, 3–4.

35. Kay Redfield Jamison, *Night Falls Fast: Understanding Suicide* (New York: Random House, 1999), 3.

36. Kay Redfield Jamison, *Night Falls Fast*, 4.

37. Kay Redfield Jamison, *Night Falls Fast*, 4.

38. Kay Redfield Jamison, *Night Falls Fast*, 4.

39. Kay Redfield Jamison, *Night Falls Fast*, 5.

40. Kevin Hines, *Cracked, Not Broken: Surviving and Thriving After a Suicide Attempt* (Lanham, MD: Rowman & Littlefield Publishers, 2013).

41. Kevin Hines's more recent book is *The Art of Being Broken: How Storytelling Saves Lives* (Brentwood, TN: Post Hill Press, 2023).

42. I thank Bruce Russell for suggesting this example, although I admittedly took some liberties with it.

43. William Styron, *Darkness Visible*, 50.

44. Edwin S. Shneidman, *The Suicidal Mind*, 61.

Chapter Five

The Significance of Charting a New Path

I hope that this little book can start a conversation about the amorality of suicide. I certainly do not intend to claim either that there are only three kinds of amoral actions or that there are only three different categories of actions of suicide (regardless of how broadly they are construed). Neither amoral actions nor actions of suicide fit into such neat little boxes. Both subjects are inherently complex, and to suggest otherwise would be both inaccurate and naive. Nevertheless, the more that I have thought about this topic, the more I have become convinced that it is a mistake to believe that actions of suicide belong in the moral domain.

To take stock, I have suggested here that, if an agent is unable to exercise deliberative agency with respect to an action—that is, if an agent is unable to have reasons for an action and to act upon the reasons that they have—then *that action* is amoral. I have further suggested that, when an agent's relational knowledge is compromised, then they are unable to act for *moral* reasons. Additionally, I have acknowledged that situational and circumstantial factors can severely limit an agent's ability to exercise either their deliberative agency or their moral agency, even if neither agency is otherwise compromised. It follows then that, for any action, if an agent is unable to exercise either their deliberative agency or their moral agency (for any reason), then that action is amoral. So, lacking such agencies is a sufficient condition for an action to be amoral.

Regarding actions of suicide, I have appealed to Thomas Joiner's interpersonal theory of suicide, while acknowledging that actions of suicide vary widely. Losing a sense of self and, thereby, losing one's autonomy seems to be at the heart of some actions of suicide—including among persons suffering from a mental illness and persons suffering from an existential crisis. The threat of losing a sense of self also seems applicable to those who make the decision to sacrifice themselves completely for another, or others, or for a cause to which they are deeply committed—indeed, to do otherwise is *unthinkable*. But losing a sense of self (or facing a clear, severe, and immediate threat to one's sense of self) compromises an agent's ability to exercise deliberative agency. Indeed, with respect to actions of self-sacrifice, the possible exercise of one's deliberative agency simply does not apply.

Additionally, experiencing a thwarted sense of belonging—such as among persons who suffer a moral injury, or who are socially oppressed or otherwise socially marginalized—can compromise an agent's ability to see a moral reason as entailing a reason to act. For example, to experience a moral injury is to experience a specific type of betrayal. It is to have one's moral compass shattered. Moral reasons lose their normative force when an agent's relational knowledge is compromised, given the relational nature of morality. That is, experiencing a thwarted sense of belonging compromises an agent's ability to exercise their moral agency. If an agent no longer sees themselves as connected with others in a community than *a fortori* such an agent no longer sees themselves as a member of the moral community. Simply put, a moral agent who suffers from a severe moral injury cannot act upon the moral reasons that they do not have.

Furthermore, situations and circumstances can be so constrained that an agent's ability to make a decision that reflects their will is no longer possible. Their action of suicide stems from a perceived necessity. *Choice*, in this context, is a misnomer. Indeed, in such cases, an agent's ability to exercise either their deliberative agency or their moral agency (or both) is compromised. It is possible, therefore, that even moral agents can be morally estranged from their actions. It is further possible that an agent can intend to do what they do not (all things considered) desire to do. Foxhole Jumper's action, for example, is an action of suicide, even though he did not desire to die. His death was intended only as the necessary means of saving the lives of others. But, as I have suggested here, any action of suicide appears to be an action in which an agent's death is intended only as a means to another aim, or end.[1]

The upshot is that, if an action constitutes an action of suicide, then an agent lacks the ability to exercise either their deliberative agency or their moral agency (or both) with respect to *that action*. An agent might lack these agencies, respectively, or find themselves encumbered by situational constraints that defeat their ability to exercise their deliberative agency. Tellingly, being unable to act from either an agent's deliberative or moral agency (or both) is a common thread that weaves through all actions of suicide—despite their variations. So, if an action constitutes an action of suicide, then either an agent's deliberative or moral agency (or both) are lacking or compromised.

Yet, as I have noted above, lacking the ability to exercise one, or both, agencies (or having one's deliberative agency compromised) implies that an agent's action is amoral. An action performed by an agent with such agencies either lacking or compromised is not an appropriate subject of moral evaluation. It follows that, if an action constitutes an action of suicide, then *that action* is amoral.

Throughout this project, I tend to focus upon *agents* rather than *persons*. My reasoning for doing so needs clarification because I certainly do not intend to undermine the personhood of those who engage in actions of suicide. Rather, I wish to leave open here the possibility that non-human animals also engage in what appears to be actions of suicide.[2] So, if it turns out that non-human animals engage in actions of suicide, then *those actions* seem to be clear candidates of actions outside of the moral domain, or amoral actions. Additionally, if it turns out that non-human animals do *not* engage in actions of suicide, then an explanation is necessary to articulate why some actions of non-human animals (namely, for instance, those actions that look self-sacrificial) are not actions of suicide. Such an inquiry, of course, will demand that we examine how we define actions of suicide, and that is a welcomed inquiry. As I previously noted, I believe that how we discuss and, consequently, how we define actions of suicide needs attention.

I believe that the thesis that actions of suicide are amoral has several merits. One merit of the thesis that actions of suicide are amoral is that it does not depend upon the further idea that persons who engage in actions of suicide are, in fact, suffering from a mental illness and, therefore, their action of suicide is amoral. While it is true that some (perhaps even most) persons who perform actions of suicide do so because they are suffering from a mental illness and that their deliberative agency could be compromised by their mental illness, it is also true that actions of suicide are various and complex. Including self-sacrificial actions as actions of suicide, for instance, implies that some actions of suicide do not need to entail a story about mental illness. To clarify, my intention here is not to shift conversations away from the connections between suicide and mental illnesses. Such conversations are greatly needed. Rather, my intention is simply not to *limit* discussions of actions of suicide to discussions regarding mental illnesses.

An additional merit of the thesis that actions of suicide are amoral is that such a thesis takes seriously the social and environmental factors in which any given action of suicide takes place. When both a *relational* account of morality and a *relational* account of actions of suicide are assumed, then a person's social and situational factors simply cannot be ignored in discussions regarding the moral status of actions of suicide. That is, it is insufficient to regard an action of suicide as an isolated action that pertains only to the person in question. While I suggest that there are some actions of suicide that are amoral due to a person's lack of deliberative agency or moral agency, I also suggest that there are some situations or circumstances in which a person does not perceive themselves as having a choice in the matter due to the severe and immediate threat upon their sense of self.

Still another merit of the thesis that actions of suicide are amoral is that it maintains that such actions are, indeed, actions—including both an *act* and an *end* for which the act is done. The upshot is that the position that actions of suicide are amoral jettisons one of the prevailing misconceptions about actions of suicide—namely, that such actions are simply acts of self-killing and, as such, they belong in the moral domain seemingly by definition. Abandoning the common tendency to equate actions of suicide with an act of self-killing opens a conceptual space for the amorality of suicide.

Yet challenges persist. One challenge is holding space for such sensitive conversations. It is an understatement to say that actions of suicide are difficult to discuss. There seems to be a recognizable and understandable desire to keep such discussions minimal and surface-level. In some situations, it might even be best to do so. My point is that, while I believe that more compassionate and deeper conversations about suicide are needed, there is also a need to be mindful of the appropriate time and space for such conversations.

Nevertheless, there is a difference between simply being mindful of how and when such conversations occur and avoiding them completely. It seems clear that a persistent failure to discuss actions of suicide has severe and devastating consequences. Among those consequences, of course, are missed opportunities for suicide prevention and intervention. Another consequence of a persistent failure to discuss actions of suicide in respectful, sensitive, caring, and meaningful ways is that it yields a kind of collective, social permission that makes it acceptable for such discussions to remain perpetually at bay. Always keeping such discussions minimal and surface-level, however, makes it easier to stigmatize such actions. Anything foreign, or unfamiliar, is easier to condemn.

It also appears that there is a deep-seated fear that if one so much as tries to understand the perspective of someone who is at-risk for suicide, then they might understand suicide a bit *too well*. Not wanting to make sense of suicide could be mistaken as a defense or safety mechanism. Such a tendency is understandable, albeit it may reside at an unconscious level. But I believe that, ironically, such a tendency to seek out such a safety mechanism has the opposite effect. Regarding suicide as simply beyond one's comprehension ignores the seemingly counterintuitive idea that all persons are a varying risk for suicide. There is no immunity against dying by suicide. For example, no one is immune to suffering from certain illnesses that could heighten one's risk for suicide and, until one reaches such states, they cannot know for certain what they might do or be capable of doing.

Moreover, no one who acknowledges that there are persons or causes worthy of self-sacrifice is immune from dying by suicide. So, there is irony here in believing that, if suicide remains an enigma, then one is somehow immune from dying by suicide. The irony is that efforts to keep an understanding of suicide at bay seemingly makes persons more alone in their pain. Hence, borrowing from Shneidman, efforts to keep an understanding of suicide at bay increases a person's suffering because it increases the isolation of one's thoughts.[3] A person might be unaware that other people have felt similarly, for instance. Remaining ignorant about suicide in an effort to avoid it misses the mark. Ignorance here is not bliss. It is deadly.

Another challenge to the amorality of suicide is that it is too often confused with the claim that actions of suicide are morally permissible. To be clear, that is *not* an implication of my thesis. Recall that stating that any action is morally permissible is stating that the action in question is in the moral domain. Because I understand the dominant view to be that actions of suicide are morally wrong, at least on occasion, I have focused upon challenging the dominant view here. Nevertheless, it remains important not to make the same mistake in the opposite direction. Namely, recognizing that it simply does not follow that actions of suicide are somehow *morally* permissible or even *morally* justified if they are not morally condemned. To make *any* moral evaluations about an action of suicide is still to place *that action* within the moral domain. Consequently, such an understanding merely repeats the mistake of thinking that actions can be regarded as within the moral domain irrespective of matters of agency.

So, in sum, I have put forth an argument for the amorality of suicide by acknowledging that, if an agent is unable to exercise either their deliberative or their moral agency, then their corresponding action is not in the moral domain. I have further appealed to Thomas Joiner's interpersonal theory of suicide, a relational account of suicide, to explain how unmet psychological needs are at the root of actions of suicide. But, again, if unmet psychological needs compromise either an agent's deliberative agency or their moral agency (as I believe that they do), then actions of suicide are not in the moral domain.

In this chapter, I wish to revisit the current landscape regarding common ways of understanding the relationship between actions of suicide and the moral domain, as I mentioned in chapter one. I also will explore what might be said with respect to different, non-deontic ethical frameworks. I will then suggest a few implications of the amorality of suicide. Finally, I will close with a brief overview of some of the areas in need of further exploration.

REVISITING THE CURRENT LANDSCAPE

In chapter one, I noted that I regard the idea that actions of suicide are amoral appears to contrast with the dominant view regarding the relationship between actions of suicide and the moral domain. The dominant view is that actions of suicide are immoral, at least on occasion. Notice that the dominant view not only assumes that actions of suicide are in the moral domain, but also that an agent who engages in an action of suicide is, in fact, a moral agent with a sufficient degree of deliberative agency, and that other, possible alternative ways of acting were clearly among their considerations. These are significant assumptions. They are assumptions that deeply influence judgments about the moral status of such actions. Ultimately, however, I believe that these assumptions are mistaken. I find the dominant view unsatisfactory for several reasons.

For starters, such a view appears to define "suicide" in such value-laden terms instead of in a value-neutral way. Defining "suicide" as self-killing or self-murder, for example, appears to be prevalent. Yet such a way of defining "suicide," confuses an act with an action. Acts are what an agent does; but, to know their action, we must also know the end or the aim for which they so act. When suicide is construed as an act, the intentionality of the agent in question is sidestepped. To be clear, the worry is not simply that, per the dominant view, conversations about the moral status of actions of suicide are closed before they have a chance to start (although that is unfortunate). Rather, the salient worry here is far more troubling. The salient worry is that common ways of discussing actions of suicide are not discussing *actions* of suicide at all.

At the very least, the dominant view does not regard actions of complete self-sacrifice as actions of suicide, for example. I believe that such an exclusion is indicative of the fact that the dominant view maintains a simplistic way of defining actions that are inherently complex. Certainly, it is not difficult to regard actions of complete self-sacrifice as meeting the definition of suicide when suicide is defined in terms of intending self-injurious behavior and intending (albeit indirectly) to die as a result of that behavior.

But the dominant view overlooks the possibility that an agent could *indirectly* intend a fatal act as a means to some other, given end. Again, the Foxhole Jumper does not want to die. He does not directly intend his death. Nevertheless, the Foxhole Jumper indirectly intends his own death as the necessary means of saving members of his platoon. I believe that an important insight is lost when actions of complete self-sacrifice are excluded from conversations about suicide. Specifically, the insight that becomes lost is the idea that all actions of suicide—or, at least all such actions that appear to meet the definition of suicide—are actions in which the agent in question *indirectly intends their death as a necessary means to some other end or ends*, when either their deliberative agency or moral agency (or both) is compromised.

Foxhole Jumper, therefore, is not an anomaly with respect to his action of suicide. Rather, Foxhole Jumper's situation highlights the idea that some persons who perform actions of suicide and who also suffer from depression, an existential crisis, a moral injury, or excruciating physical or psychological pain (or, rather, what Edwin Shneidman called excessive psychache) are like Foxhole Jumper in an important respect. Namely, it seems that such persons are indirectly intending their death as a necessary means to some other end or ends. Incidentally, such a view supports Shneidman's observation that a person would not engage in an action of suicide unless they believe that they must do so.[4]

The dominant view places actions of suicide within the moral domain, at least on occasion, and that, of course, has further unwelcome consequences. To be sure, if suicide falls *within* the moral domain, then moral evaluations are appropriate. If, however, suicide falls *outside* of the moral domain, then moral evaluations are inappropriate. I have already alluded to the idea that placing suicide within the moral domain fuels social stigma against suicide. It does so not only because moral judgments are regarded as appropriate, but also because it leaves open the possibility of (moral) wrongdoing *for any given action of suicide*. So, placing suicide within the moral domain taints any action of suicide—especially those where the circumstances or underlying factors are unknown—with the *possibility* of wrongdoing. This possibility is alone sufficient to fuel the social stigma against suicide since, by default, it implies that those persons who die by suicide are also possible wrongdoers, as William Styron observed.[5]

There is another concern with respect to placing suicide within the moral domain. The concern is that regarding actions of suicide as within the moral domain seems to compromise suicide prevention efforts. In general, there appears to be a two-prong approach to such efforts. One prong of this approach tends to focus upon individuals, and so the goal might be to make sure that people are familiar with resources, for example, or that individuals know the warning signs of suicide risk in effort to help others.[6] The other prong of this approach is community-based. Aligning mental health and intervention specialists with law enforcement, for instance, can increase the likelihood that a person suffering from a mental illness receives the care they need. The prevalence of, and access to, community resources such as support groups, help for addiction, employment opportunities, affordable housing, community spaces (such as community centers and parks), access to education, access to mental healthcare, and greater economic and social equity especially among persons who have been historically marginalized are all useful and much-needed communal actions. Such actions help to build stronger relationships within communities and, ultimately, might help to reduce the number of deaths by suicide within a community.[7] My worry, then, with regarding suicide as an action meriting moral judgments of any stripe is that, practically speaking, it may have the undesirable effect of neglecting both approaches to suicide prevention efforts—as if fueling social stigma is not reason enough to discourage such judgments.

Additionally, attaching moral evaluations to actions of suicide might inadvertently limit the promotion of resources for individuals, or even limiting the help of finding such resources. After all, if it is believed that individuals are morally responsible for their actions of suicide, then it seems to follow that there is also the associated belief that individuals are morally responsible for both finding and utilizing such resources for themselves. But, as Styron observed, a sufferer of severe depression is unlikely to be able to find and to utilize resources while in the grip of their illness. Moreover, community-based efforts of suicide prevention are also likely to be short-changed by the perpetuation of the belief that actions of suicide somehow belong in the moral domain. In general, that which is the responsibility of each person is also not something that demands the time, attention, and resources of an entire community since doing so would be redundant. Or so the thought goes.

Moreover, I also find the position that actions of suicide are morally *permissible* to be wanting. Recall that thinking of actions of suicide as morally permissible places them squarely within the moral domain. Notice, however, that such a view assumes that an agent *can* exercise their deliberative agency, and seemingly does not consider the possibility that an agent who engages in an action of suicide might not be doing so as a deliberative, moral agent. To be sure, such a view seems to assume the *absence* of a mental illness for any action of suicide. Believing that an action of suicide is (or at least that it can be) in the moral domain implies that, for at least some actions of suicide, an agent's intentionality reflects their choice. If an agent intends an outcome, for instance, then they desire *that outcome*.

But, again, I do not see how that is an accurate description of what is happening with respect to actions of suicide. As I have been at pains to explain, while actions of suicide are, indeed, *intentional*, it seems clear that intentionality need not reflect an agent's desires. In chapter one, I employed the example of intending to break a window to escape a burning building to help to illustrate this point. I certainly can intend to break a window to escape the burning building without desiring to break a window and without desiring to fuel the fire as a result of breaking a window. If an agent engages in an action of suicide because they believe that they have no choice in the matter, or because their basic psychological needs are unmet, then it is intellectually reckless to believe that their action is *morally* evaluable, as an action in the moral domain.[8]

The common tendency to regard actions of suicide as actions within the moral domain is pervasive, however. Some people, for example, might insist that an action of suicide could be morally *obligatory*, at least on occasion. Perhaps, they might claim, it is not too difficult to imagine situations (like

Immanuel Kant's illustration of a man bitten by a rabid dog) in which a person whose death is imminent could somehow save the lives of others by hastening their own death. Would such a possibility thereby place at least some actions of suicide (namely, *those* actions of suicide) squarely within the moral domain? My response is no. The moral domain is not the only mode of normativity. Even if such a person in that situation *felt obligated*, it is not a *moral* ought that demands their sacrifice. A psychological need to maintain a sense of self unto one's death as well as reasons of love offer alternative ways of understanding how they might feel so obligated.

As I previously noted, it seems as though there are limits to common sense morality. For example, when airline flight attendants remind passengers that, in the unlikely event of an emergency, they should secure their own oxygen mask before assisting others, the flight attendants are not promoting selfishness but sound reasoning. Simply put, we cannot help others if we completely neglect ourselves for either too much or too long. Per common sense morality, then, complete self-sacrifice is not *morally* obligatory. It cannot be. Only love can make that demand.

Thus far, I have addressed actions of suicide as immoral, morally permissible, and morally obligatory, and I have found each of these views to be wanting. But there is a worry that other ethical ways of thinking are being neglected here—namely, for instance, a virtue ethics approach and a consequentialist approach. Recall that, although I cannot possibly speak to all ethical theories or frameworks here, my thesis is still that actions of suicide are amoral, or outside the moral domain. But if actions of suicide are outside of the moral domain, then they must be outside of *whatever we take the moral domain to be*. It is not enough simply to state that common views about the moral status of suicide tend to assume a deontic framework.[9] So, although I acknowledge that I cannot possibly address here every way of understanding the moral domain, I hope to provide a glimpse into why I believe that actions of suicide are amoral irrespective of the ethical framework employed.

So, someone might believe that actions of suicide reflect either a virtuous or a vicious character of the agent in question, or that their action is an expression of either a virtue or a vice. For example, it is quite understandable to claim that Foxhole Jumper's action was courageous. But, if Foxhole Jumper's action was, in fact, courageous, then it seems as though his action was morally virtuous as well. The same could be said of Thomas Hart Benton—namely, that he displayed courage in his willingness to sacrifice his life for what he believed in.

I contend that, if any action is to be virtuous or vicious, then such an action needs to reflect an agent's will in an appropriate way. The fact that people like Kevin Hines, for example, later regret that they engaged in an action of suicide suggests that such actions may not reflect an agent's will in an appropriate way. At the very least, I believe that courageous actions and actions of suicide can come apart. In the former there is a choice—a person could act courageously, or they could not. Or their action stems from their habits (or character) or it does not. In the latter, there is no choice, or no perception of a choice. Their action is not stemming from the habits that they have developed. Foxhole Jumper, Thomas Hart Benton, and Kevin Hines seemingly engaged in their respective actions of suicide believing that they did not have a choice, or that they could not have acted otherwise. But even internalizing courageous actions through making them a habit, does not yet reveal what a person is willing to give their lives for; nor does it reveal when, or how, they would experience their sense of self as lost. I believe that to characterize actions of suicide as displaying courage—or, quite frankly, as displaying any moral virtue or vice—is simply failing to appreciate the kind of unique action that suicide is. Seeing actions of suicide as about either a loss of a sense of self, or about a severe and immediate threat to one's sense of self, is more basic and fundamental than already having a sense of self and proceeding to act courageously *as a moral agent.*

Additionally, I will consider one kind of consequentialist moral reasoning here, which I believe could be the most detrimental to the amorality of suicide, and that is scalar utilitarianism. Scalar utilitarianism maintains that there are morally *better* and morally *worse* actions, which need not entail that there is some kind of over-arching best, or morally superior, action (namely, the maximization of utility) that is demanded of an agent.[10] So, per scalar utilitarianism, an action of suicide could be morally worse than some other action or, in instances of self-sacrifice perhaps, morally better than other actions that an agent could do, or that are open to an agent to perform. Yet judging an action to be morally better or morally worse than some other action (or actions), assumes that an agent is, in fact, a moral agent who can exercise their deliberative agency about what they believe they ought to do, or even to calculate which possible actions that are open to them to perform would have greater utility. But an agent's capacity to exercise their deliberative and moral agency, however, must not be assumed.

Arguably, a scalar utilitarian might contend that there simply *are* morally better and worse actions that an agent could do in any given situation, even if such actions are *not* recognized by the agent in question. Yet such a response overlooks the problem of moral requirability, which Dale Dorsey's work highlights. Making a moral judgment or a moral evaluation of an agent's action (from an objective, or third-person, perspective) assumes that some actions were open to an agent to perform insofar as they could have acted differently. The problem is simply that any *moral* assessment of actions that are open to an agent to perform *must consider an agent's capacities at that time.* An agent's degree of deliberative and moral agency are not mere details that can be extracted from a moral assessment of either the actions they perform, or the actions that are open to them to perform.

As I intend to stress here, actions of suicide are unique actions. The World Health Organization (WHO), for example, recognizes that actions of suicide could be impulsive.[11] Specifically, the World Health Organization claims that "many suicides happen impulsively in moments of crisis with a breakdown in the ability to deal with life stresses, such as financial problems, relationship break-up or chronic pain and illness."[12] If at least some actions of suicide are impulsive as the WHO suggests, then there is a further reason to call into question whether agents engaging in actions of suicide are also capable of exercising their deliberative, moral agency at the time of their action.

My point here is that all ethical theories or frameworks make assumptions about *moral agents* who engage in morally evaluable actions. Additionally, all ethical theories or frameworks need to respond to the problem of moral requirability—that is, it is neither helpful nor wise for an ethical framework or theory to claim that an action that an agent simply cannot do is, in fact, somehow morally requirable of them. Hence, an alternative way of understanding the relationship between actions of suicide and the moral domain is needed.

IMPLICATIONS

There is much to be learned from the past—even the relatively recent past. For example, consider alcoholism. Misusing and abusing alcohol were thought to be simple choices that some people make. So, the difference between a person suffering from an addiction to alcohol, or alcohol use disorder, and a person who, say, chooses to binge drink on a particular weekend were simply not appreciated.[13] They were treated in the same way insofar as both were regarded as choices. Public awareness of alcohol use disorder, however, seems to help to empower sufferers of alcoholism to get help, and promotes a more compassionate response to understanding the behaviors of those who suffer from alcoholism. Divorcing alcoholism from a *choice* is an important first step to reclaiming one's life.[14]

Similarly, it could be that regarding actions of suicide not as a person's choice that is expressive of their will could likewise lead to greater compassion and humility. If nothing else, it is vital to listen to the accounts and stories of those people who have been suicidal or who have performed an action of suicide. Understanding their unique perspectives seems to count against the tendency to regard their actions as somehow within the moral domain. So, I believe that one implication of the amorality of suicide is greater compassion toward those who suffer from suicide ideation or who have performed an action of suicide.

Establishing the amorality of suicide, however, might not only eradicate possible barriers to suicide prevention efforts, but it also might help to unite very different approaches to suicide prevention efforts. There are clearly cultural differences with respect to such efforts. Of course, the lens through which I am approaching suicide in this project is informed through a Western culture, which tends to regard individualism quite highly. In general, much (indeed, perhaps too much) of the discussion about the morality of suicide focuses upon individual freedoms and competencies with less attention to one's social and political environment, as well as to one's communal citizenship. I recognize that other cultures or societies approach suicide differently, however.[15] I also acknowledge that the extent to which a culture or a society regards suicide as a public health concern informs the way people think about the relationship between suicide and morality, as well as the degree of social stigma against actions of suicide. My focus upon suicide as informed through the lens of Western culture is *not* to give priority to this way of thinking. Rather, it is simply to adhere to what has informed my thinking on the subject. In any case, I believe that regarding actions of suicide as amoral actions has pragmatic value insofar as it might help to strengthen cross-cultural efforts for suicide prevention.

A second implication of the thesis that actions of suicide are amoral is that such a view can help to change conversations about suicide, quite literally. In her book *Epistemic Injustice*, Miranda Fricker argues that some socially acceptable and prevalent ways of thinking can alienate a person within a given society either because their testimony does not match the accepted view or because there is a deprivation of language within the given society.[16] For example, the acknowledgement of actions constituting sexual harassment and domestic violence were impossible to communicate with others until such phrases acquired currency within a language.[17]

In a similar way, persons who suffer from suicidal ideation also suffer injustice in societies that lack ways of effectively communicating their experiences. As Fricker explains,

> [w]hen you find yourself in a situation in which you seem to be the only one to feel the dissonance between received understanding and your own intimated sense of a given experience, it tends to knock your faith in your own ability to make sense of the world, or at least the relevant region of the world.[18]

I believe that continuing to place actions of suicide within the moral domain perpetuates the dominant, societal understanding of such actions at the detriment of both sufferers and their loved ones.

The prevalent social stigma regarding actions of suicide has the effect of marginalizing the voices of persons impacted by actions of suicide and inducing further suffering such that, even where there are open and honest conversations about suicide, our language still fails us. In the words of Miranda Fricker, such suffering takes the form of hermeneutical injustice. Fricker writes,

> [i]f one lives in a society or a subculture in which the mere fact of an intuitive or emotional expressive style means that one cannot be heard as fully rational, then one is thereby unjustly afflicted by a hermeneutical gap—one is subject to a hermeneutical injustice.[19]

Because persons who are particularly vulnerable to actions of suicide are often regarded as suffering from either a mental illness or from bouts of irrationality, Fricker's observation of hermeneutical injustice seems applicable.[20]

The charge of injustice here is significant, since it implies more than simply that the first-person perspective of persons suffering from suicidal ideation, for example, are rendered unintelligible. The charge of injustice suggests that such experiences are unfairly denied currency within a language. Fricker explains,

> [o]ne way of taking the epistemological suggestion that social power has an unfair impact on collective forms of social understanding is to think of our shared understandings as reflecting the perspectives of different social groups, and to entertain the idea that relations of unequal power can skew shared hermeneutical resources so that the powerful tend to have appropriate understandings of their experiences ready to draw on as they make sense of their social experiences, whereas the powerless are more likely to find themselves having some social experiences through a glass darkly, with at best ill-fitting meanings to draw on in the effort to render them intelligible.[21]

My point here is that, insofar as the dominant view regards actions of suicide as wrong (at least on occasion), then one of the consequences of that view is that those who suffer from suicide ideation, for example, might experience unnecessary shame in seeking help for something that should not have moral condemnation associated with it. Perpetuating the dominant view that suicide is wrong, at least on occasion, is perpetuating a kind of injustice. Seeing excessive drinking *as* alcoholism, for example, changes the moral landscape. So too, then, seeing actions of suicide *as* excessive psychache or suffering, changes the moral landscape. In neither circumstance is a person *choosing* to hurt themselves.

Clinging onto the belief that actions of suicide belong in the moral domain is an indication of a failure to consider the experiences of certain persons.

One possible reason for discounting the first-personal experiences of persons who engage in actions of suicide (which includes suicidal ideation and attempts) appears to be that it is simply easier to blame an individual rather than to embark upon the daunting task of fixing society. In the definition of suicide that I have put forth here, I have stressed the need to recognize actions of suicide as encompassing a person's situation, circumstance, and state of mind. Maintaining the belief that actions of suicide are somehow individual *choices* that belong in the moral domain gives society a free pass. But Émile Durkheim's work noted earlier calls attention to the disturbing societal trends. The idea that suicide rates are higher in some societies than in others, and even the idea that some societal groups are more at-risk than others suggests that it is not just individuals but also *societies* that must do some work. Fricker's attention to hermeneutical injustice, therefore, helps to support the idea that persons who are more at-risk for suicide within a society might be suffering from an additional harm simply by the prevailing belief that actions of suicide belong in the moral domain. Thinking about suicide as outside of the moral domain creates the necessary space for difficult conversations to begin.

Recognizing actions of suicide as outside of the moral domain ought to lift the burdens of shame and guilt associated with moral wrongdoing. Furthermore, understanding actions of suicide as amoral places a stronger demand upon our collective responsibility—to create communal spaces that are welcoming of all persons, and to speak openly and honestly about crises that, if we are lucky to live long enough, each one of us will face. To follow Leelah's plea, I believe that fixing society entails a recognition that suffering can be mitigated when a person is not alone in their pain. So, there is a collective moral responsibility—a call to action—that remains steadfast in light of the amorality of actions of suicide. Hence, a social responsibility toward suicide prevention efforts is not only compatible with the amorality of actions of suicide, but it is also strengthened when the amorality of such actions is recognized. Fix society, indeed.

FURTHER WORK

My aim here is simply to start a path toward regarding actions of suicide as outside the moral domain, or amoral. It is merely an introduction to what it might mean, and what it might look like, to regard actions of suicide as amoral. I believe that such a thesis promotes more compassion and humility. But certainly, I could not advocate for more humility here without also exercising humility in putting forth the thesis that actions of suicide are amoral. So, with humility, I recognize that much more work here is needed. In this section, I will focus upon three different (and broadly construed) areas that need further exploration.

For starters, understanding actions of suicide as rooted in the frustration of basic, psychological needs warrants further exploration. I have noted that actions of suicide are quite varied, and so it remains to be seen whether other actions of suicide also fit the pattern of an agent lacking one or more psychological needs. Certainly, actions of suicide cannot be conveniently categorized into one of the three groups that I have mentioned here. So how (or whether) the frustration of other basic psychological needs underlies actions of suicide is worth exploration. Moreover, it seems reasonable to suggest that psychological needs are interdependent. Losing a sense of competence, for example, is akin to losing a sense of self and a sense of belonging. How these and other psychological needs depend upon each other deserves attention.

I also believe that attention to how actions of suicide are defined and how we commonly refer to such actions is worthy of exploration. I have suggested here that our language is both a barrier to our understanding and a way in which the dominant view regarding the relationship between morality and actions of suicide perpetuates. While changing language is slow-going and cumbersome, I believe that failing to do so perpetuates an injustice. In short, it prevents sufferers of suicide ideation and those persons who have engaged in actions of suicide from having a value-neutral way of framing their experiences. Ironically, however, perpetuating an injustice is *within the moral domain* and, therefore, failing to change the dominant view is a *moral* failure.

Another area in need of further development concerns the nature and scope of amoral actions. While I acknowledge three categories of amoral actions, I certainly do not intend for these categories to be exhaustive of amoral actions. So, it could be that additional actions of suicide, or actions of suicide that are not explicitly addressed here, are also amoral even if they seemingly do not fall into at least one of the three categories of amoral actions mentioned here. I recognize that one obstacle to thinking about actions of suicide as amoral is that thinking about amoral actions, in general, is rather atypical. There seems to be a tendency to assume that most—if not all—of the actions that a moral agent performs are in the moral domain. So, if it turns out that the scope of the actions that are outside of the moral domain is broader than assumed, then perhaps a person will be more inclined to acknowledge that actions of suicide are among those actions.

In closing, Albert Camus famously wrote that "[t]here is but one truly serious philosophical problem, and that is suicide. Judging whether life is or is not worth living amounts to answering the fundamental question of philosophy."[22] On the one hand, I whole-heartedly agree with Camus that suicide is the fundamental question of philosophy. In fact, in homage to Voltaire, I believe that if philosophy did not already exist when humanity first wrestled with suicide ideation, then it certainly would have been necessary to have invented it.

On the other hand, however, I believe that regarding the philosophical problem of suicide as judging whether life is or is not worth living is far too simplistic. If Shneidman was correct that actions of suicide are the result of excessive psychache, then I believe that an account of actions of suicide ought to be about how best to minimize psychache in our own lives and how best to help others to do the same. Moreover, if Shelly Kagan is correct to posit that actions of complete self-sacrifice are to be included among actions of suicide, then I believe that, for at least some actions of suicide, the mode of normativity at issue is not morality, but love. Conversations about suicide, then, are *not* conversations about death, nor are they conversations about turning away from what matters the most to us. Instead, they are conversations about the depths of human suffering and what it is that someone can value more than life itself. They are conversations about the power of both excessive psychache and of profound love. They are conversations that we cannot afford to short-change.

NOTES

1. I have focused upon two possible aims, or ends, with respect to actions of suicide in this project—namely, the aim of ending one's pain and the end of saving the lives of another or others. But I recognize that there could be many possible aims or ends with respect to an action of suicide. For example, in passing, I have mentioned the action of Thomas Hart Benton and the action of Protester. I also have mentioned actions of suicide performed by suicide bombers. So, if someone believes that they are furthering a cause or a principle of which they are deeply committed (or have internalized), then that aim is yet another possible aim with respect to actions of suicide. A rejoinder might contend that, since I cannot possibly entertain all possible ends that an action of suicide could have, then I cannot claim that actions of suicide are amoral. In response to such a concern I wish to reiterate two further ideas presented here. First, I believe that one common thread among actions of suicide is the felt loss of a sense of self, or the perceived severe and immediate threat to one's sense of self. But certainly, both deliberative and moral agency are undermined when one loses their sense of self. Second, I have stressed in chapter four that we need to be careful about the separability of actions. Simply put, there is a difference between intending to perform an action of suicide and intending, say, to participate in a larger terrorist plot where one's action of suicide is part of the plot. I maintain that the latter is within the moral domain, whereas the former alone is not.

2. See, for example, the work of Frans de Waal, *The Age of Empathy: Nature's Lessons for a Kinder Society* (New York: Crown Publishing Group, 2010). I also do not intend to suggest here that non-human animals are not persons. Indeed, I believe that

at least some non-human animals are good candidates for personhood. Nevertheless, my tendency to focus upon *agents* here is in keeping with the common (albeit perhaps mistaken) tendency simply to regard human beings—and typically *only* human beings—as persons. Philosophical discussions about personhood deserve attention elsewhere.

3. As previously mentioned, Edwin Shneidman maintained that "[s]uffering is half pain and half being alone with that pain" in *The Suicidal Mind* (New York: Oxford University Press, 1996), 119.

4. Edwin S. Shneidman, *The Suicidal Mind*, 133.

5. William Styron, *Darkness Visible*, 30.

6. For a list of warning signs compiled by the American Foundation for Suicide Prevention, please see "Risk Factors, Protective Factors, and Warning Signs" on their website: https://afsp.org/risk-factors-protective-factors-and-warning-signs#warning-signs (accessed December 13, 2023).

7. For example, in his book *Why People Die by Suicide*, Thomas Joiner postulates that when there is a sense of belonging within a community, then suicide rates suppress. Joiner even cites national tragedies as having the effect of increasing a sense of belonging within a community; and so, it seems that the reason (or reasons) as to why people come together is less important than the fact that people come together (Cambridge: Harvard University Press, 2005), 127–32.

8. First-personal accounts like of William Styron, Kay Redfield Jamison, and Kevin Hines are necessary, I believe, to lend much-needed voices to conversations regarding the relationship between moral domain and actions of suicide. I further believe that, if more first-personal accounts were explored, then those accounts also would lend some support for the idea that actions of suicide are amoral.

9. I thank an anonymous reviewer for bringing this point to my attention.

10. Alastair Norcross, *Morality by Degrees: Reasons without Demands* (Oxford: Oxford University Press, 2020).

11. World Health Organization, "Suicide," August 28, 2023. https://www.who.int/news-room/fact-sheets/detail/suicide (last access date December 13, 2023).

12. World Health Organization, "Suicide," https://www.who.int/news-room/fact-sheets/detail/suicide. There has been some push back, however, regarding the idea of believing that a person's action of suicide could be impulsive since it is believed that persons must work themselves up to the point to engage in an action of suicide. Thomas Joiner, for example, refrains from regarding suicide as impulsive primarily because of the worry that doing so will undermine suicide prevention efforts. Specifically, in his book *Myths about Suicide*, Joiner writes: "the extremely fearsome and often painful prospect of bringing about one's own death requires previous experiences and psychological processes that take months—at least—to accumulate [. . .] the idea that suicidal acts come out of the blue undermines attempts to study, assess, treat, and prevent them" (Cambridge: Harvard University Press, 2010), 84. But claiming that actions of suicide can be impulsive does not negate the idea that a person can take several steps over a period of time that increases their risk for dying by suicide. So, I do not believe that adhering to the idea that actions of suicide can be impulsive undermines the study of suicide as Joiner maintains. Indeed, Andrew Solomon also

recognizes that actions of suicide involve a degree of impulsivity (*The Noonday Demon: An Atlas of Depression*, New York: Touchstone, 2001), 244.

13. For more on alcohol use disorder, please see "Understanding Alcohol Use Disorder," as published by the National Institute on Alcohol Abuse and Alcoholism, updated April 2023, https://www.niaaa.nih.gov/publications/brochures-and-fact-sheets/understanding-alcohol-use-disorder (last access date December 13, 2023).

14. In fact, the first step of twelve-step program of Alcoholics Anonymous® is "[w]e admitted we were powerless over alcohol—that our lives had become unmanageable." https://www.aa.org/the-twelve-steps.

15. For a concise and informative overview of some of the cultural differences regarding suicide, please see Kay Redfield Jamison's book *Night Falls Fast: Understanding Suicide* (New York: Random House, 1999), 12–18.

16. Miranda Fricker, *Epistemic Injustice: Power and the Ethics of Knowing* (New York: Oxford University Press, 2007), see especially 147–75.

17. Miranda Fricker, *Epistemic Injustice*, 147–75.

18. Miranda Fricker, *Epistemic Injustice*, 163.

19. Miranda Fricker, *Epistemic Injustice*, 161.

20. With respect to hermeneutical injustice, Miranda Fricker distinguishes between two types—namely, systemic injustice and incidental injustice. Systemic injustice is more applicable to the injustices suffered by persons in need of help in societies where actions of suicide have been predominantly characterized as morally wrong. See Fricker, *Epistemic Injustice*, 158–59.

21. Miranda Fricker, *Epistemic Injustice*, 148.

22. Albert Camus, "The Myth of Sisyphus," (originally published in 1942), reprinted in *The Plague, The Fall, Exile and the Kingdom, and Selected Essays*, 489–605, translated by Justin O'Brien (London: Everyman's Library, 2004), 495.

Bibliography

Alcoholics Anonymous®. Twelve Step Program. https://www.aa.org/the-twelve-steps.

American Foundation for Suicide Prevention. "Risk Factors, Protective Factors, and Warning Signs." https://afsp.org/risk-factors-protective-factors-and-warning-signs#warning-signs.

Anscombe, G. E. M.. "Intention." In *Essays in Philosophical Psychology*, edited by Donald F. Gustafson, 30–40. New York: Anchor Books, 1964.

Berman, Jeffrey. *Mad Muse: The Mental Illness Memoir in a Writer's Life and Work*. Bingley, UK: Emerald Publishing Limited, 2019.

Bissell, Tom. "Great and Terrible Truths." *The New York Times*. Sunday Book Review. April 24, 2009.

Blackburn, Simon. *Mirror, Mirror: The Uses and Abuses of Self-love*. Princeton: Princeton University Press, 2014.

Brock, Rita Nakashima, and Gabriella Lettini. *Soul Repair: Recovering from Moral Injury after War*. Boston: Beacon Press, 2012.

Camus, Albert. "The Myth of Sisyphus." Originally published in 1942. Reprinted in *The Plague, The Fall, Exile and the Kingdom, and Selected Essays*, 489–605, translated by Justin O'Brien. London: Everyman's Library, 2004.

Cholbi, Michael. *Suicide: The Philosophical Dimensions*. Buffalo: Broadview Press, 2011.

De Waal, Frans. *The Age of Empathy: Nature's Lessons for a Kinder Society*. New York: Crown Publishing, 2010.

Deci, Edward L., and Richard M. Ryan. "The 'What' and 'Why' of Goal Pursuits: Human Needs and the Self-Determination of Behavior." *Psychological Inquiry* Vol. 11, No. 4 (2000): 227–68.

Dorsey, Dale. "Amorality." *Ethical Theory and Moral Practice* Vol. 19, No. 2 (April 2016): 329–42.

———. "Consequentialism, Cognitive Limitations, and Moral Theory." In *Oxford Studies in Normative Ethics*, Vol 3, edited by Mark Timmons, 179–202. New York: Oxford University Press, 2013.

Driver, Julia. "Meta-Cognition, Mind-Reading, and Humean Moral Agency." In *Moral Psychology & Human Agency: Philosophical Essays on the Science of*

Ethics, edited by Justin D'Arms and Daniel Jacobson, 123–36. New York: Oxford University Press, 2014.

Durkheim, Émile. *On Suicide*. 1897. Translated by Robin Buss. New York: Penguin Books, 2006.

Fairbairn, Gavin. *Contemplating Suicide: The Language and Ethics of Self-Harm*. New York: Routledge, 1995.

Fantz, Ashley. "An Ohio Transgender Teen's Suicide, A Mother's Anguish." *CNN*. January 4, 2015. https://www.cnn.com/2014/12/31/us/ohio-transgender-teen-suicide/index.html.

Frankfurt, Harry G. "Alternate Possibilities and Moral Responsibility." *The Journal of Philosophy*. Vol. 66, no. 23 (December 1969): 829–39.

———. "Autonomy, Necessity, and Love." *Necessity, Volition, and Love*. New York: Cambridge University Press, 1999: 129–141.

———. "Rationality and the Unthinkable." *The Importance of What We Care About*. New York: Cambridge University Press, 1988: 177–190.

———. *The Reasons of Love*. Princeton: Princeton University Press, 2004.

Frankl, Viktor E. *Man's Search for Meaning* (1959). Boston: Beacon Press, 2006.

Fricker, Miranda. *Epistemic Injustice: Power and the Ethics of Knowing*. New York: Oxford University Press, 2007.

Frith, Uta. *Autism: Explaining the Enigma*. Malden: Blackwell Publishers, 1989.

Gawande, Atul. *Being Mortal: Medicine and What Matters in the End*. New York: Henry Holt and Company, 2014.

Gilligan, Carol. "Moral Injury and the Ethic of Care: Reframing the Conversation about Differences." *Journal of Social Philosophy* Vol. 45, No. 1 (March 2014): 89–106.

Hecht, Jennifer Michael. *Stay: A History of Suicide and the Arguments Against It*. New Haven: Yale University Press, 2013.

Hines, Kevin. *Cracked, Not Broken: Surviving and Thriving After a Suicide Attempt*. Lanham, MD: Rowman & Littlefield Publishing Group, 2013.

———. *The Art of Being Broken: How Storytelling Saves Lives*. Brentwood, TN: Post Hill Press, 2023.

Hume, David. *A Treatise of Human Nature*, edited by L. A. Selby-Bigge. New York: Oxford University Press, 1888, second edition 1978.

———. "On Suicide," (1757) in *The Ethics of Suicide: Historical Sources*, edited by Margaret Pabst Battin, 406–411. New York: Oxford University Press, 2015.

Jackson, Frank. "Epiphenomenal Qualia." *The Philosophical Quarterly* Vol. 32, No. 127 (1982): 127–36.

Jamison, Kay Redfield. *Night Falls Fast: Understanding Suicide*. New York: Random House, 1999.

Jobes, David A.. *Managing Suicidal Risk: A Collaborative Approach*. New York: The Guilford Press, 2006.

Joiner, Thomas. *Myths about Suicide*. Cambridge: Harvard University Press, 2010.

———. *Why People Die by Suicide*. Cambridge: Harvard University Press, 2005.

Judd, Naomi, and Marcia Wilkie. *River of Time: My Descent into Depression and How I Emerged with Hope*. New York: Hachette Book Group, Inc., 2016.

Kagan, Shelly. *Death*. New Haven: Yale University Press, 2012.

———. *The Limits of Morality*. New York: Oxford University Press, 1989.

Kant, Immanuel. *Grounding for the Metaphysics of Morals* (1785), third edition, translated by James W. Ellington. Indianapolis: Hackett Publishing Company, 1993.

———. *The Metaphysics of Morals* (1797). In *Practical Philosophy: The Cambridge Edition of the Works of Immanuel Kant*, 353–603. Translated and edited by Mary J. Gregor. New York: Cambridge University Press, 1996.

Kennedy, John F. *Profiles in Courage*. New York: HarperCollins Publishers, 1955. Reprinted in HarperPerennial, 1992.

Korsgaard, Christine M. Self-Constitution: *Agency, Identity, and Integrity*. New York: Oxford University Press, 2009.

———. *The Sources of Normativity*. New York: Cambridge University Press, 1996.

Lipsky, David. "The Lost Years and Last Days of David Foster Wallace." In *Rolling Stone* 1064. Originally published October 30, 2008. Published online September 20, 2019. https://www.rollingstone.com/culture/culture-features/the-lost-years-and-last-days-of-david-foster-wallace-883224/ (accessed December 15, 2023).

Litz, Brett T., Nathan Stein, Eileen Delaney, Leslie Lebowitz, William P. Nash, Caroline Silva, and Shira Maguen. "Moral Injury and Moral Repair in War Veterans: A Preliminary Model and Intervention Strategy." *Clinical Psychology Review* Vol. 29, No. 8 (2009): 695–706.

Martin, Clancy. *How Not to Kill Yourself: A Portrait of the Suicidal Mind*. New York: Pantheon Books, 2023.

McIntyre, Alison. "Doctrine of Double Effect." *Stanford Encyclopedia of Philosophy*. Stanford: The Metaphysics Research Lab, 2023. https://plato.stanford.edu/entries/double-effect/

National Institute on Alcohol Abuse and Alcoholism. "Understanding Alcohol Use Disorder." Updated April 2023. https://www.niaaa.nih.gov/publications/brochures-and-fact-sheets/understanding-alcohol-use-disorder.

National Institute of Mental Health. "Frequently Asked Questions about Suicide." Accessed November 23, 2023. https://www.nimh.nih.gov/health/publications/suicide-faq.

Norcross, Alastair. *Morality by Degrees: Reasons without Demands*. Oxford: Oxford University Press, 2020.

O'Keeffe, Terence M. "Suicide and Self-Starvation." *Philosophy* Vol. 59, No. 229 (July 1984): 349–63.

Oregon's Death With Dignity Act (DWDA). "Frequently Asked Questions" Accessed December 10, 2023. https://www.oregon.gov/oha/PH/PROVIDERPARTNERRESOURCES/EVALUATIONRESEARCH/DEATHWITHDIGNITYACT/Pages/faqs.aspx.

Plato's *Apology*, Trans. G. M. A. Grube. In *Plato: Complete Works*, edited by, John M. Cooper, 17–36. Indianapolis: Hackett Publishing Company, Inc., 1997.

Posner, Kelly, Beth Brodsky, Kseniya Yershova, Jacqueline Buchanan, and John Mann. "The Classification of Suicidal Behavior." In *The Oxford Handbook of Suicide and Self-Injury*, edited by Matthew K. Nock, 7–22. New York: Oxford University Press, 2014.

Rosati, Connie S. "Moral Motivation." *Stanford Encyclopedia of Philosophy*. Stanford: The Metaphysics Research Lab, 2016. https://plato.stanford.edu/entries/moral-motivation/

Seemann, Axel. "Person Perception." *Philosophical Explorations* Vol. 11, No. 3 (September 2008): 245–62.

Shay, Jonathan. "Moral Injury." *Psychoanalytic Psychology* Vol. 13, no. 2. (April 2014): 182–191.

Shneidman, Edwin S. *The Suicidal Mind*. New York: Oxford University Press, 1996.

Sinclair, Jim. "Bridging the Gaps: An Inside-Out View of Autism (or, Do You Know What I Don't Know)." In *High-functioning Individuals with Autism*, edited by Eric Schopler and Gary B. Mesibov, 294–302. New York: Plenum Press, 1992.

Smyth, Bryan. "De-Moralizing Heroism: Ethical Expertise and the Object of Heroic Approbation." *Southwest Philosophy Review* Vol. 36, No. 1 (January 2020): 65–74.

Solomon, Andrew. *The Noonday Demon: An Atlas of Depression*. New York: Touchstone, 2001.

Stefan, Susan. *Rational Suicide, Irrational Laws: Examining Current Approaches to Suicide in Policy and Law*. New York: Oxford University Press, 2016.

Stump, Eleonore. *Philosophical Theology and the Knowledge of Persons*. Eugene, OR: Cascade Books, 2023.

———. *Wandering in Darkness: Narrative and the Problem of Suffering*. Oxford: Oxford University Press, 2010.

Styron, William. *Darkness Visible: A Memoir of Madness*. New York: Random House, 1990.

———. "Why Primo Levi Need Not Have Died." *New York Times*. Op-ed. December 19, 1988. Reprinted in *My Generation: Collected Nonfiction by William Styron*, edited by James L. W. West III, 189–92. New York: Random House, 2015.

———. *Sophie's Choice*. 1976. Reprint, New York: Vintage Books, 1992.

The Brittany Maynard Fund, an initiative of Compassion & Choices. https://thebrittanyfund.org/.

The Holy Bible. New International Version. Grand Rapids: Zondervan Publishing House, 1984.

The Oxford Handbook of Self, edited by Shaun Gallagher. New York: Oxford University Press, 2011.

Van Heeringen, Kees. *The Neuroscience of Suicidal Behavior*. Cambridge Fundamentals of Neuroscience in Psychology Series. New York: Cambridge University, Press, 2018.

Vargas, Ramon Antonio. "Naomi Judd Dealing with Bipolar Disorder when She Died by Suicide, Autopsy Says." In *The Guardian*. August 27, 2022.

Wallace, David Foster. "This is Water." Commencement Address at Kenyon College in Gambier, Ohio, 2005. For transcript, please see: http://bulletin-archive.kenyon.edu/x4280.html (accessed December 15, 2023).

Waller, Bruce. *Freedom Without Responsibility*. Philadelphia: Temple University Press, 1990.

West, Louis Jolyon. "Reflections on the Right to Die." In *Suicidology: Essays in Honor of Edwin Shneidman*. 359–76. Northvale, NJ: Jason Aronson Incorporated, 1993.

Williams, Bernard. "A Critique of Utilitarianism." In *Utilitarianism For and Against* by J. J. C. Smart and Bernard Williams. 75–150. New York: Cambridge University Press, 1973.

———. "Moral Incapacity." *Proceedings of the Aristotelian Society* Vol. 93 (1993): 59–70.

Wolf, Susan. "Meaning in Life." in *Meaning in Life and Why it Matters*. 1–33. Princeton: Princeton University Press, 2010.

World Health Organization. "Suicide." August 28, 2023. https://www.who.int/news-room/fact-sheets/detail/suicide. (last access date December 13, 2023).

Index

accidental actions, 62n39
accidental harm, 49
actions, 74; accidental, 62n39; acts versus, 14–23, 22, 30n7; agency and, 48; agency view of, 6; of children, 4, 7; choice and, 17; with cognitive limitations, 48–49; deliberative agency and, 31n9, 60n12, 76, 110; foresight with, 63n62; goals of, 15, 24, 101; immoral, 93–94; intentional action, 5; intentions and, 14–15; involuntary, 31n9; knowledge of, 14–15, 52; of moral agents, 13; in moral domain, 10–11, 100–101; moral evaluation of, 20; morality of, 2–3; moral reasons for, 42, 99; of non-moral agents, 56; normative judgments of, 41–42; philosophy of, 14; reason for, 49–50; reflection on, 5; rules of action, 103–4; self-conception with, 54–55; from spite, 58; voluntary, 31n9. *See also* amoral actions
actions of suicide: as amoral actions, 26, 29, 86, 123n31, 127, 136; attempts compared to, 123n32; Berman on, 76–77; choice and, 135–38; deliberative agency and, 59; Foxhole Jumper and, 77, 85; goals for, 18–22; help before, 114–15; Hume on, 39–40; inaction and, 24; intentions and, 18–19, 85; Joiner on, 125–36, 129; Kant on, 21–22; means for, 20; moral character and, 64n66; in moral domain, 25–26, 25–28, 121n6, 129–35, 138–40; moral evaluation of, 132–33; moral judgment of, 57; moral reasons for, 79–80; performing, 79; philosophy of, 104–5; relational accounts of, 127–28; relationships and, 121n7; Schneidman on, 99, 140; sense of self and, 56; suicidal acts and, 13–14, 18, 23; suicide-by-cop as, 97; in utilitarianism, 111–12
agency: actions and, 48; of animals, 4–5; assumptions about, 35n57; with death, 18, 20, 33n41, 34n45; deliberative agents, 38–39; Frankfurt on, 41; indirect, 23; means-end reasoning in, 30n6; with mental illness, 25; in moral domain, 5; with moral injury, 45; moral reasons and, 41–42; philosophy of, 32n19; view, 6, 55. *See also specific topics*
alcoholism, 135–36, 142n14
Alcorn, Leelah, 79

American Foundation for Suicide Prevention, 1, 30n2
amoral actions: actions of suicide as, 26, 29, 86, 123n31, 127, 136; deliberative agency and, 12, 37–41; moral agency and, 11, 33n31; by moral agents, 48; in moral domain, 125, 138–40; morality and, 3–13; moral judgments and, 5–6, 48–55, 74; philosophy of, 93–94; safety contracts and, 114–17; scholarship on, 41–48, 55–59; stigma of, 120
amorality. *See specific topics*
animals: agency of, 4–5; children and, 37, 60n12; cognitive limitations of, 31n10; humans and, 32n20, 140n2; means-end reasoning and, 28; as non-moral agents, 3; wild, 4, 31n8
Anscombe, G. E. M., 57–58, 77
anxiety, 45
Apology (Plato), 21
assisted living, 90n63
assumptions, 21, 30n7, 35n57
attempted suicide, 15–16, 33n35, 123n32
autism, 9–10, 43
autonomy, 28, 36n63, 36n64, 86

behavior. *See specific behavior*
Being Mortal (Gawande), 89n49
belonging (relatedness): in interpersonal theory of suicide, 65–74; need for, 29, 86; sense of, 36, 94, 99; thwarted sense of, 69, 74–80, 87n3
Benton, Thomas Hart, 58–59, 64n66, 134, 140n1
Berman, Jeffrey, 76–77
betrayal, 44–45, 44–47, 79, 99, 126
Bissell, Tom, 87n21
Blackburn, Simon, 38, 40, 42
blame, 5–6, 31n8
bodily autonomy, 28
Brock, Rita Nakashima, 45–46
burdensomeness, perception of, 36n63, 66–70, 74–75, 80–86, 87n3, 109, 115

Camus, Albert, 139–40
causality, 40–41
causation, 27
character, moral, 52–53, 63n55, 64n66, 133–34
charity, 91n66
children: actions of, 4, 7; animals and, 37, 60n12; assumptions about, 30n7; deliberative agency of, 4–5, 13, 31n11, 32n20; development of, 8; maternal love for, 76–79; moral development of, 60n13; as non-moral agents, 3
choice: actions and, 17; actions of suicide and, 135–38; for death, 77–79, 85; deliberative agency and, 120; free will and, 41; maternal love and, 76–79; in moral domain, 96–97, 135–36; moral judgment of, 99; for self-harm, 137–38; self-perception of, 127–28
Cholbi, Michael, 30n3, 54–55
circumstantial limitations, 12–13, 51–52
"The Classification of Suicidal Behavior" (Posner), 15
cognitive limitations, 11, 31n10, 48–49, 59
colloquial language, 16
common sense morality, 63n61
compassion, 29
competence (effectiveness), 29, 36, 75, 80–86, 94, 101, 139
completed suicide, 33n35
compulsory military service, 123n24
conflicting intentions, 24
contemplated suicide, 15
control, 45
correlation, 27
courage, 58, 64n66
crime, 25, 81–82, 84, 89n50, 112–13
cruelty, 62n50

Dages, Paul, 121n7
danger, 80
Darkness Visible (Styron), 16–17, 67–68

death: agency with, 18, 20, 33n41, 34n45; assisted living and, 90n63; avoidance of, 89n39; choice for, 77–79, 85; as consequences, 63n62; Death With Dignity Act, 90n51; emotional, 72–73; Epicurus on, 21; hastening, 89n50; intending to die, 23; intentions and, 63n62; means for, 19–20; Open Yale Course on Death, 23; overdoses and, 18–19, 34n44; prevention of, 69; self-harm and, 66; self-sacrifice and, 140; shameful, 40; to suicidal persons, 20; by suicide, 15–16, 45–46, 87n3
Deci, Edward L., 36n63
definitions, of suicide, 15–18, 22–23, 22–24, 33n33, 56, 130
deliberative agency, 3; actions and, 31n9, 60n12, 76, 110; actions of suicide and, 59; amoral actions and, 12, 37–41; autonomy for, 36n64; blame and, 5–6; causality and, 40–41; of children, 4–5, 13, 31n11, 32n20; choice and, 120; deficiencies in, 7–8, 10–11; deliberative, moral agency, 48–55; deliberative agents, 38–39; Dorsey on, 32n19, 37; humans and, 28; Joiner on, 94; lack of, 5; with mental illness, 127; moral agency and, 7, 126–27, 134–35; moral evaluation of, 11; moral injury and, 78–79; non-moral agents and, 3–4; reason and, 6–7, 72; relational knowledge and, 29; self and, 59, 89n48; self-conception and, 70–71; sense of self and, 59
dementia, 68
depression: external reasons for, 83; MDD, 44; mental illness and, 16–17, 67–68; moral injury and, 77–78; PTSD and, 45; scholarship on, 35n58; severe, 88n27, 88n31, 132; Styron on, 109–10, 112; suicidal ideation and, 70–71; symptoms of, 26
desire, 57–58, 60n3
despair, 107
desperation, 119
discussing suicide, 30n1
doctors. *See* physician-assisted suicide
Doctrine of Double Effect, 63n62
dominant view, 25–26, 129–31, 136, 139
Dorsey, Dale, 5–7, 6, 11–12, 11–13, 55, 59; on amorality, 32n30, 48–49, 121n9; on deliberative agency, 32n19, 37; on moral judgment, 134–35
drunk driving, 95
duration of life, 105–8
Durkheim, Émile, 24, 26–27, 66, 138

effectiveness (competence), 29, 36, 75, 80–86, 94, 101, 139
egoism, 49–50, 56
emotional death, 72–73
empathy, 10
ends. *See* goals
Epicurus, 21
Epistemic Injustice (Fricker), 136–37
ethics. *See specific topics*
euthanasia, 81–82
existential crises, 26, 55–56, 73
externalism, 42, 60n15

failed suicide, 33n35
fear of suicide, 141n12
firearms, 87n3
floodgate worry, 93–94
Foote, Henry, 58
foresight, 63n62
Foxhole Jumper: actions of suicide and, 77, 85; in Doctrine of Double Effect, 63n62; in dominant view, 130–31; in moral domain, 133; PAS and, 89n48; philosophy of, 54–57, 59; preservation of life to, 86; self-sacrifice and, 80–81, 84
fragmentation, 68

Frankfurt, Harry, 34n43, 38–39, 41, 49–50, 51, 53–54
Frankl, Victor, 72–73, 100
Freedom Without Responsibility (Waller), 94
free will, 41
Fricker, Miranda, 136–37, 142n20
friendship, 14–15

Garcia, Robert, 32n30
Gawande, Atul, 89n49, 90n63
genuine incapacities, 52
Germany, 72–73, 76–79
Gilligan, Carol, 46–47
goals, 34n45, 62n39, 105; of actions, 15, 24, 101; for actions of suicide, 18–22; scholarship on, 36n63
God. *See* religion
Golden Gate Bridge, 118
"Great and Terrible Truths" (Bissell), 87n21
grief, 10
Grounding for the Metaphysics of Morals (Kant), 22–23, 34n48, 103–7, 108
guilt, 45–46

hastening death, 89n50
Hecht, Jennifer Michael, 35n56
hermeneutical injustice, 136–37, 142n20
heroism, 55–56
hindsight, 117–20, 121n2
Hines, Kevin, 118, 133–34, 141n8
Holocaust, 72–73, 76–79
homicide, 16, 25, 97, 102, 122n15
How Not to Kill Yourself (Martin), 34n45
Hume, David, 39–40, 111
humility, 29

identity, 43, 46–47, 54, 56, 99
ignorance, 129
immoral: actions, 93–94; appeals to immorality, 122n19; means, 96–97; morally impermissible as, 1–4, 30; objectively wrong as, 101–8, 122n15; PAS as, 82. *See also* morally wrong
impulsivity, 141n12
inaction, 7, 11–12, 24, 49
indirect agency, 23
indirect responsibility, 95–96
insight, 117–20
intentions: actions and, 14–15; actions of suicide and, 18–19, 85; conflicting, 24; death and, 63n62; desire and, 57–58; intending to die, 23; intentional action, 5; intentional inaction, 24; intentionality, 16, 35n53; intentional self-injurious behavior, 23, 33n41, 97; intentional self-killing, 34n42; moral domain and, 30n7; multiple, 15; perceived, 4; self-killing and, 18, 24; of soldiers, 57; stand-alone, 19
internalism, 42, 46, 60n15
interpersonal theory of suicide, 65–74
involuntary actions, 31n9

Jackson, Frank, 8–9
Jamison, Kay Redfield, 71–72, 116–17, 141n8
Jesus Christ, 99–100
Jews, 72–73, 76–79
Jobes, David A., 115–16
Joiner, Thomas, 29, 36n63; on actions of suicide, 125–36, 129; on burdensomeness, 115; on deliberative agency, 94; on fear of suicide, 141n12; interpersonal theory of suicide, 65–74; on moral community, 141n7; Schneidman and, 80, 86, 109
Judd, Naomi, 70–72, 87n23, 88n31, 96
Judeo-Christian worldview, 97–101

Kagan, Shelly, 23, 84, 140
Kant, Immanuel, 21–22, 103–8, 133
Kazemi, Juliana, 32n30
Kennedy, John F., 58
Kenyon College, 70, 87n21

killing, 63n62, 100, 102–3, 122n15
knowledge, 8–9, 14–15, 24, 52
Korsgaard, Christine, 21–22, 42–43, 53–55, 104

legacy, of suicide, 16–17, 112–14
legality, of suicide, 25, 81–82, 84, 89n50, 112–13
Lettini, Gabriella, 45–46
LGBTQ+ community, 46–47
libertarianism, 41
life extension, 89n49
life saving, 102–3
Litz, Brett T., 44, 61n27
loss, 68, 75–76, 85–86. *See also* self
love, 50–51, 56, 59, 76–79, 99–100, 105, 140. *See also* self-love
lying, 42
Lyons, Geolon, 33n34

Major Depressive Disorder (MDD), 44
Managing Suicidal Risk (Jobes), 115–16
Man's Search for Meaning (Frankl), 72–73
Martin, Clancy, 34n45
Mary's Room experiment, 8–9
maternal love, 76–79
Maynard, Brittany, 85–86
MDD. *See* Major Depressive Disorder
Meaningful Lives (Wolf), 50–51
means, 18–22, 28, 30n6, 34n45, 62n39, 96–97
mental illness: agency with, 25; deliberative agency with, 127; depression and, 16–17, 67–68; dominant view of, 26; moral injury and, 61n31; moral wrongness and, 27–28; psychology of, 27, 95–96; relationships and, 131–32; severe, 72–74, 88n27; suicidal ideation and, 35n57; as terminal illness, 88n31; undiagnosed, 26–27
metaphysics, 38–39
Metaphysics of Morals (Kant), 107–8
military veterans, 44, 62n37
moral agency: circumstantial limitations in, 12–13; deficiencies in, 7–8, 10–11; deliberative, moral agency, 48–55; deliberative agency and, 7, 126–27, 134–35; in existential crises, 55–56; inaction as, 49; moral agents, 13, 28–29, 48, 60n15, 109, 134–35; reasons with, 126; relational knowledge and, 8–9, 41–48; for self-sacrifice, 58–59
moral attribution, 13
moral character, 52–53, 63n55, 64n66, 133–34
moral claims, 50
moral community, 47–48, 80, 111, 132, 141n7
moral deliberation, 8
moral development, 60n13
moral domain: actions in, 10–11, 100–101; actions of suicide in, 25–26, 25–28, 121n6, 129–35, 138–40; amoral actions in, 125, 138–40; choice in, 96–97, 135–36; courage in, 64n66; dominant view in, 129–30; Foxhole Jumper in, 133; intentions and, 30n7; moral community and, 80; morality in, 2, 5; moral responsibility in, 94, 138; obligations in, 56; in philosophy, 32n30; relational knowledge in, 9–10; self-killing in, 101–2
moral double-standards, 16–17
moral evaluation, 11, 20, 41, 132–33
moral incapacities, 51–53, 62n50
"Moral Incapacity" (Williams), 51–53
moral injury, 44–48, 61n27, 61n31, 62n37, 77–79, 131
moral judgment: of accidental harm, 49; of actions of suicide, 57; amoral actions and, 5–6, 48–55, 74; of choice, 99; definitions and, 22–23; Dorsey on, 134–35; of inaction, 11–12; morality and, 1–2, 5–6; in religion, 97–101; scholarship on, 29;

of self-sacrifice, 20–21; stigma from, 103; of suicide, 17
moral justifications, 129
morally impermissible, 1–4, 30
morally permissible, 1–4, 28–30, 82, 108, 113–14, 129, 132
morally responsible, 94–96, 99–101, 109, 132, 138
morally wrong, 97–98; philosophy of, 39–40, 42–44, 61n17, 108, 118–20, 129, 142n20; society and, 4–5, 12, 22–23, 28, 101–3
moral negligence, 96
moral obligations, 132–33
moral reasons, 12, 41–42, 47, 75–76, 79–80, 99
moral requireability, 6
moral requirements, 11, 48, 51
moral responsibility, 94, 138
moral sense, 4
moral significance, 12
moral wrongness, 27–28, 35n56, 118, 129
motivational judgment externalism. *See* externalism
motivational judgment internalism. *See* internalism
multiple intentions, 15
murder, 16, 25, 97, 102, 122n15
Murray, Henry, 66
Myths about Suicide (Joiner), 109, 141n12

National Institute of Mental Health, 30n1
National Suicide Prevention Lifeline, 30n4
Nazis, 72–73, 76–79
neuroscience, of suicide, 2
Night Falls Fast (Jamison), 71–72, 116–17
non-deontic ethical frameworks, 28
non-egotistical normative reasons, 56
non-human animals. *See* animals
non-moral agents, 3–4, 48–49, 56
nonmorality, 50–51
nonsuicidal self-injury, 19
The Noonday Demon (Solomon), 26, 35n58, 82–83
normative judgments, 6, 12, 41–42, 50–51

objectively wrong, 101–8, 122n15
obligations, 56, 58
O'Keeffe, Terence M., 122n13
ontology, 40
Open Yale Course on Death (Kagan), 23
overdoses, 18–19, 34n44
Oxford Handbook of Suicide and Self-Injury, 15

pain, 20, 66–69, 117–19, 129–32, 138–40
parts of speech, 33n34
PAS. *See* physician-assisted suicide
patriarchal society, 46–47
perceived intentions, 4
perception, of burdensomeness, 36n63, 66–70, 74–75, 80–86, 87n3, 109, 115
permissible, morally, 1–4, 28–30, 82, 108, 113–14, 129, 132
person perception, 9
perspectives, religious, 97–101, 122n13
physician-assisted suicide (PAS): conception of, 81–86, 99–100, 108, 112–14; in Death With Dignity Act, 90n51; scholarship on, 89n48, 89n50, 90nn62–63, 123n28
Plato, 21
Posner, Kelly, 15
Post-Traumatic Stress Disorder (PTSD), 44–45
power, 45, 61n27
practical identity, 43, 54
preservation of life, 84, 86, 105–6
principles, 58
prior action, 95
Profiles in Courage (Kennedy), 58
psychache, 66–70, 73–74, 140

PTSD. *See* Post-Traumatic Stress Disorder

quality of life, 105–8
questions, about suicide, 30n1

rationality, 10, 31n10
reason/reasons: for actions, 49–50; deliberative agency and, 6–7, 72; for despair, 107; of love, 50–51, 59; means-end reasoning, 28, 30n6; with moral agency, 126; moral reasons, 12, 41–42, 47, 75–76, 79–80, 99; non-egotistical normative reasons, 56
The Reasons of Love (Frankfurt), 34n43
regret, 119
relatedness. *See* belonging
relational accounts, of actions of suicide, 127–28
relational knowledge: compromised, 76; deficiencies in, 12; deliberative agency and, 29; internalism and, 60n15; moral agency and, 8–9, 41–48; for moral agents, 60n15; moral deliberation and, 8; in moral domain, 9–10; morality and, 42; rationality and, 10; social interaction and, 10
relational nature of morality, 65
relational trust, 47
relationships: actions of suicide and, 121n7; conversations in, 128; dominant view of, 139; mental illness and, 131–32; psychology of, 46–47; romantic, 75; suicide prevention and, 116–17
religion, 20–21, 43, 50, 97–101, 121n10, 122n13
responsible (morally responsible), 94–96, 99–101, 109, 132, 138
rights, suicide as, 112–13
risk, of suicide, 62n37
River of Time (Judd), 70–71
romantic relationships, 75
rules of action, 103–4
Russell, Bruce, 124n42
Ryan, Jack, 116–17
Ryan, Richard M., 36n63

sacredness of life, 121n10
safety contracts, 114–17
scalar utilitarianism, 134
Schneidman, Edwin: on actions of suicide, 99, 140; Frankl and, 100; Joiner and, 80, 86, 109; on moral injury, 131; scholarship from, 29, 36n63, 66–69, 73–74, 78; on suffering, 96, 129; Szasz and, 113–14; thought patterns to, 119–20
Seemann, Axel, 9
self (sense of), 37–41; actions of suicide and, 56; anxiety and, 45; Blackburn on, 42; deficiencies in, 43–44; deliberative agency and, 59, 89n48; desire and, 60n3; Frankfurt on, 38–39; loss of, 43–47, 59, 68–75, 86, 89n48, 94, 99, 101, 109–12, 125, 134, 140n1; psychology of, 53; self-conception and, 58–59; society and, 39–40
self-abasement, 38
self-awareness, 39, 60n2
self-betrayal, 79
self-conception, 42–43, 54–55, 58–59, 70–71, 85–86, 99
self-deception, 61n17
self-defense, 63n62, 100
self-determined behavior, 36n63
self-harm, 66, 137–38
self-image, 67–69, 73, 80–81, 94, 96
self-injurious behavior, 15–16, 19, 23, 33n41, 97
self-interest, 54, 105
selfishness, as vice, 108–12
self-killing, 18, 24, 34n42, 101–2
self-love, 38, 60, 104–8
self-murder, suicide as, 25
self-perception, of choice, 127–28
self-reflection, 12, 38
self-respect, 47

self-sacrifice: in common sense morality, 63n61; death and, 140; Foxhole Jumper and, 80–81, 84; heroism and, 55–56; moral agency for, 58–59; moral judgment of, 20–21; as suicide, 22, 128–29
severe depression, 88n27, 88n31, 132
severe mental illness, 72–74, 88n27
shame, 45–46
shameful death, 40
Shay, Jonathan, 44, 46, 61n27, 62n37
Sinclair, Jim, 10–11, 43, 47
Smyth, Brian, 55–56
social acquisition, 9–10
social alienation, 136
social beings, humans as, 74–75
social interaction, 10, 43
socialization, 46
social stigma, 2–3, 25, 103, 120, 131–32
society. *See specific topics*
Socrates, 21
soldiers, 45, 54–57, 56, 57, 123n24. *See also* Foxhole Jumper
Solomon, Andrew, 26, 35n58, 82–85, 114, 141n12
Solon, 26–27
Sophie's Choice (Styron), 76–79, 85, 99
Soul Repair (Brock and Lettini), 45
Sources for Normativity (Korsgaard), 42–43
spite, 58
stand-alone intentions, 19
stigma (social), 2–3, 25, 103, 120, 131–32
Stump, Eleonore, 8–9, 32n21
Styron, William: on depression, 109–10, 112; on desperation, 119; Jamison and, 141n8; literary works of, 76–79, 85, 99; on mental illness, 95–96; on stigma, 131; on suicide, 16–17, 67–68, 71–72, 86, 141n8
successful suicide, 33n35
suffering, 18, 20–21, 22. *See also* pain
suicidal acts, 13–14, 18, 23
suicidal behavior, 15–23, 33n41, 57, 65–69, 110
suicidal ideation: depression and, 70–71; in existential crises, 26; humans and, 119–20, 139–40; intentionality and, 35n53; mental illness and, 35n57; psychology of, 34n45; support for, 2
suicidality, 26–27, 82–83, 86, 100
The Suicidal Mind (Schneidman), 36n63
suicidal persons, 20
suicide. *See specific topics*
Suicide (Cholbi), 30n3
suicide bombers, 140n1
suicide-by-cop, 97
suicide intervention, 20, 78, 100–101, 113–14, 128, 131–32
suicide prevention, 17; American Foundation for Suicide Prevention, 1, 30n2; Hecht on, 35n56; morality of, 113–14; National Suicide Prevention Lifeline, 30n4; relationships and, 116–17; religion and, 101; in United States, 103
suicide survivors, 118
systemic injustice, 142n20
Szasz, Thomas, 113–14

Talk Saves Lives (American Foundation for Suicide Prevention), 1, 30n2
terminal illness, 82–85, 82–86, 88n31, 113–14, 118–19
"This Is Water" (Wallace), 70–74, 87n21
threats, 74
tobacco use, 34n42

undiagnosed mental illness, 26–27
United States, 1, 30n1, 30n2, 30n4, 103
unthinkable, 53–54, 58, 64, 125–26
utilitarianism, 111–12, 134

value-laden psychology, 23
value-neutral approaches to suicide, 30n3
vice, 108–12, 133–34

virtue, 64, 133–34
volitional necessities, 51, 53–54, 56
Voltaire, 139–40
voluntary actions, 31n9

Wallace, David Foster, 70–74, 87n21
Waller, Bruce, 94
Wandering in Darkness (Stump), 8–9
West, Louis Jolyon, 113–14
Western culture, 136
"The 'What' and 'Why' of Goal Pursuits" (Ryan and Deci), 36n63
Why People Die by Suicide (Joiner), 36n63, 65–66, 141n7
"Why Primo Levi Need Not Have Died" (Styron), 77–78
wild animals, 4, 31n8
Williams, Bernard, 51–53, 62n50, 111–12
will power, 28–29
Wolf, Susan, 50–51
World Health Organization, 135, 141n12
worldviews, 66–67, 97–101

About the Author

Robyn Gaier is assistant professor of philosophy at Gannon University in Erie, Pennsylvania. Gaier earned a Bachelor of Arts degree in philosophy from Bowling Green State University, a Master of Arts degree in philosophy from Ohio University, and a Doctoral degree in philosophy from Saint Louis University. Gaier's work has appeared in the *Southwest Philosophy Review*, the *Journal of Ethics in Mental Health*, and the *Association for the Advancement of Philosophy and Psychiatry Bulletin*.

www.ingramcontent.com/pod-product-compliance
Lightning Source LLC
LaVergne TN
LVHW091531200926
848483LV00002B/367